"An excellent book that meets an urge[?]
greatly expanded their concern for t[?]
however, we have not understood h[?]
could produce important change in the lives of the poor. This very readable,
solidly biblical book shows us how to do that. Every Christian should read it."

—**Ron Sider**, president emeritus, Evangelicals for Social Action

"A groundbreaking book for the twenty-first century, *Advocating for Justice*
blends biblical, theological, and historical foundations in presenting advocacy
as integral to the work of justice. True justice does not take place without
systemic change. The authors lead us to understand and embrace advocacy
as part of our spiritual journey and call to discipleship."

—**Jo Anne Lyon**, general superintendent, The Wesleyan Church

"This is a remarkable and much-needed book! It is robustly researched yet
deeply personal. It is focused on the character and example of God rather
than partisan versions of social strategies. The book will help me as a pastor
lead my church in a more effective public witness of Christ's love and service
and help us impact the systems of this world."

—**Joel C. Hunter**, senior pastor, Northland—A Church Distributed

"Forty years ago Ron Sider introduced us to the insidious and pervasive presence
of structural sin that generates so much of the world's poverty and hunger, but
the Christian community has yet to coalesce around a strategy to overcome
these dark structural forces. Now, in this compelling and inspiring book, the
authors present a persuasive case for advocacy as an essential tool that the
Christian community must no longer shy away from. Building on a Trinitarian
foundation to describe why followers of Christ must become advocates to the
powers and principalities of our day, the authors explain what advocacy looks
like, how it can and should be done, what organizations are currently engaged
in advocacy, and how we can resolve some major concerns, including how to
integrate evangelism into the work of justice advocacy. Well-researched, well-
written, and timely, this book will have staying power to inform, educate, and
advise the Christian community for many years to come."

—**Roland Hoksbergen**, Calvin College

"Scripture is filled with examples of God's people being called to speak up and
defend the rights of the vulnerable and oppressed. Advocacy is not an option
for us; it's a biblical responsibility and an integral part of our discipleship
and witness. But advocacy is not easy, and Christians have struggled (and
often failed) to do it well. This timely and practical resource offers a robust
vision of what faithful advocacy can look like today. Read this book if you
want to understand better how to renew our witness for justice, peace, and
the flourishing of all creation."

—**Ben Lowe**, activist and coauthor of *The Future of Our Faith*

Advocating
for
Justice

AN EVANGELICAL VISION
FOR TRANSFORMING SYSTEMS
AND STRUCTURES

Stephen Offutt, F. David Bronkema,
Krisanne Vaillancourt Murphy,
Robb Davis, Gregg Okesson

Ƀ
Baker Academic
a division of Baker Publishing Group
Grand Rapids, Michigan

Published by Baker Academic
a division of Baker Publishing Group
P.O. Box 6287, Grand Rapids, MI 49516-6287
www.bakeracademic.com

Printed in the United States of America

Library of Congress Cataloging-in-Publication Data
Names: Offutt, Stephen, author.
Title: Advocating for justice : an evangelical vision for transforming systems and structures
    / Stephen Offutt, F. David Bronkema, Krisanne Vaillancourt Murphy, Robb Davis, Gregg
    Okesson.
Description: Grand Rapids, MI : Baker Academic, 2016. | Includes bibliographical references and
    index.
Identifiers: LCCN 2016007735 | ISBN 9780801097652 (pbk.)
Subjects: LCSH: Christianity and justice. | Evangelicalism.
Classification: LCC BR115.J8 O35 2016 | DDC 261.8—dc23
LC record available at http://lccn.loc.gov/2016007735

In keeping with biblical principles of creation stewardship, Baker Publishing Group advocates the responsible use of our natural resources. As a member of the Green Press Initiative, our company uses recycled paper when possible. The text paper of this book is composed in part of post-consumer waste.

16   17   18   19   20   21   22   7   6   5   4   3   2   1

Contents

Acknowledgments

The authors of this book are a diverse bunch. Collectively, we bridge the gap between scholar and practitioner. Some of us are employed by academic institutions while others of us live and breathe in the daily world of policy and politics. We are scattered across the United States—from Washington, DC, to California. We attend different churches in different denominations. We have had different faith and life experiences. We are, in many ways, an unlikely team.

And yet we are bound together by two basic beliefs: evangelicals are actively involved in carrying out God's mission in the world and evangelicals have curiously left a very effective tool—advocacy—to one side in the midst of their efforts. Our team has come together to examine why this might be the case and to encourage evangelicals to weave advocacy into the fabric of their religious lives and communities. If evangelicals take up this call, we also believe that they can become more faithful followers of Jesus while quite possibly having a greater impact on the world around them. Some evangelicals in the global church have recently begun to move in this direction. The time is right for a book that can deepen reflection and provide some guidance for such initiatives.

Throughout the writing process, our team has sought to be led by the Holy Spirit. We have begun and ended each of our meetings in prayer. We have hoped to embody 2 Timothy 2:15, which in the King James Version begins, "Study to show thyself approved unto God." Our biblically grounded approach has had the effect of allowing the writing of this book to be a blessing to us. We have learned a great deal from each other and forged lasting friendships in the process.

A project such as this is not accomplished without accruing debts. We wish first to thank Jared Noetzel, who provided many hours of research, editing, and technical support. We are particularly appreciative of the work he did on the case studies that appear in the appendix. Second, we thank Jim Kinney and the many people at Baker who have played a part in getting this book to press. We are truly grateful for their patience, wisdom, and professionalism. Third, we thank Asbury Theological Seminary, Bread for the World, and Eastern University—three of the organizations that employ us and that have shown demonstrable support for the ideas found in this book.

We have received support and counsel for this book from our peers in academia and in faith-based relief and development organizations. Joel Hunter, Lynne Hybels, Jo Anne Lyon, and Mark Noll provided early support and encouragement as this project was getting off the ground. We are also grateful to those who shared ideas with us in round table sessions at the 2012 Accord meeting in Colorado Springs and who provided feedback on early concept paper drafts of this book at the 2013 Accord meeting at Calvin College. Chad Hayward and Jason Fileta paved the way for us to host these sessions. We have also benefited from Rachel Waltner Goosen's scholarship on John Howard Yoder, particularly that which exposed Yoder's deep personal failings. Some parts of this book are influenced by Yoder's ideas, but we do not condone his harmful actions toward others. Sandra Joireman and Ron Sider deserve special thanks for the input they provided as reviewers of the manuscript in its more finished form. The encouragement and advice we received from these leading members of our faith community increased the scholarly integrity of the manuscript. It goes without saying that we as authors are fully responsible for any errors that may appear in the pages that follow.

Finally, we thank our families for putting up with us while we have written this book. We have left our homes for in-person team meetings, we have slipped away from vacations to join in conference calls, and we have collectively logged many early morning and late night writing sessions. For your grace and support, thank you!

Part 1

The Problem
Defined

1

An Evangelical Approach to Advocacy

Definitions and Underpinnings

Rachel is a widow in present-day Uganda. She and her children are being kicked off their land because they do not have a formal land title. Laws that prioritize male inheritance allowed her dead husband's nephew to claim the house as his own. Unwilling to enter into an exploitive and abusive relationship, Rachel and her children beg on the street for food.

Rachel's story, and others like it in many parts of the globe, is strikingly similar to that of Naomi and Ruth of the Old Testament. When death took Naomi's husband and sons, it meant a life of poverty for her and Ruth, her daughter-in-law. Ruth, however, found favor with Boaz, a farm owner who allowed her to "glean" from his fields, a practice of taking leftovers from the harvest that God had enshrined into law to protect the poor (Lev. 23:22). Boaz, therefore, used this power to guarantee the application of God's legislation.

Not everyone uses power as wisely as Boaz. In fact, just about anybody who has worked with the poor (or watched the news) has witnessed power being used illegally, unfairly, or unproductively. Misuse of power in these situations either causes or perpetuates the poverty at hand. It might be a landlord who is not making needed repairs to an apartment, gangs that demand protection payments, neighborhoods that outlaw homeless shelters, police

3

who inappropriately use force or demand bribes, poor communities without funds for primary education because of structural adjustment policies in the global South, trade agreements negotiated through threats, or women being beaten with impunity. In each case, people with power are impoverishing and dehumanizing those who cannot fend for themselves and who do not have a seat at the table.

Evangelical Christians who come face-to-face with such injustices are forced into prayerful decisions: Is God calling us to become involved in the often-risky business of "advocacy"? Ought we to engage the power of the government, whether through the police, the courts, the bureaucracy, or the legislature, to right these wrongs? If so, how can we approach advocacy in ways that glorify God? Far too often, evangelicals do not know how to answer these questions. As a result, we either do nothing, thus committing sins of omission, or we do things that are neither effective nor God honoring.

We, the authors, believe that Christians are called to political engagement on behalf of others. Thus this book has two main objectives. The first is to help evangelical Christians debate, discuss, and discern more fully the nature and scope of God's call to evangelical advocacy and to open themselves up to following that call. The second is to guide evangelicals responding to that call into advocacy work that is prayerful, faithful, and wise.

To accomplish these goals, we divide the book into three major sections. First, we explain the evangelical community's current relationship with advocacy and how we came to be in this situation. Second, we lay out a theology of advocacy, exploring the nature of God as it relates to concepts of advocacy. Finally, we provide practical lessons and narrate experiences showing how a faith community might strengthen its relationship with the Triune God and be faithful in its call to advocacy. In this chapter we begin by explaining what we mean by certain words and concepts that are important to our narrative.

What Is Advocacy?

The word "advocacy," like all powerful words and labels, is used in different ways. The word has been significantly "depoliticized" in evangelical circles, especially when evangelical definitions are compared to the word's technical definition and how it is used in human rights movements around the world. The more common political definition, which we use as the basis for our approach in this book, better serves a discussion of effective, holistic advocacy.

Depoliticized Definitions

"Advocacy" in evangelical circles often signifies a personal approach. It connotes a volunteer role such as that of a donor, sponsor, or one who commits time to the cause of an organization. In these cases, the word chosen is a noun—a person may be an "advocate"—rather than a verb. Compassion International's child sponsorship program, for example, uses this definition and approach,[1] with a robust "brand advocacy" department encouraging supporters to invite others to get involved in the cause of remedying child poverty. Here advocacy is about raising awareness and encouraging others to do so, aiding one person in need, or directing one's time, talent, and resources toward a certain cause or issue. This cause-marketing approach bases its work on the premise that if more people know about a crisis, more can be done. The rationale behind personal advocacy is the belief that once an issue, in this case child suffering, is better understood, more money and resources will be dedicated to alleviating the problem. This model has been hugely successful for Compassion International, greatly enhancing its ability to lift children, one by one, out of some of the most impoverished places around the globe.

A second use of the word "advocacy" in evangelical circles is similar to the first but has a more professional orientation. Advocacy in this sense seeks support for a particular cause and begins to incorporate policy-related elements. Organizations like World Vision, for example, hire professional staff to "advocate" for government grants or to promote the interests of the organization. (We note in later chapters other innovative and grassroots forms of advocacy in which World Vision is engaged.) This implies an engagement with the state by lobbyists who are trying to win bids for important project support. Such activities are considered necessary because of the competitive process of influencing Congress and the officials of a presidential administration concerning critical budget and policy decisions. World Vision became involved in this type of advocacy earlier than most. Their office personnel in Washington, DC, started "in the early 1980s to do 'professional advocacy' and pre-position World Vision to get US government grants and bring the needs of children to policy makers."[2] In sum, depoliticized approaches to advocacy have been useful in allowing faith-based organizations to reach certain organizational objectives and, ultimately, serve greater numbers of the poor and vulnerable in societies around the world.

1. Compassion International, "Resource Guide: Equipping Your Personal Ministry with Compassion, Spring 2015. http://www.compassionmedia.com/pdf/compassion-resource-guide-spring-2015.pdf.
2. Robert Zachritz, email to Krisanne Vaillancourt Murphy, March 10, 2015.

Political Definitions

The problem with this, however, is that the use of the term "advocacy" to connote a depoliticized, primarily financial and personnel-driven approach is significantly at odds with the etymological, historical, and broader current use of the word. Indeed, the vast sector of organizations engaging governments on a whole host of economic, social, cultural, and political issues has an entirely different idea of what advocacy means. This mainstream approach to advocacy is consistent with the medieval Latin word *advocare*, which means "to summon to one's aid." The word "advocacy" appears in English, possibly for the first time in late Middle English, in the mid-fourteenth century. It is used in conjunction with the word "advocate," or "one whose profession is to plead cases in a court of justice."[3]

Advocacy of this kind is still what the term most commonly means today. Contemporary scholars have thus defined it as "organized efforts and actions [intended] . . . to influence public attitudes and to enact and implement laws and public policies so that visions of 'what should be' in a just, decent society become a reality."[4] Another technical definition argues that advocacy is "an organized political process that involves the coordinated efforts of people to change policies, practices, ideas, and values that perpetuate inequality, prejudice and exclusion."[5] Such definitions clearly take advocacy in directions that are different from how many evangelical organizations currently use the term.

The Underpinnings of the Political Definition of Advocacy

An awareness of the political dimensions of any work in social change underpins the political definition and understanding of advocacy work. Witness, for example, this testimony from an American Christian who previously spent time in Guatemala:

> I believed that if Guatemalan children needed a school, then the local church could open one, and volunteer groups could partner with local churches by assisting in construction and providing student sponsorships. However, if the community lacked a school due to corruption in the local municipality or central government, was our help just enabling the government to continue in its injustice? How should we have balanced the need to address institutional injustice, the children's immediate educational needs, and the fact that challenging government corruption could take years? Unfortunately, we did not know any

3. *Online Etymology Dictionary.*
4. Cohen, de la Vega, and Watson, *Advocacy for Social Justice*, 7–8.
5. VeneKlasen et al., *New Weave*, 23.

veteran expatriates, or even Guatemalan brothers and sisters who were wrestling with these issues. If I were in Guatemala today, the questions I would be asking would be much deeper in substance and the relational connections I would pursue would be much broader in context.[6]

Structural issues lie at the root of reflective engagement with poverty. The prevalence of these issues shows how contexts in need of relief or development also need advocacy or policy work. Without the latter set of activities, the root causes of impoverishing situations remain unaddressed. The tropes used to address these situations include extensions of the venerable proverb, "Give a man a fish and you feed him for a day; show him how to fish and you feed him for a lifetime": make room on the bank of the river for the person to fish, and finally, stop the factory upstream from dumping chemicals that are killing the fish. A more recent and popular analogy used in educational materials references townspeople mobilizing to rescue and care for babies floating through their town in the river (or youth or adults floating in the river who had been beaten) and eventually deciding to go upstream to see who is throwing these babies (or people) into the river in the first place to stop the problem at its source. The idea and label of "upstream" analysis and action also has a distinguished history in the annals of justice work and is one that we find logical, compelling, and biblical in terms of the underpinnings and nature of the complex, difficult, and challenging "political" advocacy work.[7]

The nature and practice of advocacy defined along political lines have at least five dimensions. First, advocacy is done to bring about change, and more specifically changes in policies, laws, and/or the enforcement of laws. Second, the desired change either (1) addresses a systemic injustice or personal abuse of power and authority that leads to poverty, exclusion, or human oppression, or (2) addresses unproductive policies that are not necessarily a matter of justice but that constrain human flourishing in some way, such as setting the minimum wage too high or too low.[8] Third, when injustice is an underlying cause of poverty, it may be so in at least two senses: (1) though not a proximate cause of poverty, the injustice keeps people from accessing the resources needed to

---

6. Shana Davis, Eastern University master's student, correspondence with Krisanne Vaillancourt Murphy, July 24, 2014.

7. The *Upstream Journal*, started in the 1970s, is a source for tropes such as these ("Upstream Journal," http://www.upstreamjournal.org/. Another online resource for such thinking is the Upstream website ("Upstream").

8. We realize that some people will define certain issues as issues of justice, and others will not. At the very least, we believe that the language of "unproductive policies" can help bridge the divide in a productive way, recognizing at the same time that defining whether an issue is an issue of justice or not is very much worth the conversation.

move out of poverty (a lack of income is a proximate cause of poverty, but an underlying cause might be, for example, a policy that restricts access to education needed to escape the poverty trap), and (2) though on the surface the injustice is done by an individual, it may also somehow be produced and perpetuated by the system. Fourth, when injustice is part of a system, an organized process of engaging the problem is required. This is because complex systems are hard to change but also because powerful interests may seek to maintain the status quo. And finally, the organized process of engaging the problem focuses on those who have the power to actually do something about it.

Theological Definitions

All of these definitions provide some semblance of truth. But in the big picture advocacy is seen in light of the character of God, because all reality begins and ends with God. Humans participate in God's reality through faithfulness to living (and representing) God's reign over the world. To explain this in biblical language, we image God. "God" may seem a strange place to begin talking about the political sphere, in part because Christians have perpetrated great evil through the centuries by the misguided use of God. But misuse should not imply retreat.

We state this up front because the topic of this book takes us into realms of competing ideologies and of power struggles (some of which come prepackaged with what could be called "sacred energy," where people claim holiness on their side) that polarize, conflate, and distort. Sadly, evangelicals also succumb to these temptations, lending triumphalistic, combative, or polemical energy to their advocacy work. But this is not God's way in the world.

By beginning with God, we seek to enter into an entirely different view of advocacy. As we will see in chapter 3, God's advocacy begins with the Trinity, spills over into creation, and embodies a different kind of power in the world predicated upon a different kind of kingship.[9] God graciously allows humans to participate in his rule through being "image bearers," which helps inform how we engage in the world (and thus how we do advocacy). The clearest picture for this is found in Jesus Christ, who ushers in the kingdom—that is, his rule in the world—through the Holy Spirit (our Advocate) and shares this rule with the Church[10] in order to bring all things in heaven and earth

---

9. Scot McKnight says it best: "The character of the king shapes the character of the kingdom." *Kingdom Conspiracy*, 131.

10. We refer to the church with a small "c" when speaking of local congregations and with a large "C" when referring to the universal Church (one, holy, catholic, and apostolic), spanning across time and geography.

under himself (Eph. 1:10). By talking thus, we are not implying that we want to reduce God's character (and thus his rule) to a singular concept such as advocacy, as if hijacking Scripture for our own purposes; on the contrary, we desire to understand human advocacy by looking at God's advocacy.

While the word "advocate" is not prominent in the Old Testament, biblical writers paint a multifaceted picture of advocacy taking place in the ancient Near East, whether humans stand as advocates before God, humans before other humans, God before humans, or God on behalf of humans. God advocates on behalf of humans in many kinds of situations, whether for Israel to return to the Lord in the face of idolatry; for the sake of the nations that surround Israel; or on behalf of the poor, aliens, widows, and orphans. As this implies, the entire Old Testament can be understood through the metaphor of God's advocacy as a means of "a rendering of truth and a version of reality that are urged over and against other renderings and versions."[11] God reorients Israel to himself for the sake of the nations and justice for the oppressed.

In the New Testament, the word sometimes translated "advocate" (*paraklētos*) comes into prominence, referring to one who speaks on behalf of another in court. John would use the term "advocate" to describe the work of the Holy Spirit (John 14:16, 26; 15:26; 16:7) and Jesus Christ (1 John 2:1), offering a picture of how the Persons of the Trinity testify on our behalf before the world. In the church, we embody these realities through the presence of the Holy Spirit within us. We advocate because we have the Advocate. Chapters 3, 4, and 5 will unpack these ideas with greater depth.

We believe these theological realities need to inform how we go about advocacy work. We advocate for others and learn and work with them to advocate for themselves (especially people trapped in poverty, widows, aliens, and orphans) because God advocates for us. And we do so by being faithful to the way that God advocates for the world: through service, love, weakness, and even suffering. Our faithfulness to God's nature, under the Lordship of Jesus Christ, *images* his character (and thus his rule) to the world as a means of witness. We believe this is done best through the local church (chap. 5).[12] And as we bear witness to God, we also grow in conformity to the image of the Son. Thus, if done well, advocacy becomes a means of discipleship.

11. Brueggemann, *Theology of the Old Testament*, xvii. Brueggemann even uses the word "advocacy" in the subtitle of his book: *Testimony, Dispute, Advocacy*.

12. As we will explain later, this does not mean that every church member needs to have specialized knowledge in political advocacy, but that only together as a local congregation (and working with other Christians) can we faithfully represent God before the world, inclusive of the political realm. Or as Scot McKnight explains, "What Christians want for the nation should first be a witnessed reality in their local church. Until that local church embodies that desire for the nation, the church's witness has no credibility." *Kingdom Conspiracy*, 102.

We choose to focus on problems that come under the purview of the government at the local, state, national, and international levels. We do not rule out the importance of organized action by civil society to negotiate social changes with, say, corporate leaders[13] or larger social groupings who can collectively decide to act or live differently. In fact, we would encourage these kinds of actions. However, this book focuses on engaging the state for the good of society because evangelicals so consistently shy away from doing so. Our approach demands a synthesis of theology, social theory, and practice, as will be seen in our chosen definition of advocacy in the rest of this book.

Our Definition, Focus, and Approach

In a thoroughly evangelical definition and approach to advocacy, we see good biblical and theological reasons for ensuring that the political connotations of the word "advocacy" are kept front and center. First, doing so allows us to point the spotlight on what most evangelical actors who are involved in charitable, compassionate, relief and development endeavors have overlooked: the political dimensions of the contexts in which they are operating, dimensions that almost always have a deep impact on structuring the situations of the poor and vulnerable. Second, it allows us to combine the notions of charity and justice,[14] both of which are essential to understanding

13. We are acutely aware that the private sector, too, for understandable reasons (Lindblom, *Politics and Markets*), holds significant power in society, far more than does "civil society." As a result, it has been the target of advocacy actions when it abuses its power. Methods have been used that range from the voluntaristic (boycotts, shareholder advocacy, and corporate social responsibility) to a variety of state regulation strategies. However, there is no escaping the fact that advocacy often is, and must be, directed toward policies that set the best possible context for business activities so as to enable and encourage entrepreneurial spirit, the provision of jobs, and the creation of wealth where business is fulfilling its ministry. We believe that the business world should legitimately engage in advocacy, and often it does, as when businesses hold governments accountable for laws, policies, and procedures. Therefore, much if not all of what we write in this book applies to that sector as well. Analyzing the role that business has played in advocacy efforts as well as the corresponding shifts specifically in the business sector that are required for it to engage in transformational advocacy are beyond the scope of this book. For two arguments that begin to explore that line of thinking, see Bronkema and Brown, "Business as Mission"; Bronkema, "Business as Ministry." See also Van Duzer, *Why Business Matters to God*, for a take on the role of business in society.

14. Justice is a foundational concept for this study. We argue that humans undertake justice because God is a God of justice (see Jer. 22:16); hence, we image his justice in the world. Scholars look at justice from many different vantage points, including rectifying, distributive, or what Nicholas Wolterstorff calls primary justice, which deals with the rights and dignity of others built upon the Judeo-Christian image-of-God concept. See Wolterstorff, *Justice: Rights and Wrongs*. However, digging deeply into the nature, role, and rhetoric of justice is beyond the scope of this book. Beyond Wolterstorff's two books on the subject, the other being *Justice in Love*, see also Keller for the lack of an agreed-upon definition of justice in our culture, and how

any engagement with the state and state power from a Christian perspective. Third, it helps point to essential aspects of God's character that have been ignored and that are particularly pertinent to a theology of advocacy, which is sorely missing in evangelical circles, and which we develop in chapter 3. God, as revealed in Scripture time and time again, advocates for all humanity through the Holy Spirit, the Advocate, and is an advocate for poor and vulnerable people. The God of the Bible is a God who yearns for justice for the poor in the face of unjust structures and systems. We advocate because God advocates for the world. Our advocacy must be faithful to God's advocacy for us to be faithful.

God is also a God of power, who created and structured power, giving it to individuals and institutions, including the state, with the intent of empowering all people so that they might flourish. The God of Israel set up structures of power through laws governing the economic, political, and social systems. Such laws were designed to give power and protection to all people, including the poor and vulnerable. The enforcement of these laws was a matter of justice and a matter of concern to society as a whole, especially given God's warnings about what would happen if power was used to oppress rather than empower.[15] This is seen perhaps most starkly in the inclusion of the Jubilee year in Israel's economic system, which was intended to guarantee all Israelites access to land.[16] Land is empowering; it enables people to create wealth and meet their own basic needs. The concern over how power might be misused is also seen in God's creation of the political system of laws that protected the vulnerable from exploitation and oppression by others.

Taking theological and political considerations into account, *we define evangelical transformational advocacy as intentional acts of witness by the body of Christ that hold people and institutions accountable for creating, implementing, and sustaining just and good policies and practices geared*

---

the word is at times used as a "trump card" to put an end to debates: *Generous Justice*, 149–50. See Benson and Heltzel's edited volume *Evangelicals and Empire* on "prophetic evangelicals" and how "justice within shalom" is at the center of their theology (p. 8); see Schlossberg, Samuel, and Sider, *Christianity and Economics*, for extensive considerations of the meaning and types of biblical justice and its application to issues of poverty; see Rundle's edited volume *Economic Justice in a Flat World* on economic justice from an evangelical perspective. For justice as discipleship and evangelism, see Eugene Cho, *Overrated*, 42–51. The words "social justice" no longer seem to be a taboo for many evangelicals, a process of evolution documented by Schmalzbauer, "Whose Social Justice?," with the concept of "the common good" also appearing more and more in the writing of evangelicals of all stripes: Sherman, *Kingdom Calling*; Skillen, *Good of Politics*; Gushee, *New Evangelical Manifesto*; Monsma, *Healing for a Broken World*; Volf, *Public Faith*.

15. See, for example, Jer. 22:13–17; 23:10–14; Amos 3:10; Mic. 3.
16. Lev. 25:8–54.

toward the flourishing of society. Transformational advocacy challenges in-justice and obstacles to human flourishing at whatever level it is practiced by humbly engaging with people who can address the wrong, trusting God's Spirit to change all those involved as well as the institutions themselves.

Our definition makes explicit the fact that we are directing this book toward everyday Christians, not Christians who are professionally engaged in public life. Christians in politics and government—those who formally participate in the process of legislation and policy creation—play a critical role in allowing faith to influence local, state, national, and international decisions and priorities. But other books and articles take these actors into account.[17] We instead consider the role of Christians who are part of civil society and the private sector as well as people who are part of local communities, organizations, businesses, and families.[18] We are also writing this book specifically as a call to "evangelical" Christians who have been uncertain, skeptical, or even cynical about approaching governments for God's good in the world. To that end, in what follows we look more closely at the word "evangelical" and introduce the spiritual dimensions of our approach.

What Is an Evangelical?

Given that our book is written about and for the evangelical community, we need to answer a surprisingly difficult question: what is an evangelical? We believe evangelicals are *those who feel compelled to share the "good news" or the "evangel" of Christ's death and resurrection, who hold a high regard for the Bible, and who believe the Holy Spirit is active in the world today.* To this empirical definition we add and wish to emphasize an aspirational clause: *and who are strongly committed to making disciples.* Although discipleship is not always part of evangelical life, it is certainly part of the evangelical ideal, and is always part of the equation in the healthiest and most mature evangelical

17. Some of the best recent books that describe evangelical Christians in politics include Lindsay, *Faith in the Halls of Power* and Swartz, *Moral Minority*. Books hoping to influence how evangelicals use political power include Grudem, *Politics according to the Bible* and Sider, *Just Politics*. There are also massive numbers of articles in publications like *Christianity Today*, the *New York Times*, and the *Washington Post* that have covered public servants who are also people of faith.

18. Good scholarship has also been done about approaches taken to politics by Christians who are not professional politicians. Those that are particularly helpful include Marsden, *Fundamentalism and American Culture*; Diamond, *Roads to Dominion*; Emerson and Smith, *Divided by Faith*; and Kellstedt et al., "Religious Voting Blocs." Although we draw on this literature, our goal is not to contribute to it. Rather, we are looking to improve evangelical advocacy, which is a particular form of evangelical public engagement.

communities. Thus we locate transformational advocacy within the practice of evangelical discipleship.[19]

Our definition of "evangelical" is consistent with other authoritative definitions. David Bebbington's oft-used definition of "evangelical" is centered on four principles: an emphasis on conversion or a need for change in one's life, an active bent toward sharing the gospel, a high regard for the Bible, and an emphasis on Christ's atoning work on the cross.[20] The National Association of Evangelicals approaches the term slightly differently in its statement of faith, which includes an affirmation of belief in the Trinity and the deity of Jesus Christ and a high view of Scripture, among other doctrinal points.[21] The Evangelical Alliance in the United Kingdom asserts that evangelicals are passionate about God, the Church, and the Bible. Evangelicals have committed to living their lives with Jesus, and they encourage others to do so as well.[22]

What makes our definition somewhat unique is our explicit inclusion of the practice of discipleship. We are convinced of the need to link discipleship with evangelism. We are also convinced of the need to integrate advocacy into the understanding of discipleship and to make it part of the daily and ongoing activities of the body of Christ. Discipleship means helping one another to grow in conformity to the image of God in Christ Jesus. We trust that this will happen *in the lives of others* as we give witness to the kingdom of God before the rulers and authorities and *within ourselves* as we sensitively, lovingly, prayerfully, and faithfully embody God's reign on earth. We argue that evangelicals should consider transformational advocacy as a ministry on par with any other, and one to which God may call people at any time and for any length of time. It is up to local faith communities, in naming the unique giftedness of each of their members, to prayerfully discern God's call to engage in this ministry. And we hope and pray that this combination will become part of the essence of evangelical identity.

Current State of Advocacy by Evangelicals: The Problems Defined

These are unpredictable times for evangelical engagement with the state. The global evangelical movement has grown robustly, allowing many evangelical

19. The evangelical movement has always been intentionally cross-denominational. It counts among its numbers Anglicans, Presbyterians, Methodists, and Pentecostals of various stripes, to name just a few of its different groups. Denominational and confessional traditions approach public life in different ways; we briefly explain these and how they impact our argument in the following chapter.

20. Bebbington, *Evangelicalism in Modern Britain.*

21. National Association of Evangelicals, "Statement of Faith."

22. Evangelical Alliance, "What Is an Evangelical?"

communities to become influential in their own national contexts. Political
opening and the need for responsible action has followed, but evangelicals have
responded erratically. In some countries they unite in support of dictators, while
in other contexts they join in protests for greater democracy and freedom. Still
other evangelicals, often in war-torn or oppressive societies, retreat from the
public sphere, hoping to simply survive by staying below the political radar.
Finally, there are opportunistic evangelicals; one Central American evangelical
leader, for example, earned the nickname "Pastor Bribe."[23] The type, nature,
motivation, and strategy of public engagement in the global evangelical community are remarkably diverse, and growing more so every day.

The American evangelical community exhibits a similar cacophony of approaches both to public engagement and, more directly to our interests, to
advocacy, even as the range of issues they have tackled has been quite limited.
Many have fought enthusiastically for the "moral issues" of their time, seeking
to influence policies on the Equal Rights Amendment, prayer in schools, abortion, and homosexual marriage, but they have not delved into other areas of
public debate. Other evangelicals have pursued a different list of issues, including the persecution of Christians abroad, sex trafficking, hunger, education,
the environment, and healthcare. A third group of US-based evangelicals has
rejected any involvement in politics. They are also concerned that advocacy
efforts find little to no basis in Scripture and are in any case often ineffective.
They thus conclude that their energies and resources would be more God
honoring if directed toward evangelism or other types of ministry.

Multiple issues undergird such dramatic differences within the evangelical
community. Some we celebrate and some strike us as neutral realities, neither of which we dwell on in this book. The first is political diversity, which
we celebrate. Evangelicals who live in different national contexts, who view
life from different economic strata, and who have different racial and ethnic
backgrounds are likely to have different political orientations and identify
different needs. We believe the eclectic nature of the global body of Christ is
a source of incredible energy and collective wisdom; we are grateful that the
Spirit has moved in ways that have touched such a wide variety of people.
The second issue is the organizational structure of evangelicalism. It is a
cross-denominational and cross-confessional faith community. It exists with
no central authority figure, and each congregation and even each individual
has tremendous latitude to engage or advocate according to his or her own
conscience. There are pros and cons to having a faith community organized
in such a way, and the conversation about this issue is fascinating. It is not,

23. Freston, *Evangelical Christianity*.

however, the conversation that concerns us here. We simply accept this as part of the evangelical reality and acknowledge that it does impact how evangelicals go about doing advocacy.

A third issue driving evangelical approaches to public engagement strikes us as more problematic and is the one that motivates the writing of this book. We believe that evangelicals have not developed a sufficient theological and theoretical base in which to ground their advocacy efforts. This lack is likely the reason for the skepticism about advocacy initiatives that is often found in evangelical circles.

The absence of evangelical theology and theory about advocacy is felt in at least four different intellectual spheres. First, evangelicals in the West have inherited an uneasy dichotomy between private beliefs and public facts. They have relegated God to the former and left the realms of politics, economics, and technology deprived of theological input. Second, evangelicals have not sufficiently explored how power is used and abused in society and how this relates to the notion of "powers and principalities" in Scripture. Third, evangelicals are just beginning to articulate the nature of the state in society and of the scriptural call to engage it as one of these powers and principalities,[24] and have little to say about the activity of advocacy itself. Finally, evangelicals have dwelled too little on the inherent character of God as an advocate. This element of God's character is revealed not only in the Scriptures but also in his creation of economic, political, social, and cultural systems, where he enables humanity to use power for good and to fight evil, thus working toward human flourishing and the restoration of creation.

The lack of reflection and academic rigor regarding advocacy has caused most evangelicals—those who practice advocacy and those who do not—to miss the proper relationship of faith to advocacy[25] and how the two are interconnected. We argue that advocacy's proper place is within the process of discipleship. The essence of God's character empowers humanity and makes clear that faithful discipleship includes engagement with the authorities by the body of Christ, especially when power is being used sinfully. We believe that engagement in advocacy is an issue of spiritual maturity, and that most of our leaders are not equipping congregations to respond faithfully to God's calling of the church itself or of church members to engage in this area of ministry.

Although this book is a call to advocacy, it is not a call to do more of what currently passes as advocacy among some evangelical activists. We believe

24. See the next chapter for more details on what has been done so far along these lines.
25. This has led to what Noll in *The Scandal of the Evangelical Mind* describes as a political engagement that is largely nonreflective populism and moral activism.

evangelicals must be more diligent in integrating crucial elements of Christian character into the process of advocacy. Evangelicals too often fail to exhibit demonstrable love for their opponents in the public sphere and can even forget to care for those with and for whom they are advocating. Evangelicals have too often allowed their political objectives to become primary, which not only tarnishes their witness but also causes them to be ineffective[26] and, frankly, limits the ability of the Spirit to move through their works.

Further, many (especially American) evangelicals have restricted themselves to a particular set of issues without good scriptural reasons for doing so. A complex web of cultural, ideological, racial, economic, and political legacies—two of which are the fundamentalist/modernist split and our current societal polarization—has lured evangelicals into being champions of certain sets of issues. The Bible does justify involvement in many such issues; what is less clear is the justification for ignoring issues that stretch beyond these commitments. Evangelicals on both sides of America's bitter and polarized political divide have imposed a type of self-censorship on issues not deemed important to their group. Worse, some demean the causes and aspirations of their fellow evangelicals who happen to be in the other camp. Ideological orientations have thus kept evangelicals from a more biblical process of carefully considering issues from all sides, testing all ideas faithfully and prayerfully rather than rejecting them out of hand, and holding on to what is good (1 Thess. 5:19–21). We find ourselves, therefore, in agreement with Karl Barth's argument that Christians need to say "No" to all ideologies, so that they can say "Yes" to healthy political engagement.[27] When evangelicals are guided more by ideology of any kind than by Scripture, their witness to the world is muted.

To this point, evangelical involvement in advocacy has been a source of disappointment to some very prominent evangelical commentators. As evangelical insider Dallas Willard puts it: "The heart of the question before us is quite simple: Why after 25–30 years of evangelical political involvement, with a high level of visibility and influence, is there little or no improvement in the ethical quality of American political discourse and practice?"[28] David Wells, another evangelical, places the blame squarely at the feet of evangelicals themselves. He argues that "evangelical political engagement is actually less about politics and more about moral engagement. However, this engagement is quite impossible if the needed character is not there. Until this kind of moral excellence, this deep integrity, is the first thing that comes to mind whenever

26. See Hunter, *To Change the World*.
27. See Barth, *Community, State, and Church*.
28. Willard, "Failure of Evangelical," 74.

the word *evangelical* is heard, evangelical political involvement is not going to amount to more than it does now."[29]

We agree with these authors, but argue that even their insights fall short of correcting the problem of poorly conceived and executed evangelical advocacy. It *would* be nice if evangelical advocacy had a positive effect and if evangelicals were seen as people of integrity. Yet we view three items missing from their analysis—and from contemporary evangelical advocacy—as equally or perhaps even more important: (1) a commitment to living and witnessing to the gospel as part and parcel of this ministry of political engagement and advocacy; (2) a willingness to let go of the idea of effectiveness and focus on faithfulness, leaving the results up to God; and (3) moving the role of the church as a body of believers to the center of advocacy efforts rather than putting individualistic or even parachurch efforts at the center as far as witness is concerned.

In the next chapter, we look at reasons that these problems exist in evangelical public action. This analysis will set the stage for both the theological and practical framework that we develop to attempt to overcome these drawbacks and set evangelical advocacy on a course that we think is more in keeping with what God would have us do, a course that we lay out in the last chapter. There we return to the three missing elements we have just outlined and suggest a way forward for evangelicals to embrace and undertake a truly transformational advocacy. But first we turn to a deeper analysis of how these problems came to be.

---

29. Wells, "Why Being Good Is So Political," 27. See also Danforth: "If Christianity is supposed to be a ministry of reconciliation, but has become, instead, a divisive force in American political life, something is terribly wrong, and we should correct it." Danforth, *Faith and Politics,* 14. See also Bandow: "Some politicians, many of whom claim to be Christians, friendly to the religious right and the evangelical left . . . have shown little of God's love, instead exhibiting self-righteousness, callousness, and extreme partisanship. . . . Politics is often a rough and dirty game, but if Christians really have been transformed by the Holy Spirit, we need to act differently." Bandow, *Beyond Good Intentions,* 229. Gregory Boyd, *Myth of a Christian Nation,* 11, gives another perspective on what is wrong, claiming that politics has become an idol for evangelicals: "I believe a significant segment of American evangelicalism is guilty of nationalistic and political idolatry." He does not argue, as Grudem claims he does (*Politics according to the Bible,* 39–43), that evangelicals should withdraw from politics, but rather that "citizens of God need to take care to distinguish between their core faith and values on the one hand and the *particular way* they politically express their faith and values on the other" (*Myth of a Christian Nation,* 15; emphasis original).

2

Transformational Advocacy

*Past Foundations, Current Challenges, and New Frontiers
for Evangelical Action*

> Bible-believing Protestants, approaching a third of the population,
> have been the sleeping giant of American foreign policy.
>
> Allen Hertzke, 2003

Evangelicals have been actively engaging the state, but how they have done so
and on what issues has varied based on the theological roots of their specific
confessional communities. This diversity is also connected to how the evangelical community's intellectual leaders think about poverty, an issue that tends to
influence many others and the reason for which we spend significant time on it
in this chapter, and to the primary strategies the broader evangelical community
uses to alleviate poverty. In both areas we highlight problems and offer solutions. To be truly transformational, evangelical advocacy must change radically.

Evangelical Approaches to Public Engagement

We have defined evangelicals as *those who feel compelled to share the "good
news" or the "evangel" of Christ's death and resurrection, who hold a high*

19

regard for the Bible, and who believe the Holy Spirit is active in the world today. To this empirical definition we added an aspirational clause: *and who are strongly committed to making disciples.* Although all evangelicals share these traits, the evangelical community is intentionally cross-denominational and cross-confessional. As such, it draws on traditions that have different approaches to the state and to advocacy. Four of the most influential traditions in this regard have been Calvinism, Pietism-Methodism-Holiness, Pentecostalism, and Anabaptism.[1] Each thinks about advocacy and the state differently.[2]

Confessional Influences on Evangelicalism's Public Engagement

CALVINISM

John Calvin (1509–64) did not believe that the church should have authority over government, but he did believe that the political sphere falls under Christ's

---

1. Lindsay, *Faith in the Halls of Power*, categorizes the Holiness movement with the Pentecostal movement. This is a defensible position, as a line runs from John Wesley's Aldersgate experience in 1738 to the Azusa Street Revivals in 1906, which were the birthplace of the classical Pentecostal denominations, and the Holiness movement is part of that overall history. But we see greater overlap between Holiness and Methodism, as the Holiness movement emerged from nineteenth-century Methodism and existed within it as well as alongside it for many decades. Both are antecedents to Pentecostalism.

2. We are indebted to the excellent volume edited by Sandra Joireman, *Church, State, and Citizen*, for many of the confessional descriptions in this section. A number of other works also explore different Christian traditions and their engagement with the state. See, for example, Fowler et al., *Religion and Politics in America*, who include five "themes" (Puritan, religious freedom, evangelical, populist, and individualist) and four major traditions: evangelical, mainline, African American, and Catholic. Black, *Beyond Left and Right*, breaks the traditions down into Catholic, Lutheran, Anabaptist, and Reformed, with a matrix of theological distinctives, view of government, and view of Christian political participation. And the edited volume by Kemeny, *Church, State, and Public Justice*, divides the traditions into Catholic, separation, pluralist, Anabaptist, and social justice.

Our sketches of these Christian traditions most certainly do not do justice to the variety and complexity of theological views and praxes, to the history of the development and changes in these views, and to the diversity of evangelical differences. In particular, missing in these general descriptions are the battles that were fought within denominations and traditions around having the state be the enforcer of Christian discipline, an approach known under the label of "Christendom" that some evangelicals still pine for (see Skillen, *Good of Politics*; Bartley, *Faith and Politics after Christendom*, for a detailed consideration of the implications of "post-Christendom"). For the differences in evangelical approaches to engaging the state, see Curry, "Biblical Politics and Foreign Policy," with his categories of Christian reconstructionism, politics of biblical justice, and kingdom politics; Gushee, *Future of Faith in American Politics*, with his categories of evangelical right, left, center, and black and Hispanic approaches. Our sketches nevertheless provide a helpful background to understanding evangelical behavior with regard to advocacy. Surfacing these evangelical origins will also make it easier for us to see the direction in which transformational advocacy could take contemporary evangelicalism and understand more fully what transformational advocacy should be about.

Lordship. Calvinist teaching in our time emphasizes that all of creation is part of God's handiwork.[3] Thus Calvinism sees the state as responsible for governing justly, with the acknowledgment that we live in a fallen world in which sin has warped the image of God both in the nonhuman creation and in human individuals and their institutions, including government.[4]

Based on this theology, followers of the Reformed tradition tend to believe that Christians should reach out and seek to reform all of society, that political communities should be seen in a positive light, that the state has a revelatory character just as does any other institution and sphere in society, and that particular forms of government are much less important than the fact that God has called us at all times and places to do justice, love mercy, and walk humbly. This tradition, therefore, strongly supports engagement with the state on policies of all kinds and believes in holding the state accountable to govern toward just outcomes.[5]

Wheaton College professor Vincent Bacote has written about how his own encounter with Reformed teachings helped him connect faith and political action. During his student days, Bacote discovered the writings of Abraham Kuyper (1837–1920), a renowned Dutch Reformed theologian. Bacote was particularly struck by Kuyper's explanation of common grace, the idea that Christians can bring God glory through their participation in many spheres of life. Kuyper's teachings set Bacote "on a path to an informed faith that would wed the lordship of Christ to my desire to affirm our embrace of the public aspects of life."[6] Previously worried that his evangelical faith limited political engagement, Bacote found in Kuyper a theological mandate to engage in the public sphere.

PIETISM, METHODISM, AND THE HOLINESS MOVEMENT

The Pietist, Methodist, and Holiness movements focus upon sanctification, grace, and the work of the Holy Spirit.[7] These movements sought to extend Christian experience beyond intellectual and rational explanations of Scripture without compromising those elements. John Wesley (1703–91), the father of Methodism, embodied this religious mix: he was an Oxford don who was influenced by the Pietist movement and also famously experienced a "strange

---

3. All of the various Presbyterian churches are part of the Calvinist tradition, as are the Christian Reformed Church and the many other Reformed denominations. Large swaths of Baptist and nondenominational churches also have a strong Calvinist orientation.

4. Skillen, "Reformed . . . And Always Reforming?," 2009.

5. Ibid.

6. Bacote, *Political Disciple*, 24.

7. In addition to the various strands of Methodism, these traditions include the Wesleyan denominations, the Salvation Army, the Church of the Nazarene, and others.

warming of the heart" at Aldersgate in 1738. He drew from a wide variety
of Christian traditions, including the Eastern Church,[8] Reformed thought,
Moravian pietism, and the Anglican Church, of which he was a member.

Wesley presents an intriguing case study for looking at institutional witness.
On the one hand, he was a child of his day. As a moderate Tory, Wesley held to
a form of monarchy (what Theodore Weber calls "constitutional monarchy")[9]
that saw God as appointing specific rulers who would then lead the people.
He therefore opposed the independence movement in the American colonies.
On the other hand, important seeds for a theology of advocacy lie within
Wesley's robust beliefs concerning the Trinity and sanctification. From his
trinitarianism sprang his view of the three aspects of the image of God in
humanity, which were natural, moral, and what he called "political" aspects.[10]
And sanctification, for Wesley, not only involved individuals but also extended
to communities.[11] What is more, Wesley advocated for the poor in eighteenth-
century England and fought against social, political, and economic forces
that fed the slave trade. Thus, according to some, Wesley's writings provide
a "trajectory" for institutional witness: "lobbying in the political sphere on
behalf of the poor, critiquing structural issues which exacerbate class distinc-
tions, and advocating for greater human liberty,"[12] even if he sometimes failed
to develop these fully.

In the United States, Pietism and Methodism were closely intertwined
with the first and second great awakenings of the eighteenth century, helping
Methodism to become the largest denomination in America by 1820. The
great awakenings remain high points in American spiritual history; they also
unleashed extraordinary energy for social activism.[13] Abolition of slavery was
just one of the causes that key leaders and the institutions supported, including
Charles Finney. Finney (1792–1875) was a leader in the Second Great Awaken-
ing, a Presbyterian minister, and the second president of Oberlin College, one
of the first colleges in the United States to admit African Americans.

Pietism and Methodism have not, however, generated a rich tradition of
advocacy. Indeed, the Methodist movement in early American history did

8. Maddox, *Responsible Grace.*

9. Weber, *Politics in the Order of Salvation.*

10. Wesley understood the image of God in three aspects: (1) the moral image, which pertains
to human mirroring of the love of God; (2) the natural image, which relates more to freedom,
understanding, and other human abilities; and (3) the political image, on which human stewardship of creation rests. These three facets of the image of God are laid out in Wesley's Sermon
45, "New Birth," which can be found in his complete works.

11. Along with Weber's work, see also Coates, *Politics Strangely Warmed.*

12. Coates, *Politics Strangely Warmed,* 21.

13. Dayton and Strong, *Rediscovering an Evangelical Heritage.*

not often replicate Wesley's interest in advocacy. This was partly due to its concentration in the south and along the frontier, away from the centers of power. By the middle of the nineteenth century, however, Methodism had moved into the public square for two reasons. The first was the temperance movement, for which Methodists advocated strongly.[14] The second may have been an interest in "respectability," an indication of their change in social status.[15] But these upwardly mobile Methodists did not advocate strongly for those remaining behind. In fact, lack of concern for the poor was one of several reasons for denominational splits that spawned the Free Methodist, Nazarene, and Wesleyan denominations.[16] These latter movements provided direct assistance for the poor but rarely included advocacy as part of their ministry strategies.

PENTECOSTALISM

Pentecostalism has also not habitually sought to engage the state due to an interesting mix of socioeconomic and theological reasons.[17] Pentecostals are now a massive and highly diverse group, but traditionally they were situated on the lower rungs of the socioeconomic ladder, and many remain so. Such Pentecostals seldom have social networks that extend into institutions that hold power in society, and their day-to-day lives feel far removed from places where decisions about how to organize society are made.[18] They have thus not felt empowered to engage the state. Doctrinally, early Pentecostals tended to view the state as an "institution of human presumption at best, or the enthronement of godlessness, immorality, greed, and violence at the worst."[19] Given these realities, it is no surprise that in some contexts Pentecostals continue to debate even whether or not they ought to vote.[20]

14. Norwood, *Story of American Methodism*.

15. Kisker, *Mainline or Methodist*.

16. Brian Yeich, email to Stephen Offutt, February 17, 2015.

17. Some of the most important denominations that fall into the "classical Pentecostal" category are the Assemblies of God, the Apostolic Faith Mission, the Four Square Gospel Church, and the Church of God (Cleveland, TN). "Neo-Pentecostalism" is the other primary category of Pentecostal denominations and independent churches. The Word of Faith movement along with many others populate this category.

18. Some of this may be changing as global Pentecostalism becomes mainstream and sources its adherents from all levels of society, such as we are beginning to see in Africa and other majority-world contexts.

19. Grant Wacker, *Heaven Below*, 217. Cf. Swindle, "Pentecostalism."

20. Offutt, *New Centers*, 101. In "Pentecostalism," Swindle also mentions that this was not always the case, pointing to Pentecostalism's Holiness roots, which taught societal perfection as well as individual perfection and, as a result, provided strong support for the various social movements of the day. But Swindle argues that the transition from the Holiness movement to

Pentecostals do, however, want to make a difference in the world. To do so, they emphasize the spiritual and eternal kingdom of heaven. They also employ spiritual weapons more often than "weapons of the world," such as politics. Such Pentecostals believe that spiritual weapons can bring conversions and that social reform will be effected when sufficient numbers of people change their behavior because they are now followers of Jesus.[21] And their belief in the indwelling of the Holy Spirit provides confidence (and power) for engaging in all facets of society. But today some Pentecostal communities (usually those that have moved up the social ladder) in Brazil and elsewhere do wield worldly weapons as well as spiritual ones.[22] Pentecostalism, which has always been a big tent, thus expresses multiple positions on this topic but, generally, American Pentecostals keep their distance from the state.

ANABAPTISM

Of the four traditions most important to the formation of evangelicalism, Anabaptism[23] is the most overt in its rejection of state involvement. Anabaptists see the Church as the primary allegiance for Christians. Government exists to create order, but earthly citizenship is subordinate to citizenship in heaven. For many in the Anabaptist tradition there is a prohibition against holding public office, enlisting in the military, or formally participating in law enforcement. These prohibitions stem from the strong pacifist position that is deeply embedded in Anabaptist doctrine. While there is no explicit church teaching on political action, these Anabaptist theologies make many adherents cautious about political engagement; many in this tradition even refuse to vote. Anabaptists are so intentional about fostering different concepts of public engagement that their colleges tend to have conflict-resolution programs rather than political science departments. Although the positive upshot of this is that Anabaptists are highly active around the world in issues of conflict, they frequently pursue these objectives independent of the state.[24] But none of this should suggest indifference. Their strong focus on ecclesiology, on in-

---

denominational Pentecostalism was accompanied by a shift in focus to individual rather than social perfectionism.

21. C. Smith, "Spirit and Democracy."

22. Freston, *Evangelical Christianity*.

23. The Anabaptist tradition includes Amish, Brethren, Brethren in Christ, Hutterite, and Mennonite churches, among others. Not all congregations in any of the Anabaptist denominations identify as evangelical, but Brethren in Christ (especially so) and Mennonite congregations are more likely to do so than others. See Guinness, "Golden Triangle of Freedom," 32, for clear declaration of the Anabaptist influence on evangelical approaches to the state, and his concern about the fusion of that influence with "leftist politics."

24. Joireman, "Anabaptists and the State."

tentionally living in the world as an alternative community, or polis, certainly suggests one kind of advocacy. Later in the book we will explore more of this through the writings of John Howard Yoder.

CONCLUSION ON THE FOUR INFLUENTIAL EVANGELICAL TRADITIONS

By dissecting evangelicalism into its component parts, we better understand its approaches to public engagement as well as evangelicalism's internal tensions. Three out of the four traditions that have done the most to shape contemporary evangelicalism have a history of *dis*engagement with the state. The Reformed community is the clear and rather powerful exception, as it holds its own within the evangelical community. Our brief survey of the different traditions reveals a wealth of theological resources by which evangelicals can undertake advocacy, including concepts of the Triune God, creation, the "political" image of God, the Lordship of Jesus Christ, sanctification, alternative communities living openly in the world, and the Holy Spirit. Hence, we believe that there are biblical principles not beholden to any confessional position that encourage this missing faithful witness through advocacy. Because of the historical trends toward disengagement, we recognize the challenges evangelicals face when they consider embracing advocacy as part of their DNA. We nevertheless believe it is necessary to face those challenges in order to be fully faithful to God's call.

ANGLICANISM, LUTHERANISM, AND ROMAN CATHOLICISM

We may be helped in this endeavor by other Christian traditions. Anglicans, Lutherans, and Catholics have not historically played strong roles in creating and shaping the evangelical movement in the United States. But they are also not completely absent from contemporary American evangelicalism; local congregations and parishes (and at least one Lutheran denomination) in each of these categories proclaim an evangelical identity. Their contribution arises partly from the influence of the likes of Augustine, Calvin, and Luther; more recently, theologians such as Barth, Bonhoeffer, and Newbigin, themselves influenced by those earlier thinkers, have actively taken up the task of articulating for Anglicans, Lutherans, and Catholics how the Lordship of Jesus Christ relates to politics or to other structures in society. In evangelical communities overseas, these traditions have played even more important roles.[25]

---

25. In fact, we in the West need to pay special attention to some of the theological positions coming out of the majority world, particularly as they offer a very different framework from the Enlightenment heritage for looking at the intersections between spiritual and material, sacred and secular, and private and public; and we must carefully observe the way(s) these positions and this framework inform engagement with societal structures.

The Anglicans in many African countries are just one case in point, seen for example in the life of Kenyan David Gitari.[26]

The Anglican Communion, thanks to its creation by the government of England in the sixteenth century, has always had a very close relationship with the state. Like Pentecostalism, Anglicanism is a broad and diverse community. But in its public engagement it tends to be influenced by two historical traditions: a high view of the state and an expectation that Christians should engage in politics because the state is a God-ordained entity charged with executing justice and providing peace and order. This means that the church as an institution is expected to engage political leaders as well as its own congregations on contemporary political issues, that politics is a legitimate and encouraged vocation for its members, and that the church tends to support the status quo of the state, often having difficulty speaking critically of it. The plurality of theological positions within Anglicanism, however, means that Anglicans are divided on specific issues and policies.[27]

The Lutheran tradition, coming out of the focus of Martin Luther (1483–1546) on the three core tenets of the Reformation—justification by faith alone, the Bible as the ultimate authority, and the priesthood of all believers—strongly supported the formation and existence of the modern nation-state. European Lutheranism, as opposed to the kind of Lutheranism that developed in the United States, became fully entrenched as the official religion of the state in some cases. Meanwhile, US Lutherans argued for limited government, even as they focused on developing their own educational and social service institutions. The legacy, however, of understanding themselves as citizens of a state with duties and responsibilities has led Lutherans in the United States to see the government as an ally in efforts to combat poverty through the institutions they have created.[28]

The Catholic approach to engagement with the state is quite different even as its level of engagement is similar to that of Anglicanism. Catholicism over its history has developed a strong, rich, and robust social doctrine grounded deeply in biblical theology that continues to grow through the writing of papal social encyclicals, beginning in 1891 with *Rerum Novarum*. These papal writings provide the intellectual and theological frameworks for a communal vision of politics geared toward the common good. Although Rome had serious reservations as the nation-state system began to take shape (and for centuries afterward), Catholics today see the state as a natural and necessary element of society. Catholic theology still emphasizes a global vision of

26. See Gitari and Knighton, *Religion and Politics in Kenya*; Gitari, "You Are in the World," 214–31.

27. Anderson, "Anglican Tradition."

28. Lomperis, "Lutheranism and Politics."

solidarity that eschews nationalistic approaches. Within this framework, the Church has strongly advocated for the poor and oppressed. It consistently issues "prophetic" pronouncements that criticize the state and its policies concerning issues of poverty, oppression, and other social matters, and it presses the state as well as Catholic politicians to pass and enforce legislation and policies guided by the Church's teaching on social issues.[29]

The influence of these three traditions on evangelicalism complicates the perception of evangelicalism as largely the result of four main traditions. But numerically and with respect to level of influence, that general picture still holds. Like those four traditions, Anglicanism, Lutheranism, and Catholicism are also riven with internal controversies and diversities of opinion. However, unlike three of the four main evangelical groups in the United States, all three of these Christian traditions do encourage public engagement in some important ways.

Contemporary Trends in Evangelical Public Engagement

The previous section illustrates the extent of evangelicalism's pan-confessional nature—the way it cuts across denominations and traditions—and the implications this has for its approach to public engagement. And yet, in spite of evangelicalism's diversity, there is a recognizable evangelical community that is knit together by a common set of beliefs and values, interlocking social networks, and behavioral tendencies, all of which create what we may refer to as "family resemblances." Indeed, many evangelicals today are unaware which major confessional stream or tradition most influences their faith perspective. Many individuals and congregations have in fact cobbled together beliefs and practices that draw from multiple traditions. It is thus possible to talk about a shared evangelical history, colored as it is by its various traditions, in which consistent patterns of public engagement and attitudes toward the state have emerged. In this section, we discuss the current trends in evangelical public engagement.

PRINCIPLES OF EVANGELICAL PUBLIC ENGAGEMENT

We begin with four underlying principles that shape evangelical public engagement.[30] First and perhaps most important, evangelicals instinctively seek to protect freedoms. Foremost among these is religious freedom, and particularly the freedom to practice evangelism.[31] A state that fails to protect

---

29. Shelledy, "Catholic Tradition and the State."

30. For the remainder of this chapter, we will locate this discussion within a predominantly Western and specifically American viewpoint.

31. Shah, "For the Sake of Conscience"; Grudem, *Politics according to the Bible*; and Sider, *Just Politics*, all make this point.

freedoms generally, and especially religious freedom, is one that is most likely to generate acts of civil disobedience by evangelicals.

Second, evangelicals tend to engage the state when they hope government will support and promote institutions and values that they see as foundational to a biblically based society. These include the institution of the family and the value of recognizing God's sovereignty as laid forth in Scripture.

Third, evangelicals tend to have a deep suspicion of the state, seeing it as a fallen institution that tends toward corruption. Evangelicals—at least some— fear that states always act to increase their own power, and their pursuit of power usually decreases the freedom of citizens.

Fourth, as alluded to earlier, evangelicals have rarely reflected biblically and theologically on the role of the state in God's reconciling plan.[32] As a consequence, some evangelicals seem genuinely confused about the value of engaging with the state, and at times, though not always, their opposition to using or involving the state to accomplish social ends other than those cited above seems to be based more on reflexive ideology than on careful and deep research.[33]

Evangelical Priorities in Advocacy

These crosscutting motivations have helped to limit American evangelical public engagement in its scope. The limited collection of issues evangelicals take up is unique among other religious communities and organizations. More common in the religiously diverse American environment is for religious

32. This has begun to change in the last decade and a half, during which at least four books have been written that develop an evangelical theology of engagement with the state and then apply that theology to particular issues. Grudem, *Politics according to the Bible*, applies his theology to a plethora of issues under the categories of protection of life, marriage, the family, economics, the environment, national defense, foreign policy, freedom of speech, freedom of religion, and special groups; Sider, *Just Politics*, to human rights, democracy, capitalism, the sanctity of human life, marriage and family, religious freedom, peacemaking, just war, violence, creation care, and international affairs; Monsma, *Healing for a Broken World*, to issues of church and state, life, poverty, creation, human rights, disease and poverty in Africa, and war and terrorism; Skillen, *Good of Politics*, to citizenship, family, marriage, education, economics, environment, and world politics; and Campolo, *Red Letter Christians*, to the environment, war, Palestine, gay rights, gun control, education, abortion, immigration, crime, federal budget, minimum wage, national debt, government wastefulness, political lobbyists, and campaign finance. All of these theologies at least touch on the issue of justice, and many of them make it central to their understanding.

33. We hope that this statement is not misunderstood. We share what we believe to be a healthy suspicion of the state and of giving the state any excuse to increase its mandate and scope of action in society. However, we do believe that this justified suspicion at times becomes an excuse for not carefully considering and weighing the pros, cons, and details of proposed state intervention, especially where there is injustice. Of course, we hold that the same happens for those who tend to default to state intervention as being the solution.

communities to engage the state on both domestic and foreign policy in a breathtaking array of issues, marshaling resources, studies, and people to push the state toward passing and enforcing legislation that they are convinced will significantly improve people's lives in the ways that God wishes to see them improved.

"Mainline" Christian communities provide good points of comparison. With some exceptions, especially organizations like Evangelicals for Social Action (ESA), evangelicals have concentrated the large majority of their advocacy efforts on clearly defined groups of issues. The difference between the two groups can be seen in table 1, where the shaded issues are the ones that tend to be tackled by evangelicals within the larger subset of those tackled by mainline Christians.

Table 1: Categorization of Advocacy Issues

Shaded: Issues Tackled by Evangelicals			Unshaded: Issues Tackled by "Mainline" Christians		
Economic (Resources)	**Environmental** (Nature)	**Social/Civil** (Freedoms)	**Judicial** (Law Enforcement)	**Security** (Safety)	**Governance** (Legislative Processes)
Labor Rights	Biodiversity	Indigenous Rights	Incarceration	Wars	Corruption
Land Rights	Pollution	Gun Control	Immigration	Training of Police Forces (School of the Americas)	Term Limits
Trade Agreements	Endangered Species	Abortion	Prison Reform		
Health	Climate Change	Homosexuality	Police Brutality		
Education		Prayer in Schools	Victim's Rights	Militarization	
Poverty		Trafficking	Death Penalty		
Hunger		Slavery			
Living Wage		Persecution of Christians			
Homelessness		Right to Hire/ Serve Based on Faith			
Mental Health		Equal Use of Campus Facilities			
HIV/AIDS					
Corporate Social Responsibility					
Balanced Budget					
Bailouts					
Globalization					
Debt Relief					

This table was compiled based on the authors' experiences and knowledge of advocacy by Christian actors across the board, not on any rigorous research. For quick links to mainline Christian involvement in all of the other issues, a good place to start is with the website of the National Council of Churches of Christ or of the World Council of Churches, or any of the mainline denominational websites. As stated below, these different categories are intimately related with one another, and issues can and do crosscut several categories at times.

Clearly, evangelical advocacy is concentrated on the social/civil category, composed of particular kinds of rights, freedoms, and behaviors that have historically been important to evangelicals. Recently, however, the number of evangelicals engaging issues in other categories has risen, and involvement in such areas as HIV/AIDS and human trafficking has increased debate within the evangelical community over how to understand and tackle such issues. In providing this list, we are not suggesting that evangelicals do not care about or have not acted on issues in other categories. Rather, we claim that evangelicals have been slow to use advocacy in those other categories as a way of solving the problems that they confront. In this respect, evangelicals have been quite different from Christians of other stripes.

Without fail, all Christian traditions that have engaged with the state have engaged the policies in the social/civil category, particularly the policies having to do with freedoms and with rights. This is to be expected, since this category is the arena where the moral character of these policies is the most obvious. Moreover, it is the arena in which it is easiest to apply theology, since it is here that we engage with the fundamental nature of human beings and their beliefs and behaviors. This also helps us understand why Christians would differ significantly on these moral issues. Different doctrines and theologies lead people to press the state to encourage, discourage, or even disallow different kinds of behaviors, beliefs, and practices. Since evangelicals have been at the forefront of these advocacy battles, from struggling against slavery, to advocating for Christians who are being persecuted, to the defense of Christian groups that have been prohibited from holding meetings on college campuses, this arena of advocacy has been, and will always be, a hotbed of activity for Christians, in which they will both unite and disagree, depending on the particular issue at hand.

However, there seems to be a consensus among evangelicals that the most important freedom that the state must guarantee is the freedom of religion, since it is seen as being so consonant with what God wants for the sharing of the gospel.[34] In some instances, this view is premised on a logic that views the state as an extension of the Church in terms of God's work in the world; some confessional stances within evangelicalism are more likely to take this position than others.

Evangelicals largely limit themselves to the social and civil issues, while most other Christian traditions are more expansive in their advocacy interests. What

---

34. Grudem, *Politics according to the Bible*, and Sider, *Just Politics*, agree completely on this, and both make the point independently. David Bebbington argues that even early evangelical efforts aimed against slavery were motivated in part by the concern to undertake missionary activity in the Caribbean; see "Evangelicals, Theology and Social Transformation," 5.

makes evangelicals different from other Christians in this regard? To a large degree, the other categories contain policies in which evangelicals perceive that the exercise of state power is not open to challenge, or in which the exercise of state power and state intervention to bring about change is not something that has historically been widely advocated for by any sector of the population (economic and environmental, for example).[35] Because evangelicals have always had a theology that was more suspicious of the state in terms of its involvement in society, assigning the state a very limited role, they have been reluctant to advocate for issues in these other categories.

Moreover, evangelical engagement with and analysis on economic and environmental issues were severely limited by the fundamentalist/modernist split in the early 1900s. What had been a healthy integration of evangelism and social outreach broke apart. The split led evangelicals to focus more on Jesus's divinity than on his humanity; truncated their interest in doctrines of creation, providence, and the new creation; and limited theological discussion over the way that power was structured and used by a host of actors in society in economic, environmental, judicial, security, and governance areas. Consequently, evangelical theology has often neglected the implications that an acceptance of such power structures might have for a theology of the nature and role of the state vis-à-vis those structures.[36]

The fundamentalist/modernist split was exacerbated by the polarization of the US political scene both on domestic and international issues, especially those dealing with the Cold War and the fear of communism. Evangelicals seldom questioned US foreign policy and were quick to label and dismiss any analyses of poverty, economics, security, and governance that considered the way that power was used and abused as "Marxist," including those provided by more progressive Christians. What is interesting is that such analyses were proffered *while* evangelicals demonstrated a veritable outpouring of concern for the poor, starting and sustaining a multitude of ministries both domestically and overseas.

When the cold war ended, the ideological concerns that accompanied it faded. But there emerged new challenges to a robust evangelical advocacy for the poor. Politically, many evangelicals were captured by limited-issue, socially focused party politics. These revolved around abortion, school prayer, gender rights, and homosexuality. The evangelical position in the American political

---

35. It is important to remember that Keynes's writings did not appear until the late 1930s. Environmental issues have emerged even more recently.

36. It is beyond the scope of this book to review the details of this split, which has been well documented elsewhere. See, for example, T. Smith, *Revivalism and Social Reform*; Dayton and Strong, *Rediscovering an Evangelical Heritage*.

context reinforced their tendency to set aside other issues. Questions of "poverty" and "justice" involved in the categories of economic, judicial, security, and governance policies fell outside the realms of evangelical thought, theology, and praxis. Evangelicals like Ron Sider, Tony Campolo, René Padilla, Orlando Costas, Vinay Samuel, Chris Sugden, and Nicholas Wolterstorff began to urge evangelicals in the 1970s to seriously consider the many scriptural teachings that apply to these areas; it would take some time before their messages gained traction in the larger evangelical community.[37]

Since that time, evangelicals have made strides in recovering an ability to read and act on Scripture in its totality—in a holistic way—especially as it pertains to issues of poverty and social outreach. Nevertheless, evangelical understandings and approaches to poverty still have weak points, which in turn constrain their approaches to advocacy. In what follows, we look first at the limits of the evangelical theory on poverty, most developed under what is called the "transformation" paradigm, and then at the problems with evangelical praxis on poverty that stem both from that theory and from the struggle on how to incorporate the spiritual element into social outreach.

The Evangelical Approach to Poverty

How poverty is understood can help to determine the actions deemed appropriate to address it. Partly as a result of the reasons outlined above, evangelical thinking and analysis about poverty have been confused: "Evangelicals have not achieved consensus either on the nature and causes of poverty or on what strategies are most likely to eradicate it. . . . Indeed, the analysis of global poverty is often pursued from a simplistic and moralistic perspective, and frequently is based on misinformation and unfounded beliefs."[38] Such a critique reflects the fact that evangelical colleges, seminaries, and universities have been motivated to reach out to the poor around the world, but they have done very little in the way of rigorous intellectual and research-based studies of poverty.

This confusion has two root causes. The first is what might be called the "depoliticization" of the causes of poverty by not considering causes that come from the way power is structured and used. Second, the definitions of poverty itself tend to be conflated with poverty's causes in evangelical thinking. In what follows, we trace the history and evolution of evangelical theory on poverty, an evolution of what many authors have referred to as

37. See Tizon, *Transformation after Lausanne*.
38. Amstutz, *Evangelicals and American Foreign Policy*, 97.

the "transformation" paradigm, paying special attention to these two draw-backs, even as we highlight the important contributions this paradigm has made.

Evangelicalism and Poverty: An Intellectual History

The transformation paradigm provides the dominant, and perhaps only, distinctively and fully orbed evangelical theory of poverty. This approach emerged from a dialogue sustained by strategically placed members of the global evangelical community over the course of several decades. René Padilla, Ron Sider, Wayne Bragg, and others were motivated by the challenge to awaken the social conscience of evangelicals while staying true to evangelical orthodoxy. Al Tizon outlines the history of these efforts, and shows that an important early moment occurred at the first Lausanne Congress on World Evangelization in 1974. Leaders with this perspective successfully lobbied the congress to include article 5 in the Lausanne Covenant, which outlines the biblical call to Christian social responsibility and incorporates such concerns into the global identity of the evangelical movement.[39]

The dialogue that was led by Padilla, Sider, and others continued through the 1970s, 1980s, and 1990s, bolstered by a strategically important conference held by the World Evangelical Fellowship at Wheaton College in 1983. Delegates from fifty-nine countries focused much of their energy on articulating a theology of evangelical social engagement. The participants reached an important consensus that they should rally around the idea of transformation. Ideas and theories were further refined and crystallized in the years after the conference. It was not until the 1990s that several publications codified the transformation paradigm. Authors of these publications included Vinay Samuel, Chris Sugden, David Bosch, and others, but the issue of poverty is most completely defined in Bryant Myers's *Walking with the Poor*,[40] which also draws heavily on Jayakumar Christian's work.[41]

39. Tizon, *Transformation after Lausanne.*
40. Myers, *Walking with the Poor*, 57–90.
41. See Christian, *Re-Thinking Christian Response to the Poor*; Christian, *God of the Empty-Handed*. There were some slight differences in this movement in terms of institutionalization and even terminology. Internationally, led primarily by evangelical leaders from the South, this movement was institutionalized in INFEMIT, and in the journal *Transformation*, published by the Oxford Center of Mission Studies. Again, see Tizon, *Transformation after Lausanne*, for a history of both. However, the term "integral mission," pioneered and advanced by René Padilla of the Kairos Center in Latin America, has also been in the mix and more recently has been adopted by some who follow the transformation paradigm, including the Accord and Micah networks, which bring together many evangelical relief and development agencies.

Myers defines poverty relationally.[42] He states that poverty, quite simply, is made up of broken relationships. Myers highlights four categories of broken or fractured relationships: those that exist between an individual and God, an individual and other humans, an individual and himself or herself, and an individual and the rest of God's creation. By making relationships the essence of poverty, Myers asserts that things that are often associated with poverty—low levels of income, high indexes of infant mortality, and low educational attainment, among others—are either part and parcel of broken relationships or a consequence of broken relationships.

Myers was shaped by and contributed to evangelical theory about transformation, but he was also influenced in how he thought about poverty by mainstream poverty studies.[43] Robert Chambers, for example, was influential in considering broken relationships to be an essential element of poverty and used the term "deprivation trap" to describe a web of mutually enforcing disadvantages, including isolation, vulnerability, powerlessness, and material poverty. He used the household as his unit of analysis.[44] Following Chambers, John Friedman employed a sophisticated schema suggesting that poverty is the result of lack of access to social power and political participation.[45] Ravi Jayakaran broadened the field still further by focusing on the lack of freedom to grow, with limitations in mental, physical, social, and spiritual areas.[46] Myers incorporated all of these ideas and argued that the poor are poor because their relationships are oppressive at every level.[47]

Myers's analysis contributes significantly to helping us see the importance of taking into account the relational aspects of poverty and development. However, at times his analysis confuses the definition and causes of poverty in unhelpful ways and lacks a balance in identifying the latter. First, Myers—and other authors writing under this paradigm, including, most notably, Corbett and Fikkert[48]—defined poverty both as the state of relationships themselves and as a condition caused by the state of those relationships. Not only does this go against the biblical definition of poverty, which repeatedly focuses on exclusively economic and material concerns, it also expands the definition of poverty to the point where it is close to meaningless and at times counterproductive. Some who are materially rich have a "poverty of relationships" with

42. Myers, *Walking with the Poor.*
43. Reynolds and Offutt, "Global Poverty and Evangelical Action."
44. Chambers, *Rural Development.*
45. Friedmann, *Empowerment.*
46. Jayakaran, *Holistic World View Analysis.*
47. Myers, *Walking with the Poor.*
48. Corbett and Fikkert, *When Helping Hurts.*

others, God, creation, and themselves, and in no way are they considered "poor" by any definition in current use. Moreover, those who are poor often have excellent relationships with God, others, and themselves. This kind of definition feeds the temptation of evangelicals (and many others) to view the poor as spiritually and relationally inferior, which is ironically the very thing that some of those authors warn against.

There are more straightforward ways to think about poverty that allow greater precision in discerning the role that relationships and other variables, such as structures and systems of power, play in causing it. Among the most common definitions is low income. The World Bank estimates that globally, 2.2 billion people live on less than two dollars a day, and that a remarkable 5.15 billion people live on less than ten dollars a day.[49] In the United States, a family of four qualifies as poor if its income is less than $23,850 a year, according to the US Department of Health and Human Services.[50] Such statistics reveal the pervasive nature of poverty, hint at the massive nature of global inequality, and show just how much money families need to make ends meet.

Exclusive focus on income to define poverty, though, also has drawbacks. Recently, the World Bank has created a Living Standards Measurement Study that analyzes the basic living standards of the poor, as well as a Poverty Analysis Toolkit. The United Nations Development Program (UNDP) uses indexes like the Human Poverty Index (HPI) and the Multidimensional Poverty Index (MPI). Such metrics are built on indicators that measure health, education, and basic living conditions such as access to potable water and quality of housing structures. All of these indicators look at whether or not people have access to sufficient material goods, financial or otherwise, to live with dignity and well-being. These definitions are kept separate from both the causes and effects of poverty in order to see more clearly both these causes and effects and the relationships between them; in fact, many times the causes and effects of poverty are circular, each exacerbating the other and leading to deeper poverty. Such dynamics cannot be caught by a definition of poverty that focuses broadly and in an unfocused way on poverty as relational deficit.

A second weakness of the relational approach is that it prioritizes a particular source of poverty's causes, what social scientists sometimes call "microstructures" of society. That is, Myers looks at how an individual is impacted by people and things that are in direct contact with that individual. But Myers's approach does not sufficiently take into account the "macrostructures" of

49. World Bank, "Poverty Overview."
50. US Department of Health and Human Services, "2014 Poverty Guidelines."

society, or things like nation-states and the international political economy.[51] Macrostructures' impacts on individuals are sometimes more difficult to observe, but nonetheless powerfully impact an individual's well-being. Myers draws upon scholars who do incorporate the larger structures, but his own articulation of relational poverty has a more individualistic emphasis (for example, the household is replaced by the individual as the unit of analysis). His finding that the causes of poverty lie in the multiplicity and complexity of relationships is still valuable. We are simply arguing that it does not capture the whole story.

A fuller picture would demonstrate the ways that micro- and macrostructures and the relationships contained in each often overlap, reinforcing their impoverishing elements. Such overlap creates traps for the poor, as Janice Perlman explained in her study of Brazil's famous favelas, or shanty towns.[52] Relationships that are forged among favela dwellers often keep them in favelas, meaning that good relationships with the wrong people can actually be impoverishing. Perlman also found that legality, or the formal relationship a favela has with the state, matters: the closer a community is to legality, the more likely that its residents will be treated as people who can act on their own behalf, which matters a lot as they seek to escape poverty. Perlman's findings affect relational explanations of poverty and further demonstrate the importance of taking macro consequences into account.[53]

The transformation paradigm's clouded definition of poverty and its lack of attention to macro causes of poverty contribute to some of the dynamics of evangelical advocacy that were outlined in the first chapter. Namely, they lead to the "depoliticization" of evangelical development praxis and analysis. This in turn diminishes the perceived importance of advocacy as an evangelical calling, an example of which is on display in Corbett and Fikkert's widely read book, *When Helping Hurts*. Corbett and Fikkert give a nod to "systems" that make it difficult for the poor to escape their poverty,[54] but they

51. The absence of structural analysis in Myers's work does not indicate that structural analysis was missing at the Wheaton '83 conference. Certain leaders such as Wayne Bragg and Ron Sider considered the concept of transformation to include full-blown macrostructural change. This was true both at the conference and in the work of these leaders before the conference. Sider's *Rich Christians in an Age of Hunger*, published in 1977, included two whole chapters on the structural causes of poverty and the necessity of political changes to correct things. These views and discussions spilled into mainstream evangelical discussions; *Christianity Today* ran an article on the topic in 1978.

52. Perlman, *Favela*.

53. For a recent evangelical work that does examine the micro and macro structures as they relate to mission and economics, see Cheong and Meneses, *Christian Mission and Economic Systems*.

54. Corbett and Fikkert, *When Helping Hurts*, 44–48.

shy away from analyzing the dimensions of power in these systems, and they do not include advocacy in the three action categories they detail and analyze to alleviate poverty: relief, rehabilitation, and development. Similarly, when Bryant Myers produced an otherwise excellent revised and expanded edition of *Walking with the Poor*, he also gave only a perfunctory nod to advocacy. He does expand his comments on advocacy from a page and a half in the first edition to scattered mentions on thirteen different pages in the later work. But clearly, the most widely read evangelical authors in the field continue to view advocacy as ancillary to the work of poverty alleviation.

In summary, the transformation paradigm has influenced evangelical involvement in poverty issues in many powerful and positive ways, generating constructive actions by parties ranging from churches to relief and development organizations, mission agencies, and parachurch networks. Adherents of this paradigm are to be commended also for discerning the importance of right relationships with God, with other persons, and with the environment as being essential for human flourishing.

Unfortunately, evangelicals' focus on the relational aspects of poverty—to the detriment of the variable of power as a cause of poverty—has meant that when they come up against those structures of power in practice that limit what relief, rehabilitation, and development can do, they are uncertain about whether to proceed, and if so, how, because they lack the tools to diagnose these structures of institutionalized power and how they operate. To help the poor effectively in contexts in which power structures are a predominant variable, advocates need to engage in a "differentiated diagnosis"[55]—that is, analyze each context and situation of poverty with the understanding that the causes of poverty can and do vary significantly between contexts, in this case in terms of the variable of power. After having diagnosed the situation, they must design responses grounded in the diagnosis. Evangelicals' inability to produce such analyses and corresponding action plans has severely hampered their responses to poverty. Moreover, evangelical practice in the integration of the spiritual into the social has also suffered from some weaknesses.

Practical Evangelical Approaches to Poverty

When evangelicals move from thinking about poverty to developing strategies to alleviate poverty, they use three main approaches: evangelism, development, and relief (as outlined clearly by Corbett and Fikkert),[56] but not advocacy. In

55. This argument is similar to one advanced at the national economic level by Jeffrey Sachs in chap. 4 of his *The End of Poverty: Economic Possibilities for Our Time*.
56. Ibid., 52.

what follows, we lay aside relief, given that charity is an almost universal and noncontroversial aspect of evangelical engagement, and focus on evangelism and development since they are more complicated in terms of the implications they have for how to move toward evangelical advocacy. We first briefly review how evangelicals continue to see evangelism as a cornerstone of a sound plan for alleviating poverty even as they move to talk more in terms of "making disciples" than of "making converts"; then we analyze the practice of development by evangelicals and the barriers they have encountered, and still encounter, in moving into the advocacy arena based on development practice.

EVANGELISM

Evangelicals have historically demonstrated a desire and mandate to transform society. How do they go about this kind of work? Consistent with their name, evangelicals approach the work primarily by sharing the good news of Jesus Christ, the *evangel*, with others. In evangelicals' perception, a relationship with the Trinity, made universally accessible through Christ's redemptive work on the cross, has the greatest potential for social change. They stage Billy Graham–style crusades, practice lifestyle evangelism,[57] do friendship evangelism,[58] or walk through relevant Scriptures with those who are not followers of Christ both because of the eternal implications that the evangel carries *and* because of its tremendous power to change lives in the here and now. Indeed, many evangelicals believe that any strategy geared to solving poverty or other social ills has transformational power only if it allows evangelicals to bear witness to the name of Christ.

Evangelicals believe that a person who has an encounter with Christ is freed from sinful and destructive activities. In more dramatic situations this means leaving gang life, stopping involvement in violent crime, seeking healing from drug or alcohol abuse and addiction, and leaving extramarital affairs behind. Even those not involved in such activities will experience a fundamental change in how they spend their time, who their friends are, and what motivates them. Believers should be people of deeper character and greater integrity. They should be more attentive to their spouses and children, and more interested in helping the widow and the orphan. The essence of these changes is captured in a quote from a Virginia-based evangelical pastor: "I believe that the power of the Gospel is expressed in the life of a man or a woman, that when we convert to the Lord our habits change, our interests change, our way of doing things changes and believe it or not or whether you want it or not things are

57. Aldrich, *Lifestyle Evangelism*.
58. Stebbins, *Friendship Evangelism*.

going to change in our life in the way we do business, in the way we treat our children."[59] This pastor, and many like him, do not just believe in the power of conversion; they have seen it play out in the lives of their congregants.

Social scientists agree that profound social changes do occur through religious conversion. David Martin, for example, a preeminent scholar of global Pentecostalism, calls the Pentecostal movement a cultural revolution.[60] Martin states that when people convert, "the inner transformation is that of honest dealing, trustworthiness, peaceableness, hard work, independence, self-help, mutual assistance, and the ability to be articulate and fluent in the presence of others."[61] Other scholars agree that a more productive work ethic can accompany conversion, which in turn can lift people out of abject poverty.[62] Still others have noted the way that evangelicals prohibit vices that drain personal resources,[63] and the way that evangelicalism can help the poor imagine and then attain a better life.[64] People can also leave oppressive relationships behind when they newly enter into a local congregation. Their new congregational community is likely to be characterized by more egalitarian relationships and may even open up empowering, church-based transnational and transcultural relationships.[65] Such social-scientific findings (much other scholarship supports the trend of those cited here) show the cultural power wrought by evangelism and its real potential for poverty alleviation.

More and more, however, many evangelicals have recognized that too often evangelism has overemphasized the moment of conversion and underemphasized the ensuing discipleship process, with significant negative consequences. Discouraged with the lack of fruit from those evangelized and suspicious that only a fraction of those evangelized and professing Christ were actually "born-again,"[66] they have increasingly emphasized discipleship, or helping people become more mature in Christ, more and more like him in their thinking and behavior.[67] They have also increasingly recognized that the Bible mandates integrating the social function with the discipleship function, and that the Spirit integrates the two in evangelism itself.[68] By focusing on discipleship,

59. Interview with Stephen Offutt, June 12, 2006.
60. See D. Martin, *Tongues of Fire*; D. Martin, *Pentecostalism*.
61. D. Martin, *Pentecostalism*, 73.
62. Berger, *Culture of Entrepreneurship*.
63. Brusco, "Colombian Evangelicalism."
64. Smilde, *Reason to Believe*.
65. See Brenneman, *Homies and Hermanos*; Brusco, "Colombian Evangelicalism"; D. Martin, *Tongues of Fire*; Offutt, "Role of Short-Term Mission Teams."
66. Wommack, "Discipleship versus Evangelism."
67. "Make Disciples, Not Just Converts."
68. Suttle, *Evangelical Social Gospel?*

evangelicals can move toward effective advocacy by building on their traditional exclusive focus on evangelism as the key to social transformation, because the traditional focus already understood that it is spiritual growth, or the maturation of the Christian character of the individual person, that is at the root of sustainable change in societies.

EVANGELICAL DEVELOPMENT IN PRACTICE: SPIRITUAL INTEGRATION FOR OVERALL TRANSFORMATION

Probably only a minority of evangelicals today preach evangelism as the one and only solution to social change. Most other evangelicals acknowledge that concrete "good works" in the form of development are also part of Christ's mandate and also increase the well-being of societies. In so acknowledging, evangelicals follow in the historical footsteps of evangelical missionaries who promptly became engaged in activities far beyond evangelism in the societies in which they served. These conversionary Protestants,[69] on an "errand to the world,"[70] "were a crucial catalyst initiating the development and spread of religious liberty, mass education, mass printing, newspapers, voluntary organizations, most major colonial reforms, and the codification of legal protections for nonwhites in the nineteenth and early twentieth centuries."[71] Research has shown that liberal democracies are more likely to appear in parts of the world that missionaries populated than in places where they did not,[72] and for citizens of those countries, this means that they are able to

> enjoy the rights to vote, speak, and assemble freely—while neighboring countries suffer authoritarian rulers and internal conflict. Public health and economic growth can also differ dramatically from one country to another [if one has had a missionary presence and another has not], even among countries that share similar geography, cultural background, and natural resources.[73]

Such research indicates both the historical missionary commitment to such issues and the fruit that it has yielded.[74]

Evangelicals continue early missionary practices in various ways. They have founded numerous faith-based nongovernmental organizations (NGOs) to do relief and development work around the globe, the hallmark of which has been the integration of evangelism with material outreach. More recently,

69. Woodberry, "Missionary Roots of Liberal Democracy."
70. Hutchison, *Errand to the World*.
71. Woodberry, "Missionary Roots of Liberal Democracy," 244–45.
72. Ibid.
73. Dilley, "Surprising Discovery," 34.
74. For more of the same, see Walls, "History of the Expansion."

evangelical churches, denominational structures, and mission agencies have also become heavily involved in relief and development, and not just through short-term mission trips. Evangelicals are thus engaged in efforts of creation care, disaster relief, medical care, leadership development, racial reconciliation, and improving business ethics. They minister to victims of crime and violence, alcoholics, drug addicts, gang members, and prisoners. They build schools, promote agricultural development, distribute food aid, open microfinance organizations, and propagate values about the inherent worth of all persons,[75] drawing on diverse theological resources to encourage and justify these actions. They attack poverty using programming that includes child parliaments made up of former child soldiers and sex workers, and they undertake and administer water and sanitation initiatives, community health programs, microfinance and microcredit institutions, literacy and other education projects, and efforts to procure land titles for the poor.[76] The organizations that do such work range from the very small to the enormous, and they are part of an exploding NGO sector that is so infused by religious (often evangelical) actors and organizations that at least one author has argued that the commonly used faith-based/secular dichotomy in the industry is actually a misnomer.[77]

The distinguishing contribution of evangelicals in this mix continues to be the claim of an integrated spiritual and material approach, or a "claim to be inspired by the Holy Spirit and the life of Jesus and seek to holistically address the spiritual, physical, and social needs of people in their community."[78] This is particularly true of evangelical NGOs, which are supported by tithes, offerings, and special donations from evangelical congregations for whom the spiritual dimension is at the top of their list of desired outcomes.[79] Their evangelical donor base is thus able to influence their agenda, ensuring that they maintain evangelism, saving souls, and an orthodox stand on issues of social concern as top priorities.[80] World Vision's misstep in 2014 on homosexual marriage and quick backtracking on the issue was a very powerful reminder,

75. See Amstutz, *Evangelicals and American Foreign Policy*; Miller and Yamamori, *Global Pentecostalism*; Offutt, *New Centers*; Steensland and Goff, "Introduction."

76. Reynolds and Offutt, "Global Poverty and Evangelical Action."

77. Schnable, "Frames, Modes of Action, Networks."

78. Miller and Yamamori, *Global Pentecostalism*, 2. Miller and Yamamori argue this is the claim of progressive Pentecostals (most of whom are evangelical) around the world.

79. Interestingly enough, as churches get more involved in poverty work of their own, these NGOs have become concerned that they may lose some of the support the churches have been giving them. See Gramby-Sobukwe and Hoiland, "Rise of Mega-Church Efforts."

80. It also means that they have to be very, very careful about anything that smacks of "liberalism" in their approaches to development and, of course, advocacy.

for example, of the degree to which the evangelical NGOs are connected to the evangelical base.[81]

However, some of the major evangelical NGOs have struggled with the integration of the spiritual and the material as they have sought to expand their reach both geographically and technically. In chapter 7 we explore the tensions of the integration of the spiritual into advocacy work, the call to enter into closed countries where evangelism is prohibited and local Christian staff are unavailable for hire, the hiring of staff for expertise over faith, the acceptance of funds from non-Christian sources, and the dichotomy between evangelism and discipleship itself. All of these have been sources of struggle to figure out how to maintain the spiritual as a primary goal. Nevertheless, the main way that evangelicals have tackled poverty when they are at their best has always been in a way that brings together the spiritual and the material. The problem, of course, from the perspective of this book, is that their approach to poverty has been limited by their inability to incorporate advocacy when faced with situations of poverty that demand it. And further, that their view of sanctification and/or discipleship does not naturally gravitate in the direction of structural or societal problems.

Evangelical Development versus Advocacy

Evangelicals sometimes do engage in advocacy around the issue of poverty; recently they have done so in significant ways. Evangelical NGOs including World Vision, Food for the Hungry, the International Justice Mission, the Mennonite Central Committee, World Concern, and World Relief[82] have opened up offices in the Washington, DC, area—and not just to seek funding.[83] As one authoritative commentator on evangelical engagement with the state declares:

> It is crucial to note that evangelical development groups have also moved increasingly into public-policy advocacy. The realization that small changes in US policy can sometimes dwarf the impact of private development initiatives abroad has led groups like World Vision to take a more active lobbying role. This advocacy intersects the parallel human-rights movement in complex ways, sometimes complementing and sometimes in tension with the faith-based alliance on religious freedom.[84]

81. King, "Role of Religious Identity among Evangelical NGOs."
82. Reynolds and Offutt, "Global Poverty and Evangelical Action."
83. Ecumenical and mainline denominations and organizations have for many years had such offices both in New York (before the UN) and in Washington, DC.
84. Hertzke, "Evangelicals and International Engagement," 216.

Many of these organizations have also worked with lawmakers to create new policies and have advocated for serious changes to existing unjust structures. (See the appendix for examples.)

In spite of these new efforts to take on the dimensions of power that create poverty, the bulk of evangelicals continue to rely heavily on evangelism, discipleship, and community development strategies to solve poverty. It is safe to assume that evangelicals in the pews still aren't regularly hearing about advocacy as an expression of one's faith and an aspect of discipleship.

But, as we attempt to pound home in this book through repeated examples, impoverishing power structures do not just exist *within* a community; regional, national, and global dynamics also create poverty. If evangelicals are relying on evangelism or community development to help solve these problems, then they are likely operating out of inappropriate paradigms and using incorrect tools. If, for example, rivers are being polluted from heavy industry upstream or ecologies are being destroyed through activities such as overfishing or deforestation, then state or regional actors may have a role to play. Or, if confusing property rights systems and conflicting ownership claims are creating a drag on the use of land to generate wealth, then national policies are often to blame. In a final example, if restrictive trade policies block communities from getting their goods to their intended markets, then the solution must be sought in international trade organizations or negotiations. In each of these cases and many others, efforts at restoring relationships within communities will simply address the reasons that poverty exists in those places and be limited by the larger structures of which they are a part.

Why do many evangelicals hesitate so much to become involved in the "power" dimensions of poverty work, even though they are so involved in working with, and alongside, the poor? This happens for at least three reasons. First, they still mainly approach social transformation from a highly individualistic perspective, often fed by a highly individualistic view of the gospel. This causes evangelicals to miss the larger dimensions of social problems and the power and mandate of the gospel to be involved in changing them: "Evangelicals see change as personal and individual; conversion and repentance are generic tools for transformation that are believed to be able to conquer all forms of social ills . . . [and] the pervasive focus on individualism, free will, and personal relationships renders racial injustices invisible and thereby perpetuates racial inequality."[85] This is essentially the same problem that we pointed out in Myers's work.

Second, when faced with a choice of either moving into the more political work of tackling structures of power responsible for poverty or holding back,

85. Marti and Emerson, "Rise of the Diversity Expert," 183–84.

many evangelicals are scared and not theologically or practically equipped to deal with the opportunity.[86] More often than not, Christian organizations working on poverty issues locally, whether in the United States or abroad, whether from a relief or development perspective, run up against powerful actors using their power, legally and illegally, to create and perpetuate structures that prevent those seeking to rise out of poverty from accessing the means to do so. When encountering these situations—whether the poor people in question are peasants in a rural village whose land has been seized illegally by local landlords and who have thus lost their access to productive resources that would allow them to flourish, or first-generation legal immigrants in the United States who are being taken advantage of by employers paying them less than minimum wage—these evangelical organizations face a decision: do they tackle the political dimensions of these problems of poverty, or do they skirt around them and work along other lines? Organizations working in this area face this kind of decision all the time, a decision, as David Korten puts it, of whether to move to the "third-generation" strategy of advocacy after having worked in the first two generations of strategies: relief and development.[87]

We sympathize with evangelicals facing such choices because these transitions are fraught with difficulties and challenges. Many organizations have been unable, despite their willingness, to take the step into the next "generation" of activities because of the risks of the "political" work involved, work that can quickly alienate supporters of the organization because they are unwilling to be involved in something political. In this view, there is an implicit transition from an approach of economic charity, which is highly supported, to a social justice approach that includes political involvement, which makes supporters uncertain. Such a switch can plunge an organization into a sphere of action that is full of contest, conflict, and violence of various sorts, including the violence of enforcement. Organizations that get involved may be forced to choose sides in a process that can be polarizing along many different dimensions. International organizations that engage in political advocacy also run the risk of being kicked out of countries; a dynamic that is increasingly common around the world today. All of these challenges are very real and must be navigated with extreme care.

The result is that it is much easier not to become involved in political issues that call for advocacy in order for progress to be made, and that leads evangelical churches and denominations to shy away from, say, engagement

86. John Wesley refers to the layering of multidimensional sin as "complicated wickedness," which is an apt way of expressing what most people feel when they enter into the complexity of political, economic, and social realms.
87. Korten, "Third Generation NGO Strategies."

with issues such as the use of discriminatory police force against people of color.[88] In addition to these challenges, people engaged in the political sphere also risk being co-opted by those in power or becoming captive to the allures of power. Those involved in advocacy may also fear (not without reason) that engagement in the political will lead those in power to end the good grassroots interventions that agencies are carrying out. These dangers lead to a silencing of the voice of advocacy and represent genuine risks to advocacy practitioners.

Third, many evangelicals are theologically ill-equipped to discern their calling into the advocacy field vis-à-vis the issues involved, in this case in terms of poverty issues. But some help is on the way. Some new evangelical scholarship has foregrounded Scripture passages that have heretofore been curiously missing from exegeses on economic structure and power. Such references, including the Jubilee system instituted by God in the Old Testament, seem to reflect God's will for states to play a role in ensuring access for all to the basic productive resources that allow each person to flourish. New evangelical theologies on poverty and power hold promise to enrich the debate in the evangelical community over the right and proper role of the state in each and every category of policy, even as there will undoubtedly continue to be differences of opinion over specific issues. There is growing consensus in the evangelical community that engagement with the state is not only proper but also mandated by Scripture. The question is now about the details of timing, issues, and method.

In summary, a close examination of the evangelical approach to poverty helps explain the lack of evangelical involvement in issues beyond the social/ civil ones. Evangelicalism's historical legacy has inhibited its analysis of power-related causes of poverty and constricted the development of theology to make sense of them, and has not provided guidelines for practices to address them. Situations in which the structures of power are a main factor in creating and sustaining poverty may call for action by the state. We are not saying that the state should have an expanded role across the board; far from it. Rather, we are simply saying that evangelicals have not developed a sufficiently sophisticated diagnosis that will allow them to at least consider, prayerfully, faithfully, and based on Scripture, elements that have gone previously ignored as they

88. The websites of the Southern Baptist Convention (SBC) and the National Council of Churches of Christ (NCCC) provide an interesting comparison of how one evangelical (SBC) and one mainline group (NCCC) dealt with the Ferguson, MO, uprisings in the fall of 2014. In accessing both of these websites soon after the incident that fall, on the former's website (http://www.sbc.net/) no mention of Ferguson was to be seen anywhere. On the latter's website (http://nationalcouncilofchurches.us/), while it was not front and center, a secondary page was dedicated to reporting the latest and providing opportunities to engage.

contemplate a calling into advocacy on issues that come to the fore. We also do not want to take the emphasis away from the relational and community-oriented approach that evangelicals have taken. This is not a character flaw; evangelicals *should* desire and build authentic relationships with the poor. We celebrate efforts that push in this direction. We agree with the transformation paradigm that sees the restoration of relationships as critical to development. We do not in any way hope to diminish the importance of these kinds of strategies and initiatives; rather, we seek to add to them ones that seem to be clearly indicated by Scripture and that evangelicals, so far, have been largely missing.

Mature Evangelical Advocacy: A Focus on Discipleship

What, then, given this analysis, should be the distinctive evangelical approach to advocacy? For, even as evangelicals begin to become involved in the host of advocacy issues from which they are absent, they must still ask how they should approach advocacy, what methods they should adopt, and what should drive them. The answer comes, as would be expected, from the core of evangelical identity: the focus on being and making disciples. We propose that deeper and more prayerful reflection about how and why we do advocacy—questions that must be answered through theological and theoretical inquiry—will enable evangelical advocates to be more faithful in their reflection of Christ to the world *and* be more effective in being used by God to accomplish divinely inspired purposes for the political objectives of advocacy, leaving the results in God's hands.

As detailed above, evangelicals are engaged in a host of advocacy activities, concentrated primarily in the area of social/civil policies, despite the evangelical reputation and history of withdrawal. The idea that the "evangelical church has little to say about wider social commitments, and that it offers only a narrow morality centered on family and personal life," is, according to John Wilson, simply false.[89] Evangelicals are especially active in foreign policy, "emphasizing fundamental religious and moral values and mobilizing grassroots support for specific public policy initiatives on issues like religious freedom and human rights."[90] In some areas a coalition of conservative evangelical and black congregations have campaigned together successfully, such as in the enactment of the landmark International Religious Freedom legislation against slavery and genocide in Sudan, and against sex trafficking. Evangelicals have also served as "the grass-roots vanguard of efforts to elevate human

89. Wilson, "Introduction," 9.
90. Amstutz, *Evangelicals and American Foreign Policy*, 4.

rights as a key aim of global leadership," joining leading feminists and other nonevangelical partners to do so.[91] However, even as they carry out this work, we see a fundamental struggle and discrepancy: a failure to integrate disciple making with the political objective, or, phrased in older terms, to integrate evangelism and advocacy.

It is ironic, in fact, that in all of the literature by evangelicals and by those observing evangelicals in the public square, there is no mention of seeing, and no urging to see, engagement with the state as a form of ministry whose purpose is to model Christ's love and to try to make disciples. Instead of integrating discipleship and advocacy, instead of approaching advocacy and engagement with the state holistically and placing faithfulness to the spiritual side of politics on a par with faithfulness to the material side, these writers consistently separate the two.

Why? The reasons go back again to the legacies of evangelical history that posited the primacy of evangelism over social involvement and feared that such involvement would lead to compromising the spiritual for the political. Under the Enlightenment project, the public realm was enlarged and associated with empirical realities, such as politics, economics, and science, while religion (theology or belief) was relegated to the private domain: separated and minimized in most people's minds. Evangelicalism devoted most of its energies to the private domain, but struggled to know how to bridge the divide. This has led to what Craig Calhoun refers to as a "secular imaginary," a perception held by some (even some Christians) according to which the world revolves around the this-worldly,[92] even if those holding the perception continue to accentuate the spiritual.

Evangelicals continue to debate the matter. On one side, as Mark Amstutz recently queried: "How can evangelicals pursue political engagement without compromising the church's fundamental spiritual task?"[93] From Amstutz's perspective, "rising political advocacy involves significant risks, since it can undermine the independence and moral authority of the church. Because religious groups make their most important contributions to the moral life of nations when they relate transcendent norms to domestic and international social, political, and economic concerns, public affairs advocacy can shift the church's focus from its mission of proclaiming the good news of the gospel."[94] Elsewhere Amstutz says that evangelical advocacy "has raised concerns about the efficacy of such initiatives and, more significantly, about the church's shift

---

91. Hertzke, "Evangelicals and International Engagement."
92. Calhoun, "Rethinking Secularism," esp. 38.
93. Amstutz, *Evangelicals and American Foreign Policy*, 196.
94. Ibid., 7.

in priorities from spiritual concerns to temporal affairs. Some thoughtful observers have reminded religious activists that the church is not an interest group, and that it risks losing its spiritual and moral authority when it begins to function as one."[95]

Other evangelical authors reject these fears, stating clearly that the role of the church and of evangelicals is to equip and engage the state, as evangelicals have always done in the past. These authors, however, focus primarily on bringing about particular kinds of social change, and they see advocacy as the most effective way of creating the kinds of social change that God would want, rather than seeing advocacy as a ministry in and of itself that integrates both the spiritual and the political in its way of doing things, a ministry that gives witness through its action and not just through its intended results. Authors from across the political spectrum, including Wayne Grudem[96] and Ron Sider,[97] affirm that evangelicals should engage the government around problems of civil society, providing the government with a moral compass and vision through "significant presence." Chuck Colson enunciates this vision clearly, declaring that, "like our evangelical forebears who spent decades fighting against slavery in America, we modern Christians involve ourselves in politics not to gain power, but to get politicians to do what they ought to do because it is right—because it conforms to the moral order by which we live as a civilized people."[98] One of the fathers of the evangelical movement, Carl F. H. Henry, is often cited in these arguments. Henry wrote in 1947 that "the cries of suffering humanity today are many. No evangelicalism which ignores the totality of man's condition dares respond in the name of Christianity."[99]

The problem, according to these authors, is not in whether to engage, but in the effectiveness of the engagement. And the latter is seen as having been problematic for at least two reasons. First, because of the lack of moral vision, translation, distinction, and integrity of evangelicals in politics: "We've failed to communicate a common moral vision in language that ordinary people understand. Ours isn't a failure of style or technique, but rather it's a failure of *thought* and of *character*."[100] Second, because of the lack of depth of evangelical thought, lack of coherent political philosophy, and deficient theological engagement with the public realm that has emerged on this issue: "The opportunities [for evangelical advocacy] are enormous. But the lack of

95. Ibid., 4.
96. Grudem, *Politics according to the Bible*.
97. Sider, *Just Politics*.
98. Colson, foreword to *God and Governing*, xi.
99. Benson and Heltzel, *Evangelicals and Empire*, 13.
100. Kennedy, "Justice in Evangelical Political Theology," 109.

thoughtful preparation is creating tragic failure. . . . The absence of any widely accepted, systematic evangelical reflection on politics leads to contradiction, confusion, ineffectiveness, even biblical unfaithfulness in our political work."[101]

It is not surprising, though it is remarkable, that evangelicals have focused on techniques and instrumentality in their advocacy and have separated the spiritual and the political in the process of advocacy itself. This separation, which goes so clearly against the mandates of Scripture for all of our activities, also shows up in other Christian endeavors and organizations such as relief and development organizations, mission agencies, churches, educational institutions, and businesses. Thankfully, many of these evangelical actors have been trying to recapture the holistic and integrated approach to all of these, ranging from business as mission and ministry to the "integral mission" approaches cited above. Not so, however, with efforts of advocacy, even by these institutions. When they do think about it, they are confused and they fear that integrating the spiritual side might hamper efforts to "win" on the issues in which they are involved, and so they marginalize the spiritual element because they don't know how to integrate it.

This book attempts to point the way forward for that integration. It starts with a biblical and holistic understanding of advocacy. It is committed to being a witness to the advocacy community and to all with whom one comes into contact as one carries out advocacy efforts. In action, such a witness does not put political ends above spiritual means or allow the political ends to dominate the mandate to love one's neighboring opponent; it shows this love through concrete actions, and it looks for and seizes opportunities to share the saving news of Jesus Christ and what it means to be his disciple. If Christ is Lord of all, then this certainly must include structures in society (Eph. 1:10).

Actions that do not model "the Way" set forth in Scripture will hamper this effort and need to be excised from our advocacy efforts. We must attend to errors such as lack of transparency, negative casting of people on opposing sides of the argument, the sacralization of political ideologies, and reducing opponents' arguments to straw arguments. We should be creating community in this effort, forging relationships with all, creating and engaging in Bible studies and theological reflection with them. Further, we should be seeking truth together, creating a situation where people know they can trust us to put the best forward about them. We should be committed to top-quality research and findings even if the findings contradict our dearly held beliefs and can be used as an argument for the other side. This transformational advocacy approach aims not only or even primarily to achieve the political results we

101. Sider, *Just Politics*, 3, 6.

seek—for those results are in God's hands—but to prayerfully and faithfully carry out God's call, whatever the issue, in such a way that people come to know the abundant love of God and the saving power of Jesus Christ and redouble their commitment to nurture their discipleship and struggle with their sin, just as we struggle with ours.

Part 2

—◈—

An Evangelical Theology of Advocacy

3

Theology of Advocacy

God, Power, and Advocacy

A theology of advocacy asks *why* and *how* Christians must engage institutions and structures for and with the world's poor.[1] To do so we begin with God. By starting with God, we are not trying to reduce God's nature to some preconceived understanding of advocacy, as if justifying our position according to divine warrant. God cannot be reduced to any singular characteristic. Nor do we want to suggest that salvation history can be captured by viewing it through the lenses of advocacy. On the contrary, we begin with God in order to inform and shape how we undertake advocacy in the world. If advocacy arises because of God's actions in history, then this should tell us something about how we should advocate for others.

God and Advocacy

God speaks; humans respond. Thus the beginning point for a theology of advocacy is God. But who is God, and how do we transition from such lofty,

1. Though primarily concerned with poor people and poverty, we acknowledge what Nicholas Wolterstorff calls the "quartet of the vulnerable"—widows, orphans, resident aliens, and the poor—as representing the broader scope of biblical teachings about justice. See Wolterstorff, *Justice: Rights and Wrongs*, 75–76. We also refer to the "world's poor" because of certain predilections within North America to either (1) prioritize domestic poverty at the expense of those pejoratively labeled "foreigners," or (2) focus upon international poverty through the ubiquity of short-term missions-related endeavors and forget the poor right here among us.

seemingly spiritual considerations into sociopolitical structures, especially when these appear peripheral to the kingdom of God, or worse yet, inextricably riddled with sin? To move in this direction, we must understand something of the nature of God, and why (and how) God matters.

In the first chapter we explained the etymology of "advocacy" as "a summoning to one's aid" or "interceding for another," but in the Bible the meaning broadens to involve (1) *a God who speaks*, most clearly in Jesus Christ; (2) speaking *for others*, whether the poor, marginalized, or other nations; (3) speaking *before the powers* that exist in the world, be they personal, political, or spiritual; and (4) speaking *to effect change* in the cosmos, defined most fully as "[bringing] unity to all things in heaven and on earth under Christ" (Eph. 1:10). Thus, in its broadest sense, God's advocacy begins with creation and flows through salvation history with missional purposes; or, we might say, God advocates the world into existence and thereafter advocates its re-creation. One of the benefits of beginning with such an expansive understanding is that we locate advocacy within God's redemptive agenda and avoid the mistake of making it just an add-on or appendage to something otherwise whole. However, by doing this we want to avoid the other danger of reducing God's character to a lone attribute, as if plucking a singular jewel from an ornate crown.

Such a working definition *begins with God*. The nature of Yahweh in the Old Testament informs the social, economic, and political distinctiveness of Israel; or as Chris Wright explains, "There was, in other words, an inseparable link between the kind of society Israel was (or was supposed to be) and the character of the God they worshipped."[2] In the Scriptures, God represents the Subject of humanity (as the "image of God"), and in Christ we find the essence of the world. To see Jesus is to see God.[3] And so to speak of Yahweh informing the "social, economic, and political distinctiveness of Israel"[4] is at once to look ahead to Christ as the fulfillment of these realities, to move fluidly between the Old Testament law and the embodiment of the law in the person of Christ, applied to us by the Holy Spirit, our Advocate. Thus, we see advocacy not as a technique—yet one more thing to do in our technologically crazed world, which reduces everything to efficient means—but as a theology:[5] something we enter in order to faithfully image Christ in the world.

2. C. Wright, *Old Testament Ethics*, 58.

3. Or as Karl Barth explains, "For God is not known and is not knowable except in Jesus Christ." *Church Dogmatics, Vol. 2, Part 2*, 509. Or later: "Man, this man [Jesus], is the imminent kingdom of God, nothing more and nothing in and for Himself. Similarly, the kingdom of God is utterly and unreservedly this man." *Church Dogmatics, Vol. 3, Part 2*, 70.

4. God sets up the social and political structures of Israel to function in a particular way.

5. That is, theological praxis. See Ellul, *Technological Society*; Ellul, *Perspectives on Our Age*.

The definition thereafter moves with God's nature *for the benefit of diverse human agents,* as they experience "life" through conformity to God's character (cf. Deut. 30:11–20) *before the various powers within the world,* whether they be personal, political, or spiritual. Discussions of advocacy usually revolve around the political with the intimation that the "political" is somehow independent from the "spiritual." However, the apostle Paul reminds the church that it lives before "the rulers and authorities in the heavenly realms" (Eph. 3:10). Finally, advocacy in the Bible holds *cosmological significance* as it looks ahead and articulates a vision for the future eschatological kingdom while living in the present. The scope of redemption includes not only persons but the broader contexts in which humans live. Therefore, we interpret humanity in its broadest sense, not just as atomistic marbles rattling around in a tin can called life, but as embodied, cultured, and even political beings.

All of this suggests that humans advocate because God advocates,[6] and we source our understanding of advocacy in conformity with the person of Jesus Christ, while living in the totality of our world through the Holy Spirit.

The Significance of God's Character

One initial difficulty in relating God to advocacy is that it has become unfashionable to speak about religion (no less God) in our contemporary world, where the subject of divinity has been either carefully demarcated into narrow, quarantined compartments or relentlessly pushed to the margins of society, or both. Vestiges of secularization(s) still linger, despite repeated calls by sociologists like Peter Berger,[7] Harvey Cox,[8] and Samuel Huntington[9] and philosophers such as Charles Taylor[10] to reexamine the role of religion in society. Some think of God as an archaic notion (even the "opiate of the masses"), others as a specialized commodity, while even Christians contribute to the inadvertent secularization of society by restricting God to a carefully cloistered "spiritual" realm,[11] divorced from the rest of life. Hence, a theology of advocacy must first reassert the importance of God for the world, but do so with the ethics of God's nature.

In the following section, we retell salvation history through the lenses of advocacy in order to source our understanding of advocacy from God's nature.

---

6. God advocates for particular kinds of social, economic, and other arrangements that structure society.

7. P. Berger, *Sacred Canopy;* or P. Berger, *Desecularization of the World.*

8. Cox, *Fire from Heaven.*

9. Huntington, *Clash of Civilizations.*

10. Taylor, *Secular Age.*

11. We see this in chap. 1, where only the "moral" is visible in advocacy efforts.

Alasdair MacIntyre suggests we can understand the question "What am I to do?" only if we ask the prior question, "Of what story or stories do I find myself a part?"[12] As N. T. Wright explains, "The whole point of Christianity is that it offers us a story which is the story of the whole world. It is public truth."[13] In such a light, we walk into God's story and find him advocating from the beginning: through the Trinity for the world. Even after the intrusion of sin in the world, God keeps advocating not only with regard to persons but also larger systems that emanate from human endeavors. Redemption takes many twists and turns, weaving an intricate tale through blessings, the giving of the law, and justice, until we come to Jesus Christ. Herein we find the deeper narrative that turns the entire world on its axis.[14]

Our approach to this chapter will be less exegesis (although we hope to be eminently faithful to the text) and more wisdom speech. Frank Whaling's study on early Christian uses of "theology" reveals two important facets that will guide the remainder of this study: "First, theology must relate to the divine; second, theology was an aspect of *paideia* or *humanitas*, the Greco-Roman emphasis upon forming people for public life."[15] Therefore, theology focuses upon its proper subject—God—for witness to the public sphere.

Theology as wisdom (*sapientia*) foregrounds the lived character of God in society. Such a view is important because somewhere along the way theology has become encumbered by a variety of cultural vestiges, including modernistic (and subsequently post- or ultramodernistic) assumptions, especially as theology has slowly emerged from its Enlightenment past. Kevin Vanhoozer[16] and Daniel Treier[17] (among others[18]) offer a new perspective (which they argue is very old) that explores theology as "wisdom," the knowledge of God embodied in humanity while situated within concrete circumstances of life. The advantages gained by looking at theology in this way include (1) preeminence given to God's character as the basis of wisdom, revealed most clearly in Christ,

---

12. MacIntyre, *After Virtue*, 216.

13. N. T. Wright, *New Testament and the People of God*, 41–42. Likewise Lesslie Newbigin states, "The Bible tells a story that is the story, *the* story of which our human life is a part. It is not that stories are part of human life, but that human life is a part of a story." *Open Secret*, 82.

14. And God uses humans in the process of world making; or as Trevor Hart says, "We are called not simply to enter the world of the text in some sort of imaginative retreat from reality, but, having entered this world, to recognize it as none other than our own, and to begin the complex task of reconfiguring our own world in the light of this narrative presentation of it." *Faith Thinking*, 152.

15. Whaling, "Development of the Word 'Theology,'" cited in Treier, *Virtue and the Voice of God*, 5.

16. Vanhoozer, *Drama of Doctrine*. See also Vanhoozer, "One Rule."

17. Treier, *Virtue and the Voice of God*.

18. Ford, *Christian Wisdom*. See also Ford, "Theology."

through the Holy Spirit; and (2) a focus on humans appropriating wisdom into all facets of life: not just ostensibly "spiritual" domains, but also social, political, and economic ones. By linking theology with wisdom, we avoid the unsightly caricature of theology as obtusely theoretical, confined to small, dusty libraries where nothing ever happens except the awkward creaking of chairs. Wisdom theology relates to life and moves into God's world with God's character.

When we speak of God's character, we are referring directly to Jesus Christ, through the Holy Spirit (our Advocate). The Old Testament points in this direction, albeit using a variety of languages and images, images sometimes intimated in the law or expressed in poetic language (as wisdom). However, the New Testament helps us understand that Jesus has always been operating in the world. "Through him all things were made" (John 1:3). "He is before all things, and in him all things hold together" (Col. 1:17). The author of Hebrews makes it explicit: "The Son is the radiance of God's glory and the exact representation of his being, sustaining all things by his powerful word" (1:3). Jesus is wisdom personified, even humanized.

A Theology of Advocacy: Retelling the Story of God

All throughout Scripture, advocacy-related themes flood the content of the text as God "speaks" about himself (often to human authorities) and asks humans to speak about him, as we see with Moses before Pharaoh (Exod. 7–12) or Paul before Felix (Acts 24). But God is concerned not only with speech, but with right speech, since the substance of advocacy deals with God's nature. Hence, we might argue that wrong speech in advocacy amounts to idolatry[19] since it distorts the very nature of God.[20] This is an important caution to all Christians involved in advocacy work. Unless God's character informs the process, all efforts will amount to mere technique or, at the worst, gross idolatry.

God's Advocacy in the Trinity

God's advocacy begins within the persons of the Trinity and only thereafter relates to how God engages the world. Hence, advocacy is not something new

19. Speech, the way we talk, the content we give it, has to be subject to God.

20. History reveals that whenever a people compromise their view of God, society unravels into a horrid tangle of ever-increasing distortions. Brueggemann explains, "The much greater and more pervasive problem in ancient Israel is not a refusal to speak of Yahweh—that is, not a practical readiness to dismiss Yahweh as a factor in life, but the temptation to engage in wrong speech about Yahweh, which amounts to idolatry. In that ancient community, as even now, idolatry (wrong speech about God) rather than atheism (refusal to speak about God) is the more compelling and dangerous issue." *Theology of the Old Testament*, 136.

that barges onto the scene after sin enters the world (although it certainly changes *how* God advocates); rather, advocacy remains part of God's nature from all eternity. Theologians sometimes use "economic" language to refer to the relationship of Father, Son, and Holy Spirit as revealed in Scripture (drawing upon the Greek word *oikonomikos*), but it might also be possible to do the same with political language, seeing the Trinity as a polis, a community of Beings who perfectly represent goodness, love, and beauty.[21] Of course, this would require a different understanding of power, which is often thought of as the inner essence of politics.[22] Such a trinitarian polis reframes power as a power-for-the-other, as well as a power-for-the-world.

Through the history of the Western church, discussions related to the Trinity have been limited in scope, focused almost exclusively upon either how Father, Son, and Holy Spirit appear in the pages of Scripture or how the persons of the Godhead enact salvation, or both. There are two possible reasons for this restricted emphasis. For those from an Enlightenment heritage, the sociality of the Trinity confounds human reason, leaving people with "a remote and shadowy figure that can play no part in the world of real 'facts' with which science deals."[23] The other reason relates to how culture influences how we think of God, where a singular, monarchical God tends to underwrite the kind of individualism we find prevalent in the West, authenticating rather than challenging cultural patterns. Such an individualism is the bedrock upon which most people conceptualize politics; or as Lesslie Newbigin explains, "In this way of thinking, the autonomy of the individual self is the highest value, and the business of politics is to safeguard and extend this individual freedom against the pressures of the collective."[24]

However, the doctrine of the Trinity opposes these currents, resisting the attribution of a "remote and shadowy" existence to God while confronting a view of society based upon autonomous individuals. By beginning with a God whom the Puritans understood as "within Himself a sweet society," we discover a direct challenge to reductionistic individualism, while maintaining a high view of persons. If God is three-in-one, then all efforts to construct a society (no less a politics) around autonomy will be disputed. Or as Jürgen

---

21. John Howard Yoder frames much of his ecclesiology around such a polis. He writes, "The Christian community, like any community held together by commitment to important values, is a political reality. That is, the church has the character of a *polis* (the Greek word from which we get the adjective *political*), namely, a structured social body." Yoder, *Body Politics*, vii.

22. Much of the language used in politics (such as sovereignty, justice, freedom, and authority, to name just a few) comes from the Judeo-Christian heritage and requires an inner ethic of power for its faithful employment.

23. Newbigin, "Trinity as Public Truth," esp. 3–4.

24. Ibid., 5.

Moltmann says, "The divine Trinity is so inviting and so strong that the divine life reflects itself in true human community and takes human community up into itself, 'that they may be all one; even as thou, Father, art in me, and I in thee, that they also may be in us' [John 17:21]."[25] The sociality of the Trinity, further, reframes the scope of salvation, not only applying the gospel to human personal conversion (as evangelicals have long emphasized) but also extending it into communities; or as Timothy Tennent explains, "We are not just baptized *by* faith; we are baptized *into* a faith that is shared by a *community* that exists in space around the world and back in time."[26] Not only is this significant for ecclesiology but it is also vital for engaging society around the churches.[27]

Hence, the Trinity does not just describe how God reveals himself, but prescribes the nature of the Church in the world, and even so, represents the eschatological future of the world (especially if we take the idea of "gathering together" described by Paul in Eph. 1:10 as pointing toward this kind of cosmological oneness).[28] All of this underscores the relevance of the Trinity for the public realm. As we participate in God's nature, we learn to properly live in the world, inclusive of its structures. Hence, in the pages that follow, we will frame advocacy in robust, relational terms, arguing for a trinitarian framework to guide the substance and ethic of advocacy in the world.

Advocacy in Creation

Father, Son, and Holy Spirit act through creation to visibly express his love. The Triune God speaks and life blossoms into being. From nothingness, music begins to rise from distant darkness, sung in three-part harmony as the world comes into being, shaping not only the entities of creation (birds, trees, fish, and humans) but also the underlying order and cohesion of the cosmos.[29]  God creates in a way that releases power into the cosmos, not controlling the forces of nature as an autocrat, but encouraging their proliferation. Fish, birds,

25. Moltmann-Wendel and Moltmann, *Humanity in God*, 98.

26. Tennent, *Invitation to World Missions*, 62.

27. Brian Edgar argues that the old debate between evangelism and social action is predicated upon varying views of the Trinity: "This reminds us that even now any evangelism that does not lead people to an on-going life of worship in the church is not good evangelism; maybe it is not evangelism at all. And a mission which seeks peace and justice in the world which does not equally seek to bring about the peace of God (and not just the absence of war, discrimination and injustice) is not really mission either." "Consummate Trinity," 124.

28. Ibid., 121.

29. Both J. R. R. Tolkien (*Silmarillion*) and C. S. Lewis (*Magician's Nephew*) articulate creation through the life-giving imagery of song.

and other creatures teem, which communicates something of freedom, power, and even wildness into the scene.[30] God then declares everything good. Herein we witness the first hints of advocacy in the Scriptures.[31] God advocates the world into existence.

Creation seems an unlikely place for initiating a theology of advocacy, but it helps frame the nature of divine speech. In Genesis 1 God speaks and life bursts forth from nothing, nurturing the entities, integrating the parts, and releasing creation to be fruitful. When we later take up the subject of human advocacy, the creational properties of divine speech will be critical for encountering the "powers" that exist in the world. We live in a world of distorted realities. Advocacy helps reveal the really real.

Humans do not create *ex nihilo*, but nevertheless possess some abilities to cause the world to abound into fruitfulness (Gen. 1:28–30). Brueggemann likens the notion of dominion to that of a shepherd, "who cares for, tends, and feeds the animals."[32] This corresponds to what the Bible calls shalom. Cornelius Plantinga defines shalom as *"universal flourishing, wholeness, and delight—*a rich state of affairs in which natural needs are satisfied and natural gifts fruitfully employed, a state of affairs that inspires joyful wonder as its Creator and Savior opens doors and welcomes the creatures in whom he delights. Shalom, in other words, is the way things ought to be."[33] Such a definition focuses not only on the growth of the cosmos (what Plantinga refers to as fruitfulness) but also deeper imaginative dimensions of "joyful wonder" intermixed with hints of hospitality. Shalom sings.

It is one thing to paint a picture of shalom in organic, Genesis-inspired language, which lingers as some idyllic vision of a primordial past. But what might shalom look like in modern societies, especially in light of structures such as democracies, economies, or legislative processes? Our best hint to this comes in terms of the *generative nature of speech* we find in Genesis. There is some disagreement about the source of government, whether it arises before the fall or after it. But as the discussion above implies, God not

30. Andy Crouch says, "The Creator is not seeking a world of pets, individually domesticated animals bred to be attentive to their human masters. He delights in wildness. Swarming and teeming are part of what makes the world good—the overflow and excess of life. All of this actually gives greater glory to God, who has breathed into existence the vast spaces of earth, sky and sea where these creatures can teem, than would a meticulously tended backyard. The Creator loves teeming." *Playing God*, 33.

31. For more on a theology of creation, see Snyder and Scandrett, *Salvation Means Creation Healed.*

32. Brueggemann, *Genesis*, 32.

33. Plantinga, *Not the Way It's Supposed to Be*, 10. Plantinga credits Wolterstoff's *Until Justice and Peace Embrace* (1983) for helping him shape this meaning of shalom.

only creates the entities but also bestows upon humans relevant "powers" to govern the world (as a shepherd), which suggests the introduction of institutions, whether family, economics, or politics. Wolterstorff says, "There would have been government even had there been no sin. Government represents a blend of God's providential care of his creation *as created*, and of God's providential care of his creation *as fallen*."[34] As Christians engage the modern world, they engage the speech that set the world in motion, which is not static, monochromatic speech, but trinitarian in nature. Everything in the world points back to the speech that started it. Thus, God wills not some static view of shalom whereby things hang in perfect equilibrium, like a house of cards. God's view of the world *as it's supposed to be* involves relationships and fruitfulness, because of what divine speech does within the cosmos.

We see this more fully when we come to the part of the Genesis story where God fashions humans as specific image bearers, entrusted with derivative powers for representing God in the world. Moments after creating man and woman (Gen. 1:26), God trusts humans with certain powers for the growth of all things, blessing them and charging them to "rule" and "multiply" (v. 28) in accordance with how God advocates the flourishing of creation.[35] Or as Claus Westermann says,

> Blessing is concentrated on humanity in the Old Testament; the power and dynamism of the blessing enables people to "fill the earth and subdue it," and to make, discover, and invent. The blessing penetrates far more deeply into the story of humanity; the creator does not bestow ready-made products on people, but gives them the capacity to acquire and to create.[36]

Hence, smack dab in the creation account we find power entrusted to humans. The source and ethic of these powers relate to their Giver: from God, for others, to benefit the world. All power is essentially derivational. To the extent that humans use their powers as God does, they more accurately *image* God.[37] But Adam and Eve do not just image God, they also image the world. As part of

34. Wolterstorff, "Theological Foundations," 150.

35. The text directly correlates God's rule and human rule, without usurping the fundamental distinction between divinity and humanity. Clines explains, "In Genesis, therefore, humanity takes the place of God on earth, a point that becomes clearer if we adopt the suggestion that Genesis 1:26 should not be translated 'in our image,' but 'as our image, to be our image' (understanding the preposition *beth* as the *beth* of essence)." "Image of God," 427.

36. Westermann, *Genesis 1–11*, 61–62.

37. Brueggemann explains, "The image of God in the human person is a mandate of power and responsibility. But it is power exercised as God exercises power. The image images the creative use of power which invites, evokes, and permits." *Genesis*, 32.

creation, they directly relate back to it.[38] Thus Paul explains that creation waits in eager expectation (or, literally, "stretching one's neck") for the redemption of humans to be revealed (Rom. 8:19). Thus humans live in dependence upon God's speech[39] and use that speech to grow the world around them. Advocacy work must locate itself as part of this larger story.

Sin and Its Impact on the "Powers"

When sin enters the world, it affects not only the parts but also the spaces within the cosmos. If sin is the culpable breaking of shalom,[40] then the effects of sin enter the warp and woof of creation, distorting not only the entities but also the cohesion. God fashions humans as image bearers for faithfully representing his nature (including his power) in the world. But instead of imaging God, humans want to be like him, and instead of imitating him for others, they turn the world upon themselves (what Luther calls "inward curvature unto self"). As a result, they become far less than God created them to be, misappropriating God's nature and thus confounding human identity—twisting and contorting into ingenious aberrations.

Sin first attacks God's nature, for therein everything derives its essence. When we understand God's character as Advocate and have feasted upon God's goodness, we will be better equipped to engage sin within the structures of the world. Too often, the vision of shalom described above seems like a distant dream, located in some far-off part of our repressed consciousness. Distortion has become the new normal. Hatred, abuse, manipulation of the weak, and the privileging of the self (or group) have for so long been our mainstay that it hardly seems possible we can live without them. Anyone who would argue otherwise we brand an idealist, or worse yet, an enemy of the system: this is the way that things are, rather than the way things ought to be.

How does sin affect structures in our world? Certainly in ways that reflect the nature of power. If God wills a generative shalom, predicated upon

38. This is part of the reason that creation often stands as witness to God-human covenants (see Deut. 30:19–20, where Yahweh calls "the heavens and the earth as witnesses against" Israel; cf. v. 19).

39. Karl Barth says,

Thus the creature in its totality was allied to this living divine Person, being wholly referred to it for its existence and essence, its survival and sustenance. . . . It came into being as the work of the Word of God corresponding to his utterance. So originally and intimately was it disposed for the grace of God! So little did it acquire a place from which it might legitimately withdraw itself from the grace of God! Encountered by this Word of grace, it encounters just the wisdom, kindness and power without which it could not be at all. (*Church Dogmatics, Vol. 3, Part 1*, 110)

40. Plantinga, *Not the Way It's Supposed to Be*, 16.

generative human powers, then things that arise from human agency (like institutions and structures) must likewise image the Trinity. Economics ought to function for wealth, drawing upon the etymological origins of the word "wealth" as "well-being,"[41] which should be the condition of not just a few select individuals, but everyone. Politics should likewise reflect the best interests of the citizenry, reflecting the God who rules the world with a power that creates, nurtures, and integrates.[42] This is to say that human structures receive input from human imaging. Thus when sin enters the world as the "culpable breaking of shalom," it not only affects personal elements (being expressed as lust, pride, selfishness, and neglect), but filters into the institutional fabric of society. Structures receive input from the totality of a people's collective agency. Personal sins are never just personal. Collective distortions enter into the fabric of how humans organize themselves, with effect to political, economic, or social dimensions of life.[43]

We sometimes refer to collective distortions as "powers" in order to refer to the "spirit" that such institutional forms assume. "Sin is," Plantinga explains, "more than the sum of what sinners do. Sin acquires the powerful and elusive form of a spirit—the spirit of an age or a company or a nation or a political movement. Sin burrows into the bowels of institutions and traditions, making a home there and taking them over."[44] No scholar has written more on this subject than Walter Wink. He says,

> I will argue that the "principalities and powers" are the inner and outer aspects of any given manifestation of power. As the inner aspect they are the spirituality of institutions, the "within" of corporate structures and systems, the inner essence of outer organizations of power. As the outer aspect they are political systems, appointed officials, the "chair" of an organization, laws—in short, all the tangible manifestations which power takes. Every Power tends to have a visible pole, an outer form—be it a church, a nation, or an economy—and an invisible pole, an inner spirit or driving force that animates, legitimates, and regulates its physical manifestation in the world.[45]

41. The word "wealth" derives from the Middle English word *wele*, which means "well-being."

42. Wolfhart Pannenberg says it this way: "But a state that represents only the people, or society and its antagonisms, and no longer the divine truth revealed in the cosmic order or in history does not have available to it the possibility of legitimating its political order anywhere but in itself." *Anthropology in Theological Perspective*, 472.

43. Scholars disagree about the degree to which sin works into structures, with some, such as John Howard Yoder, arguing that the structures become inextricably laden with sin, while others believe the effects of sin are far less damaging.

44. Plantinga, *Not the Way It's Supposed to Be*, 75.

45. Wink, *Naming the Powers*, 5.

Wink's description opposes a common tendency to spiritualize the powers as some kind of gnostic body, residing "up there" in the air, but without any material significance. His work highlights the reality that "principalities and powers" assume visible, outer, and material manifestations, whether in the form of a nation, political system, or laws. In his effort to make this case, he runs the risk of downplaying the spiritual significance of these entities, but his writings certainly help foreground the materiality of the powers. We will return to this discussion in the following chapter.

Advocacy in Redemption (Old Testament Contours)

How does God counter the breaking of shalom? He advocates redemption, using his nature as the fundamental resource, calling people to function as image bearers within all facets of life. While we as humans might roll up our sleeves and set the world to rights, God reveals a different ethic. He speaks, blesses, reveals, gives the law, and ultimately enters the world in the person of Jesus Christ, sending his Spirit to advocate for us.

All throughout the Old Testament, God acts to redeem a people for himself,[46] calling Israel *out of* sin, or Egypt, or idolatry, and *into* his nature. God blesses Abraham so that he will be a blessing to others, especially the surrounding nations (Gen. 12:1–3; Amos 9:11–12),[47] a task Abraham accomplishes in imperfect ways by how he deals with Pharaoh in Egypt (Gen. 12:10–20) and with the king of Sodom (chap. 14), by pleading for the safety of Sodom and Gomorrah (chap. 18), through sending Hagar and Ishmael away (chap. 21), and by establishing peace treaties with the surrounding nations (21:22–34). Abraham advocates through blessing.

The substance of blessings revolves around the character of God. We witness this in a number of ways; one is the giving of the law at Mount Sinai, by which God orders the social dimension of life, including economics and politics.[48] The law constitutes the livable expression of God's

46. Even in the Abrahamic covenant we find something of the creational nature of God at work. Chris Wright explains, "It was not that he elevated an existing people to a chosen status, but that he called Israel into existence as his people, as an entity distinct from the surrounding nation states from their very beginning." *People of God and the State*, 5.

47. For more on the missional significance of Gen. 12, see C. Wright, *Mission of God*, esp. chaps. 6, 7.

48. Chris Wright further expounds,

> At Sinai God provided the bonding and moulding institutions and laws by which they were to progress from a mass of freed slaves to an ordered and functioning society. It is there, in the Torah, that we find the bulk of those features of Israel's polity that made them so distinctive: the kinship rationale of land-tenure; the jubilee and sabbatical institutions;

character within the everydayness of life. Hence, in Deuteronomy 6 (the *Shema*) Yahweh explains to Israel that God's character should be "on [their] hearts" (v. 6) and that they are to talk about God's laws in all facets of life, placing reminders on everyday symbols or power-related objects (vv. 7–9) to signify that God alone provides the basis for human affairs. Blessings cannot be limited to some spiritual dimension but need to work into the social, political, and economic fibers of the nation, visible for all to see. In Deuteronomy 4, Yahweh explains in more detail how Israel is to live the law before the other nations:

> Observe them (laws) carefully, for this will show your wisdom and understanding to the nations, who will hear about all these decrees and say, "Surely this great nation is a wise and understanding people." What other nation is so great as to have their gods near them the way the LORD our God is near us whenever we pray to him? And what other nation is so great as to have such righteous decrees and laws as this body of laws I am setting before you today? (vv. 6–8; cf. Mic. 4:1–2)

The law was to hold public significance. By living the law in all facets of society, Israel was to represent what a society looks like when it orders its ways upon God's nature. In this sense, the Torah was a means of blessing the nations.

All throughout the Old Testament, God does not sit idle but pursues the Israelites with his unique covenantal love (Ps. 26:3; Hosea 2:19), admonishing them, as God always does, to plead on behalf of the poor, the alien, and the widow (Exod. 23:11; Lev. 19:34; Ps. 12:5; Isa. 1:17; 3:14–15) precisely because God's justice functions as the measuring line that orders the world (Isa. 28:17). God advocates[49] for the Israelites *so that* the Israelites will advocate for others, whether other nations, the weak, or the marginalized.

When sin takes root, God's advocacy confronts the "powers" in the world, as it did when Moses confronted Pharaoh (Egypt), when Daniel interacted with Nebuchadnezzar (Babylon), and when Esther pleaded with Xerxes (Persia). A more discerning gaze will also see God speaking to many of the smaller nations, such as Philistia, along with an ever-present prophetic stream directed toward the nations of Judah and Israel (see especially Amos). Space does not permit an extended treatment of how God "speaks" to the powers in the ancient Near East, for assuredly he does so in a variety of ways, from direct

---

the ban on interest; the equality of native and 'stranger' before the law; the civil rights of slaves; the diffusion of political leadership and authority among the elders; the limitation on the economic power of cultic officials. (*People of God and the State*, 9)

49. Again, because God is the state, or the state is under his power.

confrontation with Pharaoh, through dreams to Nebuchadnezzar, or through Cyrus as the prefigured Messiah.[50]

The vast majority of advocacy-related speech inveighs against Israel, and especially its kings, religious authorities, and other leaders, for how they neglect God and oppress the people. Such speech sometimes occurs within political systems (Obadiah), and sometimes from the outside (Elijah).[51] The people of God are commanded to seek the peace of the city (Jer. 29:7) but without compromising their ultimate allegiance to God. Even though both Jeremiah and Daniel saw clearly how the state could function as an enemy to God's purposes, they both "chose to serve the state at the civil-political level, but also took the opportunity to challenge that state in the name of the 'God of heaven' to mend its ways in line with a paradigm of justice derived from Sinai (Dan. 4:27)."[52] In one sense, God's critique is virulent, whether directed toward the surrounding nations or to Israel (see Amos 1–2), but his love is likewise generous, envisioning an eschatological banquet for all the nations (Isa. 25:6). Throughout the Old Testament, God advocates not only for the weak but also for the strong; not only for persons but also for governments; not only for the marginalized but also for the elite.[53]

We see a more intimate, personal advocacy when Job appeals to God in the midst of his crisis. He says, "Even now my witness is in heaven; my advocate is on high" (16:19). In common Hebraic parallelism, "witness" and "advocacy" are interchangeable as Job contemplates God's nature. He further expounds on these in the next verse by saying, "My intercessor is my friend as my eyes pour out tears to God" (v. 20), deepening the intimacy of God's advocacy.

In summary, the Old Testament reveals many different forms of advocacy, from direct ultimatums, to narratives,[54] songs and poetry, apocalyptic language, and wisdom speech.[55] The genius behind the different genres is how they envision alternatives to the distortions of power, often through song or

50. C. Wright, *People of God and the State*, 17–18.

51. Both of these examples occur in 1 Kings 18.

52. C. Wright, *People of God and the State*, 24.

53. Although, to make this point, we should not collapse God's advocacy into one generic variety. The biblical account does reveal a special care for the poor, weak, marginalized, and aliens, as the measure of a just society that embodies God's law.

54. Elsewhere Chris Wright explains, "Indeed, the skill of the Hebrew historians often lies in the tantalizing way they present a story and refrain from comment, allowing readers to draw their own ethical conclusions (which are not by any means always straightforward). But the ethical impact remains, precisely because God is at work within the narrative—explicitly or behind the scenes—initiating, reacting, leading and responding to events." *Old Testament Ethics*, 33.

55. Within Old Testament monarchy, kings often had "royal courts" whose purpose was to provide wisdom for the governance of the nation. Thus, Brueggemann explains, "There was an intellectual tradition of learned, skilled persons in ancient Israel who operated in a variety

eschatological expression—not just condemning sin but imagining something new. What is more, sometimes advocacy happens overtly, but more often in subtle, imaginative, and even subversive forms that confound the "false consciousness" of the prevailing authorities and reveal a different way of living in the world.[56] Hence, interpreting advocacy in the Old Testament requires a perceptive hermeneutic that, for example, understands apocalyptic language as a kind of protest literature, or poetry as a way of imagining something new.

The substance of prophetic utterances always points first to an acknowledgment of God, and thereafter toward others. We fall into one of the dangers of advocacy-related work when we focus upon something like justice but neglect the very foundation of all: God himself! We fall into the other when we misrepresent God's nature and end up with varying conceptions of justice, which is why every oppressive political or economic structure is founded upon an idolatrous vision of God in society. Advocacy requires a Subject.

Advocacy in Redemption (New Testament Contours)

In the New Testament, we witness the gradual yet resolute unfolding of a new humanity, previously seen in opaque forms as the people of Israel, but now comprehended with vivid brilliance in Jesus Christ. And, in continuity with Old Testament testimony, Jesus does not speak in one uniform way, but through a variety of overt, subtle, and sometimes "hidden" means (such as we find in the parables) that disclose and hide, confront but imagine a new kingdom—all founded upon God's rule.

The Son enters the world in order to demonstrate a deeper picture of this advocacy: taking on full humanity, quietly working from the inside out to reorder the cosmos, while demonstrating God's love for humans, even to the point of death, death on the cross (Phil. 2:6–11). Through such a *life* of advocacy, God's kingdom breaks into the world while disclosing the real human (Rom. 5:10). Jesus begins his formal ministry by announcing the fulfillment of Isaiah's prophecy regarding "good news to the poor," "freedom for the prisoners," and "recovery of sight for the blind" (Luke 4:18–19), and fulfills these words through acts of healing, teaching, and sacrifice, ultimately dying for the sake of the world. In such ways, Christ "images" God to perfection (2 Cor. 4:4; Col. 1:15).

---

of ways throughout society, in order to shape learning and also to impinge upon public policy formation and implementation." *Theology of the Old Testament*, 684.

56. For a good treatment of this within the corpus of Scripture, see Brueggemann, *Truth Speaks to Power*.

The first thing that stands out is that God does not advocate from a distance but comes near. All throughout Scripture, God works silently, behind the scenes, with a discourse representative of wisdom speech, in songs, parables, and other language that simultaneously reveals and hides. God's advocacy refuses to be co-opted by the "powers" in the world, but works in silence,[57] through vulnerability, and yes, in humanity, such as we find in the incarnation. With Jesus's entrance into the world, a clearer picture of God's advocacy comes into focus, one that helps us appreciate the full extent God goes to in order to advocate for humanity: he will not just advocate *for* them, but be *with* them. Every aspect of Christ's life reveals true God in authentic humanity: like viewing a complex cloth weave from the back, we see only an amorphous tangle of loose threads, until we turn it around and the true pattern is revealed to show the magnificent beauty that was always there. Jesus reveals the nature of God while also revealing the real human.

Jesus walks into all facets of the world and reorients the structures for their true, appointed purposes, reminding them of those purposes. He stands before economic systems, family units, land, agriculture, and political institutions, and brings them under his Lordship. Jesus's repeated use of the word "kingdom" implies certain sociopolitical implications, as if to say that salvation must attend not only to personal issues but also to the broader contexts in which humans live. Or, as Richard Mouw puts it, "The New Testament's use of the political term 'kingdom' to describe the sum of God's redemptive purposes indicates that the total transformation of all things which he intends for his creation includes a transformation of the political realm as well as other realms."[58] To reveal such a kingdom, Jesus attacks the symbols of his day, including such things as the temple, food laws, Sabbath, and "righteousness," while establishing new symbols through liturgies of sacrifice (Matt. 16:25), giving (Luke 6:29–30), and the forgiveness of sins (Luke 7:48).[59] Ultimately, Jesus destroys the greatest symbol of all, the Messiah, to demonstrate that the pathway to power involves suffering and death. Or as Judith Diehl explains, "With some degree of irony, then, what the Romans publicized as an emblem of fear and terror [the cross] ultimately became a symbol of true power and supremacy for the Christian believers in the empire."[60] Thus we witness the full

---

57. For an interesting treatment of silence in public life, see Malesic, *Secret Faith in the Public Square*. Such a perspective does not imply quietism, but a purposeful silence that refuses to allow the "powers" to co-opt the Bible (or spiritual authority) for their own purposes.

58. Mouw, *Political Evangelism*, 24.

59. John Howard Yoder encourages Christians to adopt forgiveness as a sacrament of the church; see *Body Politics*, chap. 1.

60. Diehl, "Anti-Imperial Rhetoric," 53.

scope of Jesus's advocacy. It is a radical advocacy, with great risk to himself. He eschews comfort, refuses to conform to the status quo, and shows publicly the extent to which God goes for humanity.

With the resurrection, Jesus continues to advocate for humanity while seated at the right hand of God the Father (1 John 2:1). The very same power that raised Jesus from the dead is at work in the lives of believers everywhere (Rom. 8:11) through the work of the Holy Spirit. The death and resurrection of Jesus declare a resounding "Yes" and "No" to the world: a "Yes" to real humanity made visible in Jesus Christ (along with the products of human agency, such as systems and structures), and a "No" to the idolatrous conceptions that twist and contort through the distortions of sin.[61] As followers of Christ who embody this new humanity, we similarly live Jesus's "Yes" and "No" before the world.

Advocacy through the Holy Spirit

The Holy Spirit continues the work of Jesus's life, applying Christ's Lordship in the entirety of human life (inclusive of institutions). He reveals God's nature (1 Cor. 2:10–16) and intercedes for Christians before the throne of God (Rom. 8:26–27; cf. John 14:15–16), raising them to the highest status as God's children, and coheirs with Christ (Rom. 8:14–17). The Holy Spirit further distributes gifts for the good of the entire body (Rom. 12; 1 Cor. 12; Eph. 4), so that the Church might represent the fullness of Jesus Christ before the fullness of the world.

For such reasons, the Holy Spirit is called the Advocate (in Greek, *paraklētos*, or paraclete), which literally means "one called alongside another" (John 14:15, 26; 15:26; 16:7). In ancient Greece, a paraclete functioned as a kind of defense attorney in legal matters.[62] Jesus uses the word "another" to stress that the Holy Spirit continues Jesus's role as advocate and will be with believers forever (v. 16). He is called the "Spirit of truth" because he "[testifies] about" Jesus (John 15:26) and "will guide [them] into all the truth" (16:13), continuing the vital linkage between advocacy and witness that we find in Scripture. Through the indwelling of the Spirit after Pentecost, Jesus tells the disciples,

---

61. Lesslie Newbigin says it this way,

> A society which accepts the crucifixion and resurrection of Jesus as its ultimate standards of reference will have to be a society whose whole style of life, and not only its words, conveys something of that radical dissent from the world which is manifest in the Cross, and at the same time something of that affirmation of the world which is made possible by the resurrection. ("Stewardship, Mission, and Development," 6)

62. Beasley-Murray, *John*, 256.

they, too, "will bear witness, because [they] have been with [him] from the beginning" (15:27).

The rise of the early Church becomes possible only through the advocacy of the Holy Spirit, granting these "unschooled, ordinary men" a powerful testimony before religious authorities (Acts 4:8–31), local people, and political leaders (chap. 24). Their advocacy bears witness to the life of Jesus applied to all facets of society, whether education, economics, or even politics. Lamin Sanneh describes the early Church as "an oriental caravanserai, with its complex baggage of exotic teachings, baffling mysteries, colourful sounds and eclectic ethical code, leaving the authorities to whistle in the dark about the unshakeable foundations that have ordered the community, fixed the beliefs and set the common practices."[63] Without the witness of the Holy Spirit, none of this would be possible. But after Pentecost, the Spirit sends this ragtag group of people into the farthest lands, encountering different cultures, languages, and a dizzying array of institutions and structures. The Spirit equips people to witness to the risen Christ wherever they go (and in all facets of life).

Humans as Image Bearers in Advocacy

As we have seen in this brief narrative, humans "image" God's nature before the world. The Holy Spirit applies to our lives (even our humanities!) the character of Christ, enabling us, along with diverse others (Eph. 2:11–22; 3:18–21), to faithfully represent God in all realms of life. All Scripture points to the testimony of the One who alone defines reality, especially for those of us who swim in a sea of conflicting distortions. God's testimony about himself, whether found in the prophets or in the songs of doxology in the Psalms, points to deeper narratives of God. Christians enter into this drama of Scripture for the purpose of retelling the story of the world and reordering its powers, based upon the person of Jesus Christ.[64]

Cultural Advocacy

In the Bible we find various texts that appear to authenticate the role of political authorities (e.g., Rom. 12:19–13:7; 1 Pet. 2:13–17). Nicholas Wolterstorff places these in a larger context of teachings dealing with the household

63. Sanneh, *Encountering the West*, 136.
64. Brueggemann explains the nature of "testimony," saying: "The role of testimony is to advocate a rendering of truth and a version of reality that are urged over against other renderings and versions. The witnesses for Yahweh in the Old Testament advocate a truth and a reality in which Yahweh stands as the leading and preeminent Character." *Theology of the Old Testament*, 65.

(such as Eph. 5:21 and Col. 3:18) and argues that they should be interpreted together as indicating how Christians should engage the various institutions in society. The key for him lies in the area of difference between the kingdom of God and Greco-Roman society, both in "how [Christians] understand the significance of those institutions and in how they conduct themselves with them."[65] Like Jesus, we must look for deeper insights into how Christians should engage society, but do so with difference, continually saying yes and no because of the cross and resurrection of Christ. Or as Miroslav Volf explains,

> Christians do not come into their social world from outside seeking either to accommodate to their new home (like second generation immigrants would), shape it in the image of the one they have left behind (like colonizers would), or establish a little haven in the strange new world reminiscent of the old (as resident aliens would). They are not outsiders who either seek to become insiders or maintain strenuously the status of outsiders. Christians are the insiders who have diverted from their culture by being born again. They are by definition those who are not what they used to be, those who do not live like they used to live. Christian difference is therefore not an insertion of something new into the old from the outside, but a bursting out of the new precisely within the proper space of the old.[66]

Elsewhere, Volf refers to this as "diverting without leaving," to imply something of the dual allegiances that Christians inhabit.[67] But to speak of "dual allegiances" is not to imply a dualism; instead, it invokes an active, intentional engagement, where new birth in Christ leads to a new way of living in the world, but without any of the gnostic overtones of rejecting our earthly habitation.[68] Any effort to resolve Christian identity that involves carving the world into nice, neat categories will likely miss the incarnational impetus of what it means to live as "aliens" in the world, while also full citizens of culture. The greater challenge is to live fully in this world, including its structures, while living differently because of our new identity.

Advocacy through Christ

What does this mean for how humans undertake advocacy work? Initially, God's image comes with certain rights and responsibilities. Through the Holy

---

65. Wolterstorff, "Theological Foundations," 142.
66. Volf, "Soft Difference," 18–19.
67. Volf, *Public Faith*, 93.
68. Ellul prefers the concept of dual citizenship, or that the Christian is an ambassador sent to represent the interests of a sovereign. *Présence au monde moderne*, 46.

Spirit, we represent Christ before the world. If humans are the image of God, then we undertake this identity with faithfulness to God's image. Like those with sleepy eyes who continually focus upon an object after a long, hard night's slumber, we must relentlessly look upon God in the person of Jesus Christ. For he alone is the only true Image of God (John 14:9).

Advocacy is creational as it emanates from Christ. We do not approach the "powers" within the world for the sake of tearing them down, but for envisioning them anew through the resources of Christ's nature. The biblical narrative teaches us that whenever God's agents wanted to confront the powers in the world, they did so with imagination (and oftentimes through doxology or song). Praise language unleashes resources by which to enter God's world for the sake of reimaging God in the world. Or, as Brueggemann says, "Doxology is the ultimate challenge to the language of managed reality, and it alone is the universe of discourse in which energy is possible."[69] Inasmuch as God's advocacy begins with creation and flows to the re-creation of the world, so Christians should locate themselves within such a narrative. Advocacy should sing.

Advocacy with Humanity

Advocacy is also relational. We build intimate relationships with others because the Trinity informs the world: "that they may be one as we are one" (John 17:22). Undoubtedly, some ways of doing advocacy may bypass people, such as clicking a mouse to communicate our stance on a particular issue. But we believe that the best ways of doing advocacy involve intentional relationships with others.

God does not advocate from a distance, but comes near in the person of Christ, revealing the real human nature. As Christians, we sometimes think of humanity as a tiresome, faulty appendage to our real selves: something that gets in the way of our work here on earth. And so we seek to overcome humanity, or posit ourselves (or others) as superhumans, somehow "more" like God and less like humans. We marvel at the likes of William Wilberforce or Martin Luther King Jr., forgetting selectively that they were people just like us. We hide everything weak, vulnerable, or seemingly finite, trying to stand before the "powers" on their terms, as superhumans.[70] But Christ's humanity

---

69. Brueggemann, *Prophetic Imagination*, 18.
70. Marva Dawn queries,

> If the Church is most faithful to its true vocation as a created power through the weakness that gives way to God's tabernacling, then we must ask such questions as these: Why have we turned pastors into successful CEOs instead of shepherds for the weak? Why do

tells us something different. As Vinoth Ramachandra states, "Our humanity is not something that comes between us and God. On the contrary, it is precisely in our humanity that we are called to be bearers of the divine glory, the means by which God is made known."[71] Advocacy demands authentic humanity, faithfulness to our humanity, which is always defined by Christ's humanity, and ever located within the broader community of diverse "image bearers" around the world. Our world needs fewer heroes and more people who will dare to be truly human. Therefore, advocacy cannot take place only in highly sanitized halls of Congress or in pristine local civic buildings, but it requires connection with the very lives of people trapped in poverty: in Section 8 housing, slums, or rural landlessness. Location matters.

A focus on Christ's humanity is also critical in light of predilections within evangelicalism to accentuate Christ's deity (often to the detriment of Jesus's humanity). If we focus upon the deity of Christ (which we must!) to the detriment of his humanity (which has been our deficiency), our efforts in the world will want to mirror Christ, which often means being more like God and less like humans. We will want to deify leaders and sacralize institutions (political or economic) as we hold tenuously to our humanity as with a soiled garment. But if Christ is not only divine but also human, then we must work for a healthy "humanization" of the structures in the world, predicated upon the new humanity emerging in Jesus Christ. Jesus dwelled with the poor, those called in Hebrew the *am ha'aretz*, the oft-marginalized "people of the land"; visited gentiles; sat with "sinners"; and went out of his way to connect with the Samaritan woman. He also met with religious leaders and tax collectors. Jesus held a private conference with Pilate just before his crucifixion, in which he gently rebukes Pilate with regard to the real state of power (John 19:10–11). Advocacy not only engages the powers at the structural level, but attends to what is taking place at the grass roots, where injustices, marginalization, and harmful "social imaginaries" abound. Jesus reminds us of a new way of being human in the world, which, if we will allow it, has the potential to work its way into the structures of society through the agency of the Church.

---

we search for pastors who are handsome, sophisticated, charismatic—instead of models in suffering? Why do our churches adopt practices of business life and its achievement models? Why do we resort to gimmicks, or what Jacques Ellul calls Technique, instead of practicing an "unadulterated handling of the Word"? (*Powers, Weakness*, 57)

In such a light, we also need to be careful of Christian triumphalism, which makes us confidently proclaim: "We will change the world!" Jesus was tempted at many points with triumphalism, whether to worship Satan and receive all the kingdoms of the world (Matt. 4:8–9), or call down fire from heaven (Luke 9:54), and ultimately to forego the cross. We *should* change the world, but the pathway to such a change has nothing to do with triumphalism.

71. Ramachandra, *Recovery of Mission*, 252.

Advocacy by Means of Power

All throughout Scripture, the persons of the Trinity redefine power, expressed in love, fidelity, and generosity for the "other," as power is exercised in giving, hosting, serving, and sending. We witness this through creation, redemption, the incarnation, and the Spirit's indwelling of believers. William Schweiker explores similar ideas by investigating the moral nature of power. He describes how in a modern, technological age, "power" has come into its own as an independent entity, divorced from any theological underpinnings and thus, in most people's minds, constitutive of reality itself. Entities such as wealth, weapons, or technology (even politics) assume anthropomorphic properties: we say, "Money speaks" or "The camera likes me," and the lines between animate and inanimate become blurred. Meanwhile, human identity gets redefined. Those "in power" have more of it, and those "without power" have less. Life in this moral ontology (or "social imaginary") revolves around the acquisition of power; or in Schweiker's words, "Power does not serve a value beyond itself, because it is believed to be the source of value."[72] However, such an understanding represents only partial truth (as most lies tend to do) for power can be the source of value only if we locate power in God. By reframing the starting point we discover a deeper ontology of power that begins within the Trinity, overflows to creation, nurtures life, blesses the nations, protects the weak, and subsequently suffers, even dies, for the "other." God redefines life by redefining the essence of power.

In a world where competing power interests contend for greater shares of human identity, the powerless feel less human and subsequently suffer from the actions of others. An African proverb states, "When two elephants fight, the grass suffers." In other words, in a world of power, those without power languish from abuse or neglect. Sometimes they aren't even seen. The purpose of advocacy is not to enter the fray, rolling up one's sleeves to flex one's muscles, but to nurture a *new kind of power* within the political structures that takes its essence from God's moral ontology. Hence, "the basic human problem is not that of exercising of power in the creation of civilization but fidelity to a power that grounds and limits human power—the divine."[73]

Advocacy and Seeing the "Other"

This means we need to *see* others, especially those trapped in vicious cycles of poverty, marginalization, or hopelessness. Many of the world's problems

72. Schweiker, "Power and the Image of God," 207.
73. Ibid., 217.

happen because of failure of sight. Advocacy is more than words; it is dramatized wisdom, knit within the fabric of everyday life. Jesus defends the adulterer, sits with sinners, draws children to himself, and heals the outcast. He sees them![74] But he also sees political leaders. Any posture of advocacy that vilifies such people or treats them as objects neglects the way that Jesus dealt with others.[75]

But to do so requires an underlying ethic of advocacy for the "other," especially the diverse, sometimes onerous, always exceedingly different, and, with kingdom eyes, eternally beautiful "other." The cross of Christ destroys every wall of hostility that divides us from others (Eph. 2:13–21). Meanwhile, the Holy Spirit appropriates Christ's nature within humans: nurturing grace within the spaces of the cosmos, while calling forth a power that heals, brings together, and creates a new humanity, in which Christ is Lord over all. In the eternal generosity of the Godhead, the divine community calls believers to *advocate with*, not by coercive power or by retreating into Christian ghettos, but through conformity to the image of the Son. We advocate for others by living in the world. And by living in the world, we become more like Christ.

All of this is possible because God includes humans in the inner love of the Trinity, or, drawing upon an analogy of Saint Irenaeus, wraps them in divine embrace. Hence, Jesus teaches, "Anyone who loves me will obey my teaching. My Father will love them, and we will come to them and make our home with them" (John 14:23); and later he prays, "Father, I want those you have given me to be with me where I am, and to see my glory, the glory you have given me because you loved me before the creation of the world" (17:24). Thus God's advocacy does not just sit idle, encased within sterile, judicial language, but flows from the Trinity to humans and subsequently into the lives of others with cosmological influence.

Advocacy and Symbols

Finally, like Christ we need to challenge not only the visible structures of our day, but more important, the underlying symbols (and narratives) that influence how these receive their input. Re-creating the symbolic involves a more subtle and gradual form of advocacy by which we shape the institutions through the ways we live. N. T. Wright explains it this way: "Your task is to

---

74. We find simple statements of "sight" throughout Jesus's life—cf. Matt. 4:18, 21; 9:2, 9, 36; 14:14; Mark 2:5; Luke 5:27; 7:13; 15:20; 19:41—but perhaps nowhere as poignantly as with the woman with the flow of blood in Matt. 9:22: "Jesus turned and saw her. 'Take heart, daughter,' he said, 'your faith has healed you.'"

75. Thanks to an advance reader of the manuscript for this good reminder.

find the symbolic ways of doing things differently, planting flags in hostile soil, setting up signposts that say there is a different way to be human. And when people are puzzled at what you are doing, find ways—fresh ways—of telling the story of the return of the human race from its exile, and use stories as your explanation."[76]

Much of what we have shared in this chapter points toward these deeper, more imaginative understandings of advocacy. To bring about cultural change requires hard, disciplined, often behind-the-scenes work. Transformational advocacy might borrow a page from mission history and understand that quick, leveraged changes from the outside often bring about more damage than good. Deep cultural change requires countless little changes wrought by agents from the inside, whether they be from legislators, aides, analysts, or a host of other "political" persons including the broader citizenry—where each member exerts his or her respective powers and giftings for the common good. If structures come about through the efforts of humans, then cultural change needs to occur in the same way. But the kind of change we envision cannot happen without dramatizing the nature of God.

Christians in advocacy will constantly feel tempted to use power as the world uses power, justifying any coercive actions by the obvious injustices done against countless people. But we may take consolation in the fact that Jesus also experienced these temptations in the wilderness and doubtlessly many other times in his life. In the face of such temptations, Jesus did the unthinkable—in a manner of speaking—he sang.[77] And ultimately, he suffered, died, and rose again.

Learning to Image God's Advocacy

Throughout this chapter we have reflected upon advocacy as a metaphor for God's nature, with implications for what it means to faithfully "image" God. We have feasted upon a host of biblical and theological resources for looking at God through these lenses, framing such a theology in narrative form as a kind of lived wisdom. We believe that such an activity is not only faithful to Scripture but also necessary for living in our ever-changing world.

Such a retelling of advocacy does two related things. First, it enlarges our understanding of God beyond predetermined categories, to look, with wisdom

76. N. T. Wright, *Challenge of Jesus*, 186. The point being made here is key to how spiritual concerns are integrated into the process: it opens doors to share the gospel.

77. If the Psalms represent songs, Jesus's quotation of the Psalms in the temptation experience can be seen as a way of singing.

eyes, through the entire corpus of Scripture to grasp God's advocacy in ways that transcend the explicit use of the term. Such a narrative takes seriously the biblical text but focuses instinctively upon the nature of God through creation, redemption, and re-creation (eschatology) to discern the myriad of ways that God's advocacy takes place in the world. Hence, we allow God to define the term, not content for it to be compromised by specific, cultural readings, but alert to the fundamental reality that *advocacy includes a God who speaks for others before the powers that exist in the world and for the growth of all things in conformity to the image of the Son.*

Second, by entering into God's story we develop the imaginative ability to improvise within ever-new sociopolitical circumstances, being true to the narrative of Scripture while faithful to our diverse, contemporary settings.[78] Improvisation requires fidelity to the person of Jesus Christ, through the ministry of the Holy Spirit, our Advocate, as we seek to live God's nature faithfully within a world of competing, distorted structures. God doesn't allow us the luxury of a one-size-fits-all template for how to engage the world, but God does freely bestow upon us the Holy Spirit for the purposes of applying the Lordship of Jesus Christ to all facets of our world, even to structures and institutions.

In the next chapter, we will look more closely at the institutions and how Christians should relate to them, continuing the themes explored above, but with a tighter focus upon the "powers." And then in chapter 5 we will talk about what this means for the Church.

---

78. Vanhoozer, *Drama of Doctrine*, 32.

4

Transformational Advocacy and Power

The State and Social Institutions

God speaks. He does so most clearly in Jesus Christ, who is represented in our day in the work of the Holy Spirit through the body of Christ, which is comprised of believers all over the world. Therefore, in speaking out with and *for* poor and marginalized people, *we* live out our identity as God's image bearers on earth. But here is where it gets difficult. As evangelicals we possess robust theologies for dealing with personal sin but limited resources for facing structural or institutional forms of sin. Yet as we noted in the last chapter, the breaking of shalom filters into the institutional fabric of society—affecting political, social, and economic dimensions of life.

Our lack of an engagement with structural elements is compounded by the influence these entities have upon life. For many people, institutions such as politics, economics, or technology define reality in this world. Further, these institutions—states, corporations, universities, nonprofits, churches, etc.—are not "neutral" in their fallenness, but represent spiritual powers: entities that hold power that can either enhance, limit, or even destroy hints of shalom in the world.

In this chapter we consider the nature of these powers, these institutions before which we speak, and the people within them. We distinguish the concept of "power" from "powers" and analyze what Scripture suggests about the nature of these institutions. We argue that God has given these institutions for good and that despite their current fallenness, they too are part of God's redemptive plan. This does not imply that our goal is to redeem every institution via our advocacy but rather to suggest that *in speaking before them we are bearing witness to the truth that God desires their good contribution, and we are challenging them to fulfill their God-given role.*

Given the singularly important role of the state (indeed some might argue that most institutions in the world derive their power in a very real sense from the state), we focus on it to analyze the implication of its fallenness for our advocacy work. Specifically, we examine the role of the statesperson within the state given the fact that our advocacy is never addressed to a disembodied entity but to the people within it. In examining the state/statesperson nexus we acknowledge that the state, as a power, is more than the sum of the collective will of the people who work within it. But despite the larger whole, we acknowledge that our advocacy is always addressed to human beings who have the ability (albeit with difficulty) to reform and change the institutions of which they are a part.

We close with a brief consideration of other—nonstate—institutions before moving on, in the next chapter, to consider the Church's role in advocacy given these realities.

A Fallen World: The Locus of Our Advocacy

We examined in some detail in the previous chapter the reality of our fallen world and the way (per Plantinga) sin "burrows into the bowels of institutions," co-opting them for ends other than those intended by God. One way to think about the fall is that it represents a human quest for autonomy—a desire to establish "reigns" independent of God—to become gods.[1] This "autonomy quest" not only explains individual behavior but also helps us understand the workings of complex institutions.

God bestows gifts on humans for the common good,[2] and this good is realized to the extent that each person offers his or her giftedness to the whole. However, this goodness is not just aesthetic but actually points to the nature of the Trinity. In other words, institutions arise because God shares his nature

---

1. Karl Barth disagrees slightly with this interpretation. He sees the state becoming "demonic" when it loses sight of its true substance, dignity, and purpose. The reason for this is that "power, the State as such, belongs originally and ultimately to Jesus Christ." See "Church and State" in *Community, State, and Church*, 118.

2. This is clearly true for the Church per Paul's writings in 1 Cor. 12, but we would argue that it represents a prefiguration of God's ideal for all human communities.

with the world. We may even think of the Trinity as the very first institution if we define it as a "stable structure of social interaction."[3] But sin distorts persons and corresponding larger social entities. Institutions made up of individuals in search of personal autonomy thus become loci of divisiveness in which common goals (typically articulated in mission and vision statements) for good become subordinated to selfish ends. The authors' experiences suggest that the fall affects institutions, at least in part, because the good to which institutions aspire is corrupted by individuals seeking their own way. Fallen people create fallen institutions. Ironically, we also observe that despite this divisiveness, institutions develop clear collective identities around which they seek to mobilize allegiance. In the end, the institutions themselves participate, as collectives, in the same "autonomy quest" as the individuals within them.

This is the reality of the institutions before which we speak in our advocacy work. It is important that we also acknowledge that God's reconciliation plan is cosmic—it embraces people, cultures, and institutions. As Paul wrote in Colossians:

> [God] has delivered us from the dominion of darkness and transferred us to the kingdom of his beloved Son, in whom we have redemption, the forgiveness of sins. He is the image of the invisible God, the first-born of all creation; for in him all things were created, in heaven and on earth, visible and invisible, whether thrones or dominions or principalities or authorities—all things were created through him and for him. He is before all things, and in him all things hold together. He is the head of the body, the church; he is the beginning, the first-born from the dead, that in everything he might be pre-eminent. For in him all the fullness of God was pleased to dwell, *and through him to reconcile to himself all things, whether on earth or in heaven, making peace by the blood of his cross.* (1:13–20 RSV; emphasis added)

It is with this assurance that we now consider the nature of power and the reality of the "powers" in our world today.

Power and "the Powers"

While the words "power" and "powers" differ by only one letter, this letter makes a great deal of difference for our analysis. The basic definitions of advocacy we have laid out suggest that we Christians direct our advocacy efforts to those in power, because we assume that they can and should do

3. Volf, *After Our Likeness*, 235.

something about the injustices we're concerned about. The concept of "the powers" focuses not merely on those who hold power but also on the systems, ideologies, and structures (institutions, for example) in which they work and in which we all live—and their influence on creating or maintaining justice.

Talking about *power* acknowledges that certain individuals and institutions are given (or take upon themselves) the right to make decisions that affect the lives of other people. However, stating that institutions (states, corporations, churches, universities, voluntary organizations, etc.) are *powers* acknowledges that they have an identity and force that represent more than the sum of the individuals who work within them, and points to a "spiritual" reality about their ability to constrain or promote human flourishing (or shalom more broadly defined). C. S. Lewis talks about a similar reality observed in families, sports teams, clubs, and trade unions, in which these entities develop a "spirit" that plays itself out in "particular ways [their members have] of talking and behaving which they would not have if they were apart."[4] While much of this is natural, the "spirit" can easily become demonic when it asserts autonomy from God and creates injustices that prey upon the lives of the weak and vulnerable.

While the idea of *powers* is not a uniquely Christian concept (in the film *The Corporation*, for example, corporations are presented as suprahuman entities that transcend the full control of the individuals who work within them and who have an identity of their own), in this section we will examine institutions in light of the biblical concepts of "principalities and powers" (among other terms). But let us push the distinction between power and powers a bit further first. Gary Haugen of the International Justice Mission speaks about power and its relation to justice in this way: "What does it mean to say that ours is a God of justice? Is there anything that we can usefully understand about justice in the Bible? I believe there is. Fundamentally justice has to do with the exercise of power. To say God is a God of justice is to say that he is a God who cares about the right exercise of power or authority."[5] Theologian Hendrik Berkhof talks similarly about Paul's conception of the powers: "They are the linkage between God's love and visible human experience. They are to hold life together, preserving it within God's love . . . as bonds between God and man. As signposts toward the service of God, they form the *framework* within which such service must needs be carried out."[6] Elsewhere Berkhof refers to them as the "framework of creation, the canvas which invisibly supports the tableau of the life of men and society."[7]

4. Lewis, *Mere Christianity*, 136.
5. Haugen, *Good News about Injustice*, 71.
6. Berkhof, *Christ and the Powers*, 29; emphasis added.
7. Ibid., 23.

We will explore more about the powers below. But at this point it might be enough to say that human power is always exercised within the powers (the "frameworks"). As we address humans in positions of power, we must recognize they are part of structures that have meaning and purpose that transcend the individual participants' personal influence. Clearly the concepts of power and the powers are related, but we wish to argue here that they are distinct, that the concept of the powers helps us think more clearly about the reality of the institutions that make up our world and clearly affect humans' ability to flourish.

The Concept of the Powers

Let us more formally consider the concept of the powers, drawing on the work of several theologians whose exegesis of Paul's writing has made the apostle's ideas relevant to contemporary thinking. The Scriptures most relevant to this analysis are the following (per Berkhof), with added emphasis placed on key terms:

> For I am convinced that neither death nor life, neither angels nor demons [or *nor heavenly rulers*], neither the present nor the future, nor any *powers*, neither height nor depth, nor anything else in all creation, will be able to separate us from the love of God that is in Christ Jesus our Lord. (Rom. 8:38–39)

> We do, however, speak a message of wisdom among the mature, but not the wisdom of this age or of the rulers of this age, who are coming to nothing. No, we declare God's wisdom, a mystery that has been hidden and that God destined for our glory before time began. None of the *rulers of this age* understood it, for if they had, they would not have crucified the Lord of glory. (1 Cor. 2:6–8)

> Then [when believers are raised from the dead] the end will come, when he [Christ] hands over the kingdom to God the Father after he has destroyed all *dominion*, *authority* and *power*. For he must reign until he has put all his enemies under his feet. The last enemy to be destroyed is death. (1 Cor. 15:24–26)

> I pray that the eyes of your heart may be enlightened in order that you may know the hope to which he has called you, the riches of his glorious inheritance in his holy people, and his incomparably great power for us who believe. That power is the same as the mighty strength he exerted when he raised Christ from the dead and seated him at his right hand in the heavenly realms, far above all *rule*

and *authority*, *power* and *dominion*, and every *name that is invoked*, not only in the present age but also in the one to come. (Eph. 1:18–21)

As for you, you were dead in your transgressions and sins, in which you used to live when you followed the *ways of this world* and of the *ruler of the kingdom of the air*, the spirit who is now at work in those who are disobedient. (Eph. 2:1–2)

Although I am less than the least of all the Lord's people, this grace was given me, to preach to the Gentiles the boundless riches of Christ, and to make plain to everyone the administration of this mystery, which for ages past was kept hidden in God, who created all things. His intent was that now, through the church, the manifold wisdom of God should be made known to the *rulers* and *authorities* in the heavenly realms. (Eph. 3:8–10)

For our struggle is not against flesh and blood, but against the rulers, against the authorities, against the *powers of this dark world* and against the *spiritual forces* of evil in the heavenly realms. (Eph. 6:12)

For he rescued us from the dominion of darkness and brought us into the kingdom of the Son he loves, in whom we have redemption, the forgiveness of sins. The Son is the image of the invisible God, the firstborn over all creation. For in him all things were created: things in heaven and on earth, visible and invisible, whether *thrones* or *powers* or *rulers* or *authorities*; all things have been created through him and for him. (Col. 1:13–16)

When you were dead in your sins and in the uncircumcision of your flesh, God made you alive with Christ. He forgave us all our sins, having canceled the charge of our legal indebtedness, which stood against us and condemned us; he has taken it away, nailing it to the cross. And having disarmed the *powers* and *authorities*, he made a public spectacle of them, triumphing over them by the cross. (Col. 2:13–15)

The highlighted terms in these passages (as translated in the NIV) include "heavenly rulers," "powers," "rulers of this age," "authorities," "dominion," "ways of this world," "ruler of the kingdom of the air," "powers of this dark world," "spiritual forces," and "thrones." It is not our purpose here to explore the Greek words from which these have been translated nor develop their meaning in detail. While Walter Wink has provided helpful details on the historical meaning of these terms,[8] it might be enough to conclude that the powers occupy a prominent role in Pauline writings and that Christian witness must speak to the powers (esp. Eph. 3:10–11).

8. See Wink, *Naming the Powers.*

Marva Dawn begins her insightful review of recent scholarship on the concept of the powers[9] by noting that the notion of principalities and powers is common in religious and broader societal discourse and is used to point to the "immensity" of the influence of forces that transcend the merely human. She goes on to develop the idea that among Christian theologians in recent times there are two broad schools of interpretation concerning the meaning of these concepts: the *demythologizers*, who "too easily identify the powers only with human structures, and the *personalizers*, who insist that the powers should be identified with angelic beings."[10] Dawn quotes a variety of authors to argue that for the writers of the biblical texts in question, the distinction was probably meaningless, and that, in some sense, both ideas were intended.

Dawn and many others argue convincingly that whatever else these terms might refer to, they do include the idea of "structures" that provide (as already suggested by Berkhof) a framework for the good functioning of society, and that they include the state and other institutions. Yoder summarizes his understanding in this way: "We might say that we have here an inclusive vision of religious structures . . . intellectual structures (-ologies and -isms), moral structures (codes and customs), political structures (the tyrant, the market, the school, the courts, race, and nation)."[11]

The Nature of the Powers

From this point on we limit the discussion to the powers as "structures" including the state, and although we will not go into great detail about them, we might include institutions such as corporations and multilateral agencies such as the various UN bodies. This is not to deny the importance of viewing the concept of powers as referring at least in part to created beings. Rather, we narrow the focus to institutions and other structures because they are more closely related to advocacy work. This implies that we do not accept the idea that "demonic beings" merely use human structures (institutions) as instruments in their work. We disagree with an instrumentalist view because we don't see evidence for it in Scripture—aside from certain apocalyptic references made concerning angels of certain locations. However, even these usages do

9. Dawn, *Powers, Weakness*.

10. Ibid., 11. There is perhaps one more danger, the *divinizers*, who associate the state with God, because of cultural predispositions, political leanings, and/or hermeneutical readings of Rom. 13.

11. Yoder, *Politics of Jesus*, 143.

not imply that "angels" or "demons" merely dispose of nations or states as instruments to fulfill their designs.

With these points in mind let us return to Paul's writing on the subject. We see three broad themes emerging in the texts quoted above: (1) in a positive sense, Christ has created the powers for his purposes; (2) the powers have gone astray and do not serve Christ's purposes in this age; (3) in the cross, Christ has triumphed over the powers, and a time is coming when they will again (being dethroned) serve the purposes for which they were created. As Walter Wink has summarized: the powers are good, the powers are fallen, the powers will be redeemed.[12]

Let us examine these three points in more detail, because together they are critical not only for an understanding of the institutions we face in our advocacy work, but because they also provide us with important insights into how we might think about our approach to these institutions given the creative and redeeming work of Christ.

Created for Good

Since God's advocacy begins in creation, the early beginnings of institutions can be seen in Genesis, with God's mandate to humans to be fruitful, rule, name, and bless. Dietrich Bonhoeffer describes God's creating two institutions, family and work, which then give rise to other institutions such as politics.[13] Other scholars, such as Karl Barth and John Wesley, begin earlier, with God's nature, while a few argue that institutions arise only after the fall. The Old Testament continues to promote institutions such as family, state, and economics as agents of good in the ancient Near East, seen most poignantly in Jeremiah's admonition for the Israelites to "build houses," "plant gardens," "marry," and "seek the peace and prosperity of the city" and "pray . . . for it" while in exile (Jer. 29:5–7).[14] We find in these statements the validation of institutions (such as economics, family, and politics) for God's purposes in the world. And as we will see in the next chapter, the Church serves as an institution for the purposes of redeeming earthly institutions in the world.

Moving ahead to the New Testament, after describing the rabbinic and Greek cosmologies surrounding Paul at the time of his writing, Hendrik Berkhof draws some initial conclusions about Paul's use of the terms:

12. Wink, *Engaging the Powers*, 65.

13. Bonhoeffer, *Ethics*, 344–46. Bonhoeffer defines the state as "an ordered community; government is the power which creates and maintains order." Ibid., 332.

14. Some scholars suggest that "exile" continues to be the theme of the New Testament people of God, continuing to the present.

Paul observes that life is ruled by a series of Powers. He speaks of time (present and future), of space (depth and height), of life and death, of politics and philosophy, of public opinion and Jewish law, of pious tradition and the fateful course of the stars. Apart from Christ, man is at the mercy of these Powers. They encompass, carry, and guide his life. The demands of the present, fear of the future, state and society, life and death, tradition and morality—they are all our "guardians and trustees," the forces which hold together the world and the life of men and preserve them from chaos.[15]

Later, in a passage already alluded to above, he adds: "The Powers serve as the invisible weight-bearing substratum of the world, as the underpinnings of creation. By no means does Paul think of the Powers as evil in themselves."[16] In drawing these conclusions Berkhof is referring not only to the Colossians 1 passage but also to Galatians, where Paul talks about tradition and the law as "tutors" (*paidagōgos*, Gal. 3:24–25; NIV: "guardian"). Colossians 1 makes clear that "all things" come from Christ and are held together by him (vv. 15–17). Barth even holds that the state can be an instrument of grace in the world to the extent that it functions as a sign, or allegory, of what God is accomplishing in history.[17] In discussing Paul's writing in Romans 13, Yoder argues that even the fallen power of the state has a continued role in God's plan, because "even tyranny . . . is still better than chaos and we should be subject to it."[18] Wink states that "the Powers are inextricably locked into God's system, whose human face is revealed in Christ."[19]

We should pause here to consider the import of these ideas. While none of these authors suggests that *every* human institution is good (think of the mafia, for instance), they express a strong sense that God has given institutions (and traditions, customs, and systems, for example) to humans to provide them with order, with frameworks, with structure in the absence of which life would be unpredictable, chaotic, and profoundly dehumanizing.

As we engage in advocacy addressed to institutions in ways already suggested—to bring a "corrective" message to them—we can do so with confidence because we understand that God desires them to play a role that enables humans to live and to flourish, to be what God intended them to be. (This may be why

15. Berkhof, *Christ and the Powers*, 22.

16. Ibid., 28–29.

17. Barth, *Community, State, and Church*, 156–59. He continues later, "Its existence is not separate from the Kingdom of Jesus Christ; its foundations and its influence are not autonomous. It is outside the Church but not outside the range of Christ's dominion—it is an exponent of His Kingdom." Ibid., 156.

18. Yoder, *Politics of Jesus*, 141.

19. Wink, *Engaging the Powers*, 67.

Yoder writes, in relation to the state, at least, "that the Christian church knows why the state exists—knows, in fact, better than the state itself.")[20] Berkhof suggests this very role, and with it we transition to the current reality about the powers—their fallenness. He writes: "Therefore the believer's combat is never to strive *against* the Orders, but rather to battle for God's intention for them, and against their corruption."[21]

Bonhoeffer, for his part, sees the Church as the center of history, and thus tasked with speaking to the state. Similarly, Barth argues: "If the Church takes up its share of political responsibility, it must mean that it is taking that human initiative which the State cannot take: it is giving the State the impulse which it cannot give itself; it is reminding the State of those things of which it is unable to remind itself."[22]

Fallen

Despite the affirmations in Colossians 1 and elsewhere about the "goodness" of the powers, other passages reveal a current reality that is far less positive.[23] This reality—the fallenness of the powers—is one of the great faith challenges of our time. For if, indeed, Christ has triumphed over the powers, how then can they continue to cause such suffering in the world? Why do they fail to achieve God's plan for them in the present? The answers to these questions are beyond the purview of this volume, but the broader question of the meaning of fallenness for our advocacy is important. And perhaps as we analyze, below, this reality and the redemption of the powers, we will also gain some insights that enable us to answer these difficult questions.

So what, in practical terms, does it mean for the powers to be "fallen"? In simplest terms it means that the powers—the institutions and structures created to provide order—fail to fulfill their responsibilities in these areas. However, and worse, not only do they fail to be what they were meant to be but they also take on other roles that enable them to do great harm. In other words, their fallenness is not merely a "neutral" phenomenon but takes on a demonic identity in the world.

20. Yoder, *Christian Witness to the State*, 16.
21. Berkhof, *Christ and the Powers*, 29.
22. Barth, *Community, State, and Church*, 170.
23. Theologians disagree about the extent of the powers' fallenness, and even the extent of their effectiveness in the world. For example, Barth argues that not all political systems are despotic by nature, and some "may also manifest a neutral attitude towards Truth." Or, in one of his more famous passages: "Thus there is clearly no cause for the Church to act as though it lived, in relation to the State, in a night in which all cats are grey." Ibid., 119.

While we have purposefully avoided a full analysis of all the concepts and terms related to the powers, it is useful to discuss one particular term—*stoicheia*—which a number of authors discuss. This term, which Berkhof translates as "elemental things" or "elemental principles" in Galatians 4 and Colossians 2, refers to one form of the powers—their reality as human laws and traditions. Though this concept differs slightly from that of "thrones" or "principalities," most writers view all of these as part of the seamless "ordering" powers of the world, created by God for good, but fallen. Indeed, it is in these passages that we see how, rather than enabling order and flourishing, they enslave humans. What Paul says of them and how their purpose has been perverted is thus instructive as we consider what has happened to all the powers of the world. Willard Swartley argues that these "principles" are structures that are "deemed good and that provide the basis for natural or social order that enables life (for the Jews, the law) [but that] are turned into ultimate values, ends in themselves, and thus elevated to powers over one's life and then worshiped as gods."[24]

Berkhof extends Swartley's ideas about principles to the powers more generally:

> The Powers are no longer instruments, linkages between God's love, as revealed in Christ, and the visible world of creation. In fact, they have become gods (Galatians 4:8), behaving as though they were the ultimate ground of being, and demanding from men an appropriate worship. . . . No longer do the Powers bind man and God together; they separate them. They stand as a roadblock between the Creator and His creation.
>
> The Powers still continue to fulfill one half of their function. They still undergird human life and society and preserve them from chaos. But by holding the world together, they hold it away from God, not close to Him. They are "the rulers of this age" (I Corinthians 2:6). In their desire to rule they are in enmity towards the Lord of glory, who can suffer them only as instruments, not as lords.[25]

The reference to the 1 Corinthians 2 passage in the foregoing is critical because it points specifically to the role of the state and leaders. Paul's message is that the powers have fundamentally lost track of their identity and purpose in the world. And the results are not neutral. In losing their way they even went so far as to crucify the Lord of glory. Newbigin goes further in describing the implications of their fallenness. After recognizing that we cannot live without the powers because of their ordering function in the world, he argues

24. Swartley, "Jesus Christ: Victor over Evil," 103.
25. Berkhof, *Christ and the Powers*, 30.

that "they are corrupted, become demonic, when they are absolutized, given the place which only belongs to God."[26] They define reality for people.

We are left here with an image of powers that are bent on their own survival—as ends in themselves—and engaged in practices that create allegiance toward themselves so as to ensure that survival (recall our previous discussion of their autonomy quest). In focusing on their own survival they end up enslaving and dehumanizing the creation they were intended to protect and nurture. Again, let us reflect on this reality for a moment as we consider our advocacy work. Understanding the reality of the fallenness of the powers should not lead us to fear (as we will see below), but it should act as a sobering reminder of the extent to which they will go to ensure their existence as an end in itself, even to the point of demanding love! The individuals with whom we deal in our advocacy efforts operate within systems they do not fully control, systems that have imperatives that are at odds with God's intended purpose for them.

Some may object that in saying the foregoing we have turned nonpersonal institutions into persons and have given them moral responsibility they do not have. We will acknowledge here that it is not fully clear to us (nor to many of the authors cited here) exactly the sense in which these institutions bear responsibility or have a "will of their own." It is true that we deal with flesh and blood in our challenge to injustice. However, as Paul said in Ephesians 6, our true struggle is *not* against flesh and blood. Jacques Ellul is less ambiguous in suggesting that powers such as mammon and "technique" (roughly a sociocultural norm that represents the totality of means having absolute efficiency in every domain of human life) have "designs" of their own. In relation to mammon he says this about what Jesus was describing in Matthew 6 and Luke 16:

> Here Jesus personifies money and considers it a sort of god. . . . What Jesus is revealing is that money is a power. This term should be understood not in its vague meaning, "force," but in the specific sense in which it is used in the New Testament. Power is something that acts by itself, is capable of moving other things, is autonomous (or claims to be), is a law unto itself, and presents itself as an active agent. . . . Jesus is not describing a relationship between us and an object, but between us and an *active agent*. He is not suggesting that we use money wisely or earn it honestly. He is speaking of a power which tries to be like God, which makes itself our master and *which has specific goals*.[27]

The foregoing illustrates a sociological view of the "agency" of a power that extends beyond the state, which illustrates that even secular approaches

---

26. Newbigin, *Truth to Tell*, 75.
27. Ellul, *Money & Power*, 74–76; emphasis added.

to powers understand them as having agency. Whether or not one accepts uncritically Ellul's personification of this particular power, in the broadest reading of Paul's use of these concepts, and keeping in mind their fuller meaning, we must acknowledge that some structures in our world act and mold human behavior in ways that demonstrate their autonomy from individual human decisions. Indeed, this might be one way to think about what it means for them to be "spiritual" powers.

As we must acknowledge the fallenness of the structures when we address injustice, so also we must approach the individuals in them with the understanding that they are part of structures that, while created for good, are capable of truly monstrous and dehumanizing acts. Indeed, we may assume that the injustice—the improper use of power—is directly related to their fallenness and its attendant behaviors, including the desire to be worshiped. This should not lead us to fear, for, as we will see shortly, Christ is victor, having triumphed over the powers. However, this understanding should remind us of our need to engage in advocacy prayerfully, seeking God's wisdom and patience. William Stringfellow, writing in the 1970s on the US state as a power, warned about the danger of not acknowledging the powers:

> The principalities and powers have received little attention in American Christendom. In that context the customary propositions of moral theology concern individual decision and action and the supposed efficacy of the conviction of the individual for social renewal and societal change. . . . As a social ethic, this concentration upon the efficacious potential of individuals . . . suffers the distortion of any partial truth. That is, what it overlooks or omits is more significant than that which it asserts and affirms. What is most crucial about the situation, biblically speaking, is the failure of moral theology, in the American context, to confront the principalities—the institutions, systems, ideologies, and other political and social powers—as militant, aggressive, and immensely influential creatures in this world as it is. . . . Americans—including professed Christians, who have biblical grounds to be wiser—remain, it seems, astonishingly obtuse about these powers. . . . Yet to be ignorant or gullible or ingenuous about the demons, to underestimate the inherent capacities of the principalities, to fail to notice the autonomy of these powers as creatures abets their usurpation of human life and their domination of human beings.[28]

Simply put, let us not be naive about the capacity of the powers for evil. Yet that is not the end of the story. For us the good news is that Christ is victor, and while our advocacy work must be done with an eye to the fallenness of

---

28. Stringfellow, *Ethic for Christians and Other Aliens*, 17–18.

the powers and their capacity to perpetrate great injustice—enslaving not only humans in general but also the humans who work within their structures—we can approach them with great hope that our "witness" will bear fruit. This is so because Christ has triumphed over the powers and God will restore them to what God intended them to be. We turn to this final issue now.

To Be Redeemed

As the Bible quotations at the beginning of this section indicate, Christ has "disarmed" the powers and in time will have "abolished the rule" of all of them (Col. 2:15). After a careful analysis of the 1 Corinthians 15 passage and Colossians 1, Berkhof concludes that God does not intend to destroy the powers but to return them to their originally intended functions after reconciling them to himself along with everything else.[29] Karl Barth, in analyzing issues of church and state, concludes the same thing. He states that "the destiny of the rebellious angelic powers which is made clear in Christ's resurrection and parousia [appearing] is not that they will be annihilated, but that they will be forced into the service and the glorification of Christ, and through him, God."[30]

Redemption means that the powers will be "liberated" to be that which they were intended to be. This is good news. The passages listed above, however, go a bit further, with Ephesians 3 making it clear that the existence of the Church itself is to be used by God to reveal to the powers the full mystery of their role in God's plan. Jacques Ellul suggested one way this happens in relation to technique: by the Church's refusal to deify the powers—indeed by its destroying the myth of their godlike status. For Yoder, the most important thing the Church can "do" in relation to the truth of Christ's victory is to "be" what God intends it to be. This does not mean that the Church presents an ideal social plan to the state (or other institutions) but rather that it lives faithfully as itself—as a reconciling, loving, servant community, calling the state to be what it is intended to be (more on this in the next chapter).

Marva Dawn, without going into the details of exactly how it works in practice, says the following concerning the present work of the Church vis-à-vis the powers:

> The sovereignty of the principalities and powers has been broken, and it is the task of the Church to proclaim that. The working of the powers is limited, and it is the task of the Church to display that. Finally, this broken sovereignty and

29. Berkhof, *Christ and the Powers*, 36.
30. Barth, *Church and State*, 27.

limitation are signs of the ultimate defeat of the powers, and the Church is the place where those signs are celebrated.[31]

Dawn goes on to write about the imperative of "weakness"—of recognizing the end of our power in the face of these realities so that God's power might be manifested in the world. This would seem to provide an important directive for the attitude we should maintain as we engage in advocacy.

That the powers are still acting in rebellion should not discourage us. We live in an "in-between" time in which the consummation of Christ's reign is not yet complete but in which it is the Church's task to embody the reality of this reign and, in so doing, to remind the powers in deed and word of the limits of their role and their responsibilities to fulfill that role. The Church, in its being, reveals the mystery of what God is about in the world. So, rather than ask why evil continues, it would seem more appropriate for the Church to get on with following its Lord in being and becoming what that Lord asks it to be. This includes living out its identity as "alien ambassadors" (a theme to be explored in the next chapter).

We argue that this embodying includes speaking to the state about its role and correcting its excesses. In this sense, our advocacy is built upon the knowledge that God is using the Church to reveal God's will of reconciliation to the world—including the powers. Advocacy can, therefore, take many forms but is essentially a witness to what God is about in the world. We examine later the *ways* in which we can speak to the state using a language it can readily understand. In other words, we will see that it is not necessary to use the language of "powers," "reconciliation of all things," or "reign of Christ" in order to be faithful advocates, faithful witnesses, so long as we are faithful to these realities.

Thus we see that God has created the structures and systems of our world for good. They have a role to play, and we can approach them with the confidence that God desires to use them to achieve God's plan. However, we cannot be naive about what the powers, in their fallenness, are capable of. When separated from God's purposes, they become demonic and injustices follow. Old Testament writers frequently associate injustice with idolatry, which is why justice requires a return to God's character. Or as Jeremiah says, "'Is that not what it means to know me?' declares the LORD" (22:16).

However, we can be confident in approaching the powers because we understand both that Christ has triumphed over them and that God will redeem them and cause them to fulfill the role for which God created them. Thus, the

31. Dawn, *Powers, Weakness*, 27.

Church can live in freedom and with the clear conviction that speaking is a role that God has assigned it so that it may participate in God's great reconciling plan (Eph. 3:10). This full understanding of the powers should help to make us as wise as serpents but as humble as doves.

The State as a (Fallen) Power

The foregoing has already laid out the idea of the state as among the powers referred to in Scripture. Further, as we have already seen in the previous chapter, Jesus's own use of the concept of "kingdom" and "church" demonstrates God's desire to redeem the political realm along with the entirety of creation. The state that forms the backdrop of the New Testament story is the empire of Rome. Paul calls out its fallenness (and that of the Jewish religio-political culture that cooperated with it) in noting that it is the rulers of this age who crucified Jesus (1 Cor. 2:6–8). And yet Paul, writing in Romans 12 and 13, also calls Jesus's followers to be subordinate to the same state.[32] While the modern state has taken on roles that were unknown during the New Testament period (the breadth of the modern welfare state, or social system whereby government programs and policies ensure the well-being of its citizens, is of relatively recent origin, for example), it would seem appropriate to accept scriptural teaching concerning the state as normative for our times.

And thus, while we see Paul's call to be subordinate to the state, we also see the monstrous acts of which the state is capable in the crucifixion—and in the post–New Testament history, of martyrdom of the faithful by Rome. Perhaps no other author has laid out a more stinging indictment of the modern state than William Stringfellow in his 1973 volume *An Ethic for Christians and Other Aliens in a Strange Land*. In it Stringfellow lays out the stratagems of the powers—of which he considers the state preeminent.[33] He describes the stratagems of powers as the denial of truth, doublespeak and overtalk, secrecy, surveillance and harassment, exaggeration, deception, and usurpation. Whether he overstates the case or not, it is clear that a fallen state holds a great deal of destructive power in its hands. A fallen state seeks autonomy from God, seeks allegiance to itself—indeed, it seeks an "eternality" that belongs to God alone, and sometimes even demands love! Indeed, to understand the full

---

32. Yoder (*Politics of Jesus*) prefers subordination to "submission" on the basis of analyzing the full context of Rom. 12 and 13, which lays out first and foremost the church's call to nonconformity vis-à-vis the world—suggesting a singular allegiance to God's reign. He argues that God "orders" (rather than ordains) the state—essentially establishing it within the order of creation to accomplish specific tasks.

33. Stringfellow, *Ethic for Christians and Other Aliens*, 97–114.

force of the fallen state, we must redirect our gaze from the state God orders in Romans 13 to the "beast" described in Revelation 13. The juxtaposition makes clear both what God intends for the state and that which a fallen state (empire) is capable of.

The reality of the fallenness of the state should not, however, lead us to despair. Christ is the victor. At this point, it might be helpful to explain some recent contours in New Testament scholarship dealing with empire criticism, probing whether New Testament writers envisioned Jesus's kingdom as a direct challenge to the Roman emperor, especially when confronting the ubiquitous imperial cult throughout the region.[34] Certainly, biblical writers draw upon an impressive array of language to suggest that Christ inaugurates a rival kingdom, referring to Jesus as Lord, or King, or speaking of "Christ's triumphal procession" (2 Cor. 2:14–16) to reposition empire language within a new soteriological framework.[35] But in other instances, Paul flashes his Roman citizenship badge to get out of violent situations (Acts 22:22–29).

The Gospels, too, portray a multifaceted view of Roman presence, sometimes referring to imperial agents in a favorable light, such as tax collectors or the centurion (Luke 7:1–10), but elsewhere recounting the story of John the Baptist's death at the hands of Herod Antipas (9:7–9), or of Jesus standing before Pilate. Luke, in particular, mentions Jesus's Lordship more than any of the other Gospels, with more than two hundred direct references to *kyrios*.[36]

Assuredly, to confess "Jesus as Lord" implies an allegiance to a different king than Caesar (see Acts 17:6–7). Or as N. T. Wright explains, "To come to Rome with the gospel of Jesus, to announce someone else's accession to the world's throne, therefore, was to put on a red coat and walk into a field with potentially angry bulls."[37] But it is one thing to say that Jesus's kingdom contrasts starkly with the Roman Empire and quite another to say that New Testament writers stoke anti-empire sentiment. If that was their intent, then why would Paul tell readers to submit to all governing authorities (Rom. 13:1–7)? Doesn't this call to submit clearly show, rather, that he saw God's kingdom as far greater than any human rule, and saw all "powers" as defeated

---

34. S. R. F. Price states, "Travellers in the empire would not have been surprised to meet the cult wherever they went: they would have found the cult located both in local communities and in the associations formed of these communities in particular Roman provinces." *Rituals and Power*, 2–3.

35. For an interesting treatment of how Paul draws upon overt, imperial images to describe Jesus's ministry, see Hafemann, *Suffering and Ministry*.

36. Pinter, "Gospel of Luke," 106.

37. N. T. Wright, "Romans," 158.

by Christ's death (see Rom. 8:38–39; 1 Cor. 2:8; 15:25; Col. 2:15)?[38] So any polemic against Rome must take into consideration a different kind of kingdom, one that enables Christians to resist, submit, create, obey, and even die in light of the eternality of Jesus's rule.

Some scholars suggest the biblical texts offer anti-empire polemic in quieter, more subversive language of resistance built into the writings of the Gospels to disclose a polemic against Rome, but accomplished in ways that would not court political reaction. This is possible: subtexts are an important part of biblical interpretation, and Rome should not be neglected in the New Testament context.[39] But we should not see anti-empire everywhere, especially when more obvious readings of Scripture exist.

The challenge in reading the New Testament is to neither overtly spiritualize the biblical texts and run away from the very obvious political implications of the kingdom of God, nor hyperpoliticize the Scriptures and see empire criticism everywhere. There can be no doubt that Jesus's teaching challenges all rival kingdoms and thus conveys sociopolitical import. But it would also be a stretch to suggest anti-empire as the primary meaning of the New Testament, as if reading postcolonial interpretation back into the text. God's kingdom refuses to conform to any orchestrated agenda. Jesus can undress Pilate about the true nature of power, and he can die on the cross to establish a new way of power.

This reality is critical to keep in mind as we transition to the question of how the Church practices transformational advocacy. Our advocacy is carried out in a fallen world, often before a fallen state. However, we recall that the state is to be redeemed as part of God's fuller redemptive plan. We also note that our advocacy efforts are always (as noted previously) addressed to human beings—human beings who work within fallen structures that constrain and mold them, but human beings nonetheless.

38. Bird, "One Who Will Arise," 159.

39. Christopher Skinner, in "John's Gospel and the Roman Context," offers a good summary of the New Testament milieu:

> The experience of Roman occupation was a lived reality from which those in the New Testament era could not escape. This does not mean that every element of Jewish or Christian expression, especially their sacred literature, was intended as a response to Roman imperialism, only that the specter of the Roman Empire cast a shadow over daily life in first-century Palestine in a way that cannot and should not be ignored. (117)

Or later: "The modern, mainly Western insistence on separating politics and religion would have been foreign in the context of first-century Palestinian culture. One's view of God (or the gods) had immediate implications and practical relevance for the development of one's political views and vice versa" (118–19).

This stance provides a preview of the Church's practice of transformational advocacy, which we take up in the next chapter.

Other Powers

We have outlined the nature of the powers—created for good, fallen, but to be redeemed as part of God's plan—and have examined in particular the realities of the state. While a significant part of our advocacy may be before the state (at various levels), there are other structures, other powers before which we will also speak. We would argue that these institutions share the same fallenness as the state and are, therefore, ordered for good but prone to fail in achieving that good.

Other powers (in addition to broader systems or principles like the "market," mammon, or "technique") include corporations, multilateral agencies such as the World Bank, the International Monetary Fund, the various agencies of the United Nations, and even nongovernmental organizations (NGOs). We will not treat these powers separately from the state but note three points that influence our approach to them:

1. Among the various institutions (powers), the state is the only one with a "monopoly on the use of force" (as asserted by Max Weber). The ability of the state to raise a police force, an army, and an array of intelligence-gathering agencies means that its ability to do physical harm to people surpasses that of other institutions.

2. The other institutions, arguably, exist at the pleasure of the state or states. Corporations receive charters from states, multilateral agencies are formed by the coordinated efforts of various states, and NGOs are given status by the state. In a very real sense, then, these entities' power is derivative and bound by the state's power[40] (although there is a multidirectional nature to these relationships).

3. While these entities may implement policies, advise states, influence large numbers of people, and do harm (as well as good), they typically do not possess the authority to enact legislation or confront wrongdoing to ensure that wrongs are made right (judicial action). The state possesses this authority.

Despite these differences, on some occasions our advocacy must be conducted before these other powers. The methods we use to speak to these

---

40. Jürgen Moltmann, however, argues it is now the market that is dominating all the other institutions, even politics. He says, "Politics has deregulated the economy, and is now itself controlled and regulated by the economy. This means that political life is now the subsystem of a greater economic system." "Political Theology," 41.

institutions (or, more properly, the people within them) may be different from those we use with the state because our expectations of what they can and must do will be different from our expectations of the state. We explore some of these differences in a later chapter.

We will now discuss the principles that should guide our practice of transformational advocacy, focusing first on our identity as followers of Jesus living in this time and place.

5

The Role of the Church

In the last chapter, we looked at the "powers," viewing them in terms of their created goodness, distortion under the effects of sin, and ultimate redemption under Christ. In chapter 3 we laid a framework for advocacy by tracing God's advocacy in the world. We advocate for others as God advocates for humanity.

We now consider what this means for the Church. In Ephesians 3 Paul makes a profound statement: "His [God's] intent was that now, through the church, the manifold wisdom of God should be made known to the rulers and authorities in the heavenly realms, according to his eternal purpose that he accomplished in Christ Jesus our Lord" (vv. 10–11). Evangelicals have often neglected these words. We possess robust theologies for dealing with personal sins and impressive resolve for witnessing to individuals. These kinds of things should continue. But what do we do with structural sin, and how do we witness to the powers?

Our answer begins with God's nature. The Church mirrors (or images) the Trinity to the world. Father, Son, and Holy Spirit inform not only the nature of humanity ("that they may be one as we are one," John 17:22) but also the mission of God ("so that the world may believe that you have sent me," vv. 21, 23) as well as the underlying essence of the cosmos: "to bring unity to all things in heaven and on earth under Christ" (Eph. 1:10). Hence, the Trinity does not just describe how God reveals himself but also prescribes the nature of the Church, and even so, represents the eschatological future of the world:

pointing toward the shalom that undergirds the entire cosmos, the flourishing of all things under God's rule.

Two immediate implications arise from these comments that will frame the practice of transformational advocacy. First, theology informs the nature of our advocacy. People often think of theology (or doctrines) as dry, crusty propositional truths, reified in time and space, casting a scowling eye upon the world. But we would rather see theology as wisdom, which Walter Brueggemann refers to as "a genuine reckoning with the character of this God, who wills life in terms of responsible relatedness to the whole fabric of creation";[1] alternatively, we can see theology as what Derek Kidner calls "godliness into working clothes."[2] By locating human advocacy within the story lines of salvation history, we walk into something much larger than ourselves. God's advocacy begins with creation, flows through God's providence (guiding, protecting, and integrating),[3] and relates to the redemption of all things under the Lordship of Jesus Christ.[4] Thus, we understand advocacy as dramatized wisdom lived in the context of speaking of, for, and within God's redemptive plan.[5]

Second, the relational aspect of transformational advocacy derives from the Trinity. God wills for humans to enjoy community even as the Godhead enjoys community. For these reasons, institutions such as family and politics (if understood as how humans govern according to power) actually precede the fall,[6] rooted in the relational fiber of humanity. God's nature informs the character of these institutions, along with the capabilities of humans to love,

---

1. Brueggemann, *Theology of the Old Testament*, 388.

2. Kidner, *Proverbs*, 35.

3. The correlation between creation and providence is compelling. Brueggemann says, "The one who creates is the one who governs in a quite specific way. Thus the Creator has ordered, and continues to order, a world marked by a particular ethic." *Theology of the Old Testament*, 155.

4. Readers will differ in their comfort with talking about redemption and political engagement. But if redemption relates to all life, we must inevitably move in these directions. Marva Dawn says it this way: "It makes an enormous difference in the way individuals and churches live if we recognize that the entire atoning work of Christ (including his life, suffering, death, resurrection, and ascension) has already made the cosmos his. Then our political involvement operates not from the need to change things, but from the desire to make clear what really is the case." *Powers, Weakness*, 26. Or as Richard Mouw explains, "Christ's atoning work offers liberation for people in their cultural endeavors, in their family lives, in their educational pursuits, in their quests for sexual fulfillment, in their desire for physical well-being. It also offers liberation in the building of political institutions and the making of public policy." *Political Evangelism*, 14–15.

5. The idea of "drama" has been advanced by a number of theologians for the purposes of moving away from some of the modernist trappings of propositional truth and into a view of theology that is embodied, performed, and lived with others, within specific contexts or stages. See Vanhoozer, *Drama of Doctrine*.

6. Ronald Sider also makes this point. See "Justice, Human Rights," 168. He later reminds the reader that government is not the first and greatest institution, but serves an important

serve, send, bless, receive, and advocate for one another because of how the persons of the Trinity offer this to the world. In drawing upon Wesley's understanding of the "political" image of God, Coates states: "Because humans are made in the political image of God, they share in the Trinity's mission of redemption. Politics is thus participation in the order of salvation as it is revealed in God's triune nature."[7]

But sin distorts human relationships even as it worms its way into the fabric of the world. The beauty seen in God's shalom becomes distorted by sin and afflicts everyone (and everything). In the oft-quoted statement by Alexandr Solzhenitsyn, "The line separating good and evil passes not through states, nor between classes, nor between political parties either—but right through every human heart—and through all human hearts."[8] What is more, the effects of sin do not sit sequestered within atomistic selfhoods, but spill into public spaces in society, eventually becoming reified in such things as ideologies or human structures. John Wesley refers to this as "complicated wickedness,"[9] revealing a more complex kind of wickedness, whose layers don't just sit on top of one another like a stack of pancakes, but burrow, conflate, and harden over time.

The Church, with all of its own inconsistencies, frailties, and paradoxes, can become the vessel by which fallen, corrupted structures rediscover their moorings and become servants of human flourishing, defined by God's rule.[10]

The Nature of the Church

And so the question at this point might be: who exactly are "we"? Further, what is the basis of our speaking? How do we decide what to say? How do we approach those in power? What is the content of our message? And, what do we expect will happen when we speak?

A few basic principles should guide the body of Christ as it speaks *with* and on behalf of poor, oppressed, and hungry people *before* those in power to name the injustices that keep people marginalized and vulnerable in our world. From the start we must humbly follow the Holy Spirit's leading—that

---

function in providing "a good, accepted framework in which all the other institutions can both enjoy their own freedom and also work together effectively." Ibid., 186.

7. Coates, *Politics Strangely Warmed*, 49.

8. Solzhenitsyn, *Gulag Archipelago*, part 4, chap. 1.

9. Wesley, *Works of John Wesley*, vol. 6, sermon 67, "On Divine Providence," p. 354.

10. Hence, transformational advocacy is not just anti-sin, but pro-life. It sees the entire world through God's eyes, not with some romanticized view of the primordial past (like calling people back to the garden of Eden); thus it anticipates (by living into) the day when God's life will once again define all things.

is, be faithful to our calling as Christ's church and allow our words to flow from acts of "living into" God's kingdom. Such acts are not herculean tasks for the body of Christ, but rather natural and logical components of the mission of the Church in the world—the natural outworking of the Church simply being the Church. As such, they are critical elements of our identity as followers of Jesus that situate our advocacy within a reliance on the power of the Holy Spirit to work in the hearts of men and women.

What then is the nature of the Church?

In English translations of the Bible, the word "church" normally translates the Greek *ekklēsia*, which means a gathering or assembly of people. In biblical terms, the Church is the people of God (Titus 2:14; 1 Pet. 2:9–10), the body of Christ (Rom. 12:5; 1 Cor. 12:27; Eph. 4:12), and those who emerge from the fellowship of the Holy Spirit (2 Cor. 1:22; Eph. 1:13–14). Drawing from these biblical metaphors, we can say that the Church is a community of people wrought and hewn by the Trinity,[11] a community that images the nature of God in its relationships, and does so openly before the world.[12]

Focusing on the Trinity is critical because the subject of this book pertains to Christian witness (or discipleship) before institutions, and it may be possible to think of the Trinity as the very first institution, if, as we saw earlier, by an institution we mean "a stable structure of social interaction."[13] None of this implies that the Trinity is an institution in the same way a human institution is, but it underscores the relevance of the analogy: we learn about healthy models of institutions from the persons of the Trinity, and especially how they distribute power and integrate with one another.[14] This helps the Church live by a different identity and ethic in the world.

The Lordship of Jesus Christ defines this particular assembly. As Dietrich Bonhoeffer says, "The church is not a religious community of those who revere Christ, but Christ who has taken form among human beings."[15] The

---

11. See Volf, *After Our Likeness*.

12. Karl Barth defines the church as "the common life of these people in one Spirit, the Holy Spirit, that is, in obedience to the Word of God in Jesus Christ, which they have all heard and are all needing and eager to hear again." "Christian Community and Civil Community," in *Community, State, and Church*, 150. William Cavanaugh explains how the term *ekklēsia* not only pointed to the corporateness of the church but also its public presence: "When the early church borrowed the Greek word ekklesia for itself, it took on some of the resonances of the Greek body politic. . . . The church thus claimed to be more than a club organized around private interests; it was a fully public gathering concerned with the whole of life." "Are Corporations People?," 132.

13. Volf, *After Our Likeness*, 235.

14. Ibid., 236. Volf describes institutions according to these two criteria: how they distribute power and how they integrate together.

15. Bonhoeffer, *Ethics*, 96.

Church lives out its identity by worshiping God, growing in the fullness of Jesus Christ, and it witnesses to the world through the power of the Holy Spirit. Christians sometimes think of these as separate movements, with worship, discipleship, and witness functioning as distinct activities, but worship encompasses everything the Church does, while sanctification is essential to witness. And, what is more, even witness relates back to discipleship, as Paul explains to Philemon: "I pray that your partnership with us in the faith may be effective in deepening your understanding of every good thing we share for the sake of Jesus Christ" (v. 6).

These points are critical for transformational advocacy since the "transformational" part can come only from Christ through the Holy Spirit. The Church embodies these kinds of relationships (along with the power dynamics) openly before the world through a process of giving and receiving gifts.[16] Hence, we see advocacy as an outflow of witness, which the Church embodies as it lives out its identity through the persons of the Trinity, and by which it grows.

All of these comments underscore the public nature of the Church in the world. Public, in this sense, does not mean the Church spurns private matters;[17] nor should it imply a betrayal of the "spiritual" nature of the Church.[18] But by using the word "public" we mean that the Church exists for others in much the same way that the persons of the Trinity do, and that the Church lives its witness openly for the good of the world. Lesslie Newbigin says it best: "We are called, I think, to bring our faith into the public arena, to publish it, to put it at risk in the encounter with other faiths and ideologies in open debate and argument, and in the risky business of discovering what Christian obedience means in radically new circumstances and in radically different human cultures."[19] For the purposes of this book, "public" must pertain to political

16. Muck and Adeney refer to this as "giftive mission" in *Christianity Encountering World Religions*.

17. For an interesting treatment of the private or secretive nature of the Church, see Malesic, *Secret Faith*.

18. Jacques Ellul says,

> The review of successive historical betrayals by the Church through political involvement does not signify that the Church ought to be spiritual, that the faith is a matter of the personal and inward, that revelation is purely abstract, that the contest for truth has no political implications and that the love imperative has no spiritual significance. All that spirituality is just as false, treasonous and hypocritical as the taking of political sides condemned above. It is a negation of the incarnation, a forgetting of the lordship of Jesus Christ. (*Political Illusion*, 126)

19. Newbigin, *Truth to Tell*, 59–60. He continues,

> We have a gospel to proclaim. We have to proclaim it not merely to individuals in their personal and domestic lives. We do certainly have to do that. But we have to proclaim it as part of the continuing conversation which shapes public doctrine. It must be heard in the conversation of economists, psychiatrists, educators, scientists, and politicians. We have

structures, especially as they restrict, impede, or injudiciously harm the application of God's justice in the world.

The Church and Transformational Advocacy

What does all this mean for how the Church engages (or witnesses to) political structures? Of the host of historical responses to this question, many afford useful wisdom from which principles for godly transformative advocacy can be drawn, specifically concerning (1) the nature of the Church with regard to politics, (2) how the Church embodies power in the world, and (3) what this means for advocacy—with and for the most vulnerable within the world.

The Church's Identity vis-à-vis Politics

We start with the most problematic of issues. The Church's relationship with the state is problematic for several reasons, including the ambiguous (if not sometimes disagreeable) heritage Christians have borne with the state throughout the millennia, which often keeps Christians paralyzed with regard to the political sphere. In this sense, politics functions as a kind of "social imaginary" that lingers as with a bad taste in the mouth. On the one hand, the sordid history of Christian engagement with politics remains fresh on people's minds; and on the other, people tend to think of anything to do with the political realm as inextricably dirty.[20]

But the topic is also problematic due to the different ways that people around the world (in varying cultural and ecclesiastical traditions) understand the nature of the Church and how it relates to the state. No one occupies privileged seating. We all see the world (and ourselves) through theologically and culturally informed lenses, often blind to the ways that cultural background, social location, or personal experiences inform our reading of the text of Scripture and the world. And so to talk about the Church's identity vis-à-vis the state is immediately to locate oneself in time and space; it is to interpret from our own theological heritage.[21] What follows then is not an exhaustive treatment on the subject but rather an introduction that (we hope)

---

to proclaim it not as a package of estimable values, but as the truth about what is the case, about what every human being and every human society will have to reckon with. (Ibid., 64)

20. Mathewes says, "We cannot imagine politics as more than the agglomeration of power by individuals or groups for finally selfish ends." *Theology of Public Life*, 148.

21. And we, the authors, acknowledge that we approach this subject from a largely Western, Caucasian perspective and ask that others in North America and around the world strengthen what we have presented here.

helps frame the practice of advocacy. And it acknowledges that people in other places and traditions have valuable insights to strengthen (or correct) what we offer here.

We begin our discussion by noting that Jesus himself fully engaged the political processes of his day, challenging the status quo in the temple (e.g., Matt. 24:1–3; Mark 11:15–16), confronting the authority of the Pharisees (e.g., Luke 11),[22] or by directly engaging with the Roman Empire as he stood before Pontius Pilate concerning the real nature of power in the world (see John 18:28–19:16).

It is not uncommon, in a noncontextualized reading of Scripture, to describe the life of Jesus in undersocialized or apolitical terms, as if he dropped into history only to die on the cross and then promptly left when this work was done. Such a reading ignores the fact that both his disciples and the leaders of his day understood his intentions in fully political terms, even if they did not grasp the vision Jesus had for his eternal reign. Jesus's statements about the kingdom were not spiritualized by his hearers but understood in plain terms as expressing his intentions to establish his rule.[23] In sentencing Jesus to death, Pilate was not merely God's tool to accomplish God's plan; he was responding to a politically charged situation, responding with power to crush a perceived threat to Roman rule.

Jesus's Lordship foregrounds not only his own example but also, at once, the "spiritual" mandate of the Church, though never in such a way as to separate it from the "material." The desire to keep the two apart continues to tempt Christians. Quite simply, separate is neat and clean, while togetherness is messy and complicated. Christians often settle for easy solutions to theological quandaries, such as the persons of the Trinity, Christ's human and divine natures, being in the world but not of it, and especially the perceived relationship between spiritual and material realities. Lesslie Newbigin has chronicled the history of Western Christianity's move toward a private, spiritual gospel and away from public and material antecedents.[24] There were, of course, solid reasons for talking about the difference, especially as the Church came out of the ecclesiastical wars of the sixteenth century and then encountered the ensuing Enlightenment project with its totalizing (and often reductionistic)

---

22. From the perspective of modernist assumptions about the separation of church and state, it might seem odd to describe the temple or the Pharisees as political entities, but in Jesus's day the temple represented kingdom aspirations (not merely a location of worship), and the Pharisees were part of the political ladder of patronage that flowed up and down Roman society in Palestine.

23. N. T. Wright, *Challenge of Jesus*.

24. See especially Newbigin, *Gospel in a Pluralist Society*. Yet to be fair to the West, Christianity's engagement with the Enlightenment project also benefited the world, as is well articulated by Ramachandra, "Learning from Modern European Secularism."

view of the world through science and empirical positivism. However, such a separation not only left Christians deficient in theological resources (often avoiding topics such as creation, providence, power, or the humanity of Christ, which were being discussed by "liberals") but also restricted the effects of transformation, limiting the sphere of the gospel to private, individual matters and drawing it away from public, social issues.

The central task of the Church, however, is to live the Lordship of Jesus Christ in all facets of life, seeing the "spiritual"—that is, God's cosmic plan of redemption—in everything, while acknowledging that in the present ("already but not yet") the two will remain in tension. Dietrich Bonhoeffer challenges how we articulate the notion of separation. He sees everything under the Lordship of Jesus Christ, saying,

> There are not two realities, but only one reality, and that is God's reality revealed in Christ in the reality of the world. Partaking in Christ, we stand at the same time in the reality of God and in the reality of the world. . . . The whole reality of the world has already been drawn into and is held together in Christ. History moves only from this center and toward this center.[25]

As the center of history, the Church plays a prominent role in the world. Bonhoeffer sees the Church as both the center of the state and, at the same time, its boundary marker (in the sense of giving the state meaning defined by Christ).[26] None of this suggests that the Church usurps the functions of the state. For Bonhoeffer, the government represents an "order of preservation"[27] or "penultimate goal" of God's purposes. The role of the Church is to help the state understand ultimate things, not in a way that delegitimizes the penultimate (i.e., the state), but rather keeps it on course.[28] Later in *Ethics* Bonhoeffer wrestles with the quandary of direct engagement with the state; he muses:

> It is the sole task of the church to exercise love within the given worldly orders, i.e., to animate them as far as possible with a new way of thinking, to compensate for hardships, to care for the victims of these orders, and to establish within the church community its own new order; or does the church have a mission in regard to the given worldly orders themselves, in the sense of correction, improvements, that is, of working toward a new worldly order? I.e., is

25. Bonhoeffer, *Ethics*, 58. On these and other points, we are indebted to John Stackhouse's helpful synopsis of Bonhoeffer's key arguments in *Making the Best of It*, 131–41.
26. Bonhoeffer, *Christ the Center*, 63–64.
27. Bonhoeffer, *Creation and Fall*, 139–40.
28. Bonhoeffer, *Ethics*, 125–33.

the church merely to pick up the victims, or must the church take hold of the spokes of the wheel itself?[29]

These words imply a stance vis-à-vis the state that hints at structural witness. Barth says something similar, especially in the context of the marginalized of society: "The poor, the socially and economically weak and threatened, will always be the object of its [the Church's] primary and particular concern, and it will always insist on the State's special responsibility for these weaker members of society."[30]

We won't take the time to tease out the many differences between scholars, or the multitude of other variances seen throughout church history. We emphasize instead the central point of this section; Christ's Lordship was never meant to be limited to small, restricted spheres, but claims the entirety of the world (which is God's world).

Living out this Lordship requires humility, following in the pathway of Jesus. But it also requires theology, framed as wisdom. Unlike tactic, wisdom resists a clear-cut method, as if to pander to contemporary tendencies to make technique the idolatry of our day.[31] Wisdom requires dependency upon the Holy Spirit and humility in the way of Christ, dancing with improvisation to the music of the gospel in unique contexts and circumstances around the world.[32] On the one hand, Christians give ultimate allegiance to God alone and resist any inclinations to sacralize the state or align themselves with any particular political ideology.[33] But on the other hand, the Church resists the danger of forcing its agenda on others or, worse yet, restricting its witness

29. Bonhoeffer, *Conspiracy and Imprisonment*, 541. Readers familiar with Bonhoeffer will know he participated in a plot to assassinate Hitler. He did so with a great deal of agony and deliberation. His political theology did not readily lend itself to this kind of extreme action, but it does show the seriousness with which he took the evil of Hitler's regime.

30. Barth, *Community, State, and Church*, 173.

31. For much more on the totalizing demands of "technique," see Ellul, *Technological Society*, and especially his theological comments on technique as a power in Ellul and Vanderburg, *Perspectives on Our Age*, 85–111.

32. Brian Howell describes gospel and culture in this manner: "Contextualization is a complex dance of music and movement in which choices are made moment by moment and each new circumstance requires new response. Contextualization, then, is a transitive verb, rather than a simple noun." "Contextualizing Context," 24–25.

33. Newbigin says it this way:

We have to reject ideologies which give to particular elements in God's ordering of things the central and absolute place which belongs to Christ alone. It is good to love and serve the nation in which God has set us; we need more, not less true patriotism. But to give ultimate commitment to the nation is to go into bondage. . . . The free market is a good way of balancing supply and demand. If it is absolutized and allowed to rule economic life, it becomes an evil power. (*Truth to Tell*, 80–81)

to things apolitical. Rather, it lives as yeast within dough (Matt. 13:33). Its identity is that of a "chosen race, a royal priesthood, a holy nation" of persons who live as "aliens and exiles" within a foreign land (1 Pet. 2:9–11 NRSV).[34] And part of its witness to the state comes in the form of lament: a posture of identification with the sufferings of others (within a sinful world) along with a living hope that looks to God's final redemption of the world.

This identity places the follower of Christ in a critical position of being an ambassador of a sovereign carrying out the sovereign's wishes, representing the sovereign's wishes within the nations of this world. But it is also an identity that aligns with humanity.[35] Thus even as the Church is a polis, its members' solidarity with other humans provides a strong rationale for walking with and speaking out on behalf of other humans. Our identity requires that we use our understanding of the human plight to speak and act in a very particular way. We Christians represent the desires of our sovereign. We obey the laws of the nations of our residence but dare not defend (or uncritically accept) their interests or policies. Instead, we speak to the powers from the perspective of our sovereign, living our "alienness" in solidarity with the suffering of the many alienated people—outcasts, homeless, stateless—of our world.[36]

The Church and Power

The Church addresses the powers against the backdrop of both their created goodness and their fallenness. Although people often think of power as a lurid, noxious thing that destroys rather than builds, God's power created the world and God shared his power with image bearers, bestowing upon them "powers" to care, govern, and till the earth so that it will flourish (what might be termed the "political" image). As human beings exercised these God-given powers, certain structures arose, such as the state, economics, or tradition,

---

34. A word of caution is, perhaps, in order here. While Peter is clearly challenging us to consider the importance of living as aliens, it is doubtful that most readers of this volume live into that reality. In a useful critique in the *Christian Century* titled "White Protestants Aren't Aliens: Resident Aliens at 25" that looked back at the twenty-five years since Stanley Hauerwas and William H. Willimon's book *Resident Aliens: Life in the Christian Colony*, Jennifer McBride writes the following concerning this theme:

> Given the dominance of white Protestantism in our liberal-capitalist-democratic culture and given the privilege that naturally follows, the first step toward a more faithful existence is not to deem ourselves alien to this society but to name our complicity as residents in its sin and repent in concrete ways: by becoming allies in our everyday lives or joining coalitions working to undo racist structures like prisons.

35. James Davison Hunter refers to this as "faithful presence" to situate the incarnation within a theology of cultural engagement; see *To Change the World*.

36. See Ellul, *Présence au monde moderne*, 46–49.

which are referred to as "powers" in the Bible; they are part of the goodness of the creation and provide a framework for the good functioning of society but become unmoored from God's basic design and take on a reality that is greater than their material essence, such that Paul tells the church of Ephesus, "Our struggle is not against flesh and blood" (Eph. 6:12).[37] The Church must keep this history clearly in mind when deciding how to engage the powers.

How, then, and by what power does the Church address the powers? Beginning with the first question, Paul argues that the Church stands before the powers in the world with a specific mandate to witness to them: "[God's] intent was that now, through the church, the manifold wisdom of God should be made known to the rulers and authorities in the heavenly realms, according to his eternal purpose that he accomplished in Christ Jesus our Lord" (Eph. 3:10–11). Hence, the Church speaks not only to individuals but also to the larger entities; and it does so by the power of the Holy Spirit, who is our Advocate. Unlike the powers in the world, the Church does not seek autonomy, or subscribe to the prevailing belief that power equals force. Rather, it lives by the conviction that God's power is creational. Only in conformity to Jesus Christ will we really live.[38]

During his earthly life, Jesus explains the fundamental misunderstanding of the kingdom of God by addressing the subject of power on many occasions. According to Matthew, Jesus reveals to his disciples that he will meet his death at the hands of the Roman authorities. Within this same passage, a disagreement breaks out among the disciples regarding who will be greatest in the kingdom of God. Jesus responds by revealing the underlying ethic of the kingdom:

> You know that the rulers of the Gentiles lord it over them, and their great ones are tyrants over them. It will not be so among you; but whoever wishes to be great among you must be your servant, and whoever wishes to be first among you must be your slave; just as the Son of Man came not to be served but to serve, and to give his life a ransom for many. (Matt. 20:25–28 NRSV)

Similar teachings are conveyed throughout Jesus's ministry, such as when he washes the feet of the disciples (John 13) or when he tells the disciples that "whoever wants to save their life will lose it, but whoever loses their life for

37. Newbigin likewise says, "And these powers, while created in Christ and for Christ, having therefore a positive function in God's economy, can be and have been corrupted. They are corrupted, become demonic, when they are absolutized, given the place which belongs only to God." *Truth to Tell*, 75.

38. This is an important point, because history shows us that the Church can also become a fallen institution.

[Christ] will find it" (Matt. 16:24–26). Jesus reveals a kingdom that operates on a different kind of power, because there is a different King.

This is clearly a story his disciples were not prepared to hear. And so it is in our day. The way of "the gentiles," or hardball politics, cannot be accepted as the modus operandi of Christians engaged in politics. Rather, our comportment must be to engage in advocacy from a position of weakness, suffering, and service. We embody a different power because we serve a different King. This does not mean we relinquish power (as if it is a dirty thing), or eschew any association with political structures, but we dramatize a different kind of power in the world for the growth of all things.[39] And to move into a world in which the main currency is power requires that we faithfully represent Christ, inclusive of the incarnation, life, death, and resurrection. As N. T. Wright concludes:

> The cross is the surest, truest and deepest window on the very heart and character of the living and loving God; the more we learn about the cross in all its historical and theological dimensions, the more we discover about the One in whose image we are made and hence about our own vocation to be the cross-bearing people, the people in whose lives and service the living God is made known. And when therefore we speak . . . of shaping our world, we do not—we dare not—simply treat the cross as the thing that saves us "personally," but which can be left behind when we get on with the job. The task of shaping our world is best understood as the redemptive task of bringing the achievement of the cross to bear on the world, and in that task the methods, as well as the message, must be cross-shaped through and through.[40]

The apostle Paul clearly understood the cross in such a way, seeing it as the means by which Jews and gentiles were reconciled to become one new humanity (Eph. 2:11–22). Paul talks about boasting in weakness so that Christ's power would dwell within him (2 Cor. 12:9–10), and he tells the church in Corinth that his authority was meant for building others up, not tearing them down (2 Cor. 13:10).

Marva Dawn describes kingdom weakness in terms of "tabernacling," which draws its meaning from the incarnation, where Jesus takes on flesh and

39. Stackhouse says something similar: "As attractive as the option always is to eschew power and glorify weakness, maintain one's sanctity without compromise, and denounce both worldly institutions and one's fellow Christians who participate in them, we must return to these questions: When we are now members of the royal court, so to speak—indeed, when some of us are members of the royal family—who are we, for Jesus Christ, today?" *Making the Best of It*, 312.

40. N. T. Wright, *Challenge of Jesus*, 94–95.

"tabernacles" among humans (the literal meaning of "made his dwelling" in John 1:14). Weakness in the kingdom of God is therefore not a denial of our humanity, but precisely an embodiment of it in the world. She explains: "To be Christian churches is to resist being swept up into the values and powers of our cultural milieu. On the other hand, the role of the Christian community is to supply what is missing in that milieu—namely, the tabernacling of Christ."[41] And the new humanity of the body of Christ calls forth a new humanity in the world, defined in part by weakness and service.[42]

Transformational advocacy, as such, requires not less humanity but more of it, especially the kind revealed in Jesus Christ. And it requires a different kind of power inserted into the world through the incarnation of Jesus Christ. Therefore, any mention of "powerlessness" should not imply the abdication of power but the "tabernacling" of God's power within the structures of this world. As we stand before the "powers," we do so *with* Christ's humanity *for* the humanity of the world. And we do so from the resources of our frailty and weakness because we are living into the kingdom of Jesus Christ.

The Church's Advocacy: Witness to, Along with, and For

If we truly believe that Christ is relevant for the entire world and not just the world to come, and if we believe his Lordship is relevant for actual life, not just privatized, spiritualized vapors of reality that linger only inside the walls of the Church, and if we believe that power is creational in nature and redeemed by Christ through his humanity (punctuated by the cross) and bestowed upon the Church through the Holy Spirit, then we must move with these ideas into the hard landscape of human realities, and especially with regard to institutions and structures in society.

THREE PRINCIPLES OF FAITHFUL PUBLIC WITNESS

In its witness to the public realm, the Church must be faithful to three principles. First, advocacy is about living into the kingdom of God. The things we do today are directly related to the coming kingdom of God. The Church exists today as a foretaste of what God is completing in human history; it leans into that identity by embodying kingdom practices in the present[43] and thus demonstrating to the world that God is the Ruler of all. Its worship

41. Dawn, *Powers, Weakness*, 119.

42. In a profoundly prophetic way, Dawn says, "It seems to me that if we eat the body and blood of Christ in expensive churches without care for the hungry, the sacrament is no longer a foretaste of the feast to come, but a trivialized picnic to which not everyone is invited." Ibid., 99.

43. For more on this, see J. Smith, *Imagining the Kingdom*.

prepares it for properly engaging the world,[44] even as its witness helps train its affections for the kingdom.[45]

Second, the Church must therefore live out the Lordship of Jesus Christ so it can be an effective witness to the world. The Church's witness to the state is grounded in its existence as a "society" (polis, as we have seen) that lives differently, following the law of love as it advocates with and for others as God advocates for the world. Even before a word is uttered, the Church speaks through its life, to the extent that such a life is grounded in repentance and faith. John Howard Yoder sees this being played out in how decision-making structures within the church undermine hierarchies, how mutual admonition leads to accountability, and how consensus-based decision making displays openness and transparency. In addition to these community practices, Yoder points to the creativity—the "constant inventive vision"[46]—of the Church as critical to its witness. Given that the followers of Jesus live in society just like everyone else, the Church has the opportunity to live an alternate lifestyle in (and for) the world. It has been common among younger evangelicals to eschew institutional forms of the Church in favor of more organic, kingdom representations. While we certainly understand the reasons for talking thus, one of the ways the Church witnesses to the state is through its institutional nature. The Church witnesses to the state through embodying a different kind of institution in the world, one predicated upon the Trinity.

Liturgical practices, therefore, are not spiritualized activities, divorced from witness, but ways of training the Church for effective witness in the world. James K. A. Smith says, "The postures of our bodies spill out beyond the sanctuary and become postures of existential comportment to the world."[47] Worship relates to advocacy as it trains us to become kingdom people, pushing beyond narrow, restricted views of liturgy to see fluidity between what we do inside the walls of the church and what takes place in the streets, courts, playgrounds, and public offices. By leaning into the kingdom of God, the Church applies present activities with future realities. N. T. Wright says it best:

44. Smith says, "Christian worship and spiritual formation have long known and affirmed *in practice* that gestures are not just something we do but that they also do something to us—that kneeling for confession is a kind of cosmological act that inscribes in us a comportment to God and neighbor, a way of being-in-the-world that sinks into our bones and becomes sedimented into the core of our being through the crackle of our old knees." Ibid., 167.

45. Charles Mathewes says, "Properly undertaken, public engagement can be a struggle for conversion, conversion of one's loves and the loves of one's interlocutor." *Theology of Public Life*, 297.

46. Yoder, *Christian Witness to the State*, 20.

47. J. Smith, *Imagining the Kingdom*, 167.

What you *do* in the present—by painting, preaching, singing, sewing, praying, teaching, building hospitals, digging wells, campaigning for justice, writing poems, caring for the needy, loving your neighbor as yourself—*will last in God's future*. These activities are not simply ways of making the present a little less beastly, a little more bearable, until the day we leave it behind altogether. . . . They are part of what we may call building for God's kingdom.[48]

The fundamental basis for change begins with Christ lived within local congregations, and this congregational life subsequently trains the people of God for witness in society, where we engage political or economic structures.[49]

Third, John Yoder argues that the Church's witness must be based on its own experience and that this would distinguish witness from traditional "lobbying" efforts of Church and interchurch agencies.[50] To Yoder, witness must represent the Church's clear conviction; it must be consistent with the Church's own behavior, and witness should concern only those issues that the Church itself is demonstrably and ethically working on. (For example, a racially segregated Church has nothing to say to the state about the topic of integration.)

These three criteria narrow greatly the focus of the Church's witness efforts but ground them in the lived reality of the community of faith. This itself narrows the scale of the witness effort and raises the question of what one is to do with larger "justice issues." We would suggest that speaking "locally" based on an observable way of living in that local context would present the most straightforward way to begin to engage in witness. Some may question whether this way of being and speaking is even possible in the world. This question is born out of a deep sense of frustration (cynicism?) we sense about whether the Church is really acting like the Church. But Scripture is clear that God has provided what the Church needs to live this way: that God has given the Church a variety of gifts and sent God's Holy Spirit to lead it into truth. This provides a foundation for the Church living, confessing, and speaking.

Clearly, without the kingdom of God thriving within the Church, we lack the resources (and credibility) for transformation. And without a vision for the Lordship of Jesus Christ as a public reality, we restrict our influence to what happens between individuals, or within the walls of the Church. Not only *can* our experience inform our advocacy efforts but also, in a real sense, it *must* and *will* push us to speak in the public realm. Transformational advocacy

48. N. T. Wright, *Challenge of Jesus*, 193; emphasis original.

49. Witness, thus, is not just what the people of God do outside the Church, but also what we do inside.

50. Yoder, *Christian Witness to the State*, 21.

helps the church fulfill its biblical mandate to speak to the "principalities and powers" (Eph. 3:10 RSV).

We live between the times. Our future hope plays itself out in the here and now. The life and practices of the Church relate to the future kingdom. By straddling the two realms, the Church relates God's justice with contemporary realities,[51] and helps connect worship or discipleship with public matters. This is an important point for many who would divide the Church's "social" mission from its mission to "evangelize" the world. For Yoder this distinction is meaningless. He explains the meanings of *gospel* and *evangelism* at length to demonstrate that witness to the statesperson is, indeed, a call to discipleship. After discussing the use of these terms in the Gospels, he says, "It is clear that the good news announced to the world has to do with the reign of God among men in all their interpersonal relations, and not solely with the forgiveness of sins or the regeneration of individuals."[52] Later, he continues: "On whatever level we find a man in the effort to speak to him, what we ask of him is that he accept the gospel. . . . What we ask of him does not cease to be gospel by virtue of the fact that we relate it to his present available options."[53] Here Yoder is laying out a key understanding of the concept of witness.

Advocacy is about witness to the state, but most notably toward the statesperson—a real person who works within a real structure. It is far too easy to rest upon common caricatures given of the state—where politics assumes attributes that make it a god, or a demon—and therefore treat the political realm as one of these; or else to speak about the state in impersonal terms. But behind structures and institutions exist people, with names, identities, and histories. These are people whom God loves and for whom Christ gave his life.

The earlier emphasis upon the Trinity foregrounds the importance of relationships for transformative advocacy: we relate to others from within the arms of Father, Son, and Holy Spirit; and we extend to others the same embrace. But we also touched on the importance of Christ's humanity and how this should influence how we treat others "in power" and advocate for those who feel dehumanized by structures in society. This means we build relationships with people in political offices, not just for the purposes of changing policies or influencing legal protocols, but because we are linked in our humanity with

51. The Church needs to engage in God's justice in all the ways spoken of in Scripture: healing the sick, releasing the captive, providing sight for the blind, proclaiming the reordering of economic systems, living peace, reconciling broken relationships, providing food for the hungry, etc. The Church's witness must be consistent with its behavior. Only if it is living these realities within the congregation can it faithfully speak to political structures about them.

52. Yoder, *Christian Witness to the State*, 23.

53. Ibid., 25.

them. We pray for them, love them, and resist any inclination to deify or de-monize them. Much in the way of Jesus, we sit with people, tell stories, listen, and learn. Advocacy is not a one-way alley, but a two-lane highway, where change happens through a process of giving and receiving gifts. We need not fear that this exchange will lessen our influence or detract from our message; for to be open before the "other" comes with its own powers.

THE IMPORTANCE OF LOCAL CONGREGATIONS

Finally, we stress again the importance of the local congregation in trans-formational advocacy. For most of this chapter we have talked of the Church in large, universal terms (one, holy, catholic, apostolic) to emphasize the corporate interconnectedness of the people of God across time and space. Such a larger panorama unites us around a common identity, which is urgently needed in our contemporary day of fragmentation, specialization, and dizzying cultural diversity. But an emphasis upon the Church universal should not overshadow the importance of local congregations in advocacy work.

What specific advantages do local congregations have with regard to ad-vocacy? Initially, they have all the gifts of the Holy Spirit necessary "to equip his people for works of service, so that the body of Christ may be built up until we all reach unity in the faith and in the knowledge of the Son of God and become mature, attaining to the whole measure of the fullness of Christ" (Eph. 4:12–13). This is no small thing, for as Bonhoeffer and Yoder both un-derscore, these gifts are not just for themselves but also for the broader society.

Furthermore, churches exist in actual locations, where their contextuality, proximity, and relational resources foster the kind of fruitfulness we envision for transformational advocacy. Local congregations speak out of their relation-ships, with intimacy, and from their own contexts. Yet they do not just speak for themselves but also represent the broader expanse of the global Church around the world, moving across ethnic, denominational, and even socioeco-nomic lines. As Newbigin explains, "The local congregation is not a branch of the universal Church, but it is the place where the universal Church is made visible."[54] That kind of visibility must faithfully reflect the needs and resources of Christians around the world. For many in America, words such as "foreign" haunt people's imagination, conjuring up fear, threat, or abhorrent otherness. However, the people of God subscribe to a larger identity whereby the cross of Jesus Christ has "destroyed the barrier, the dividing wall of hostility," to create "one new humanity" through the Holy Spirit (Eph. 2:14–18). Thus, our advocacy should be deeply rooted in our location, but spilling over to the

---

54. Newbigin, *Truth to Tell*, 88.

issues facing other congregations (i.e., the Latino/a community, or inner-city black congregations), and ultimately to the broader needs of people around the world (Palestinian, Syrian, South Sudanese, etc.).

Our social location allows us to envision actual, contextual relationship with the state, not just some disembodied ideal. All advocacy work, as we have seen, seeks change—change in policies, practices, attitudes—that reduces injustice and allows for human flourishing. What is the nature of the change we are requesting when we speak to the statesperson? Here is an area where Yoder says some very useful things to the church—especially the "empowered" Church of the global North, which lives a privileged existence that assumes its "right" to be relevant: "The Christian witness to the state will not be guided by an imagined pattern of ideal society. . . . [It] will express itself in terms of specific criticisms, addressed to given injustices in a particular time and place, and specific suggestions for improvements to remedy the identified abuse."[55] Yoder uses the idea of the Church speaking in a "corrective" way and suggests that its work is actually an ongoing social critique—what he refers to as "critical witness."[56] All of this is consistent with the idea that the Church does not seek to "cover the field" in its witness but rather speaks into that with which it has direct experience.

But there is a caution. Advocacy should not be about solving problems in our Western sense of the term, but rather building relationships, envisioning new realities, and working together to foster the kind of change that emanates from the Lordship of Jesus Christ.[57] This doesn't mean the Church neglects problem solving, but that it does not approach change with some kind of technological bias that sees the world as some kind of mechanical unit in which, if we can just pull the right lever, the whole world would purr. The point might seem insignificant, but it remains foundational for transformational advocacy. We undertake advocacy because God advocates for the world. And we undertake advocacy in the way of God, through Jesus Christ, by the power of the Holy Spirit. Advocacy is therefore not a movement away from the gospel but a fundamental response to it.

In biblical terms, we are gardeners, people entrusted with creational powers to till, build up, and cause to flourish.[58] These activities are not restricted to

55. Yoder, *Christian Witness to the State*, 32.
56. Ibid., 36.
57. For more on the creativity and imagination needed for this approach to human problems, see Lederach, *Moral Imagination*.
58. John Stackhouse says, "We human beings were put in charge of the world to cultivate it—indeed, to subdue it. We are not to succumb to the lure of 'natural rhythms,' of letting things be, however beautiful they are and however ashamed we feel about our previous mismanagement. We are to garden the world, to take its potential and improve it. We are not to abandon

what we do with land, or cultures, or persons, but they extend to structures. Lesslie Newbigin says it well:

> All human traditions, institutions, and structures are prone to evil—including religion and including Christianity and the Church. They are all part of this present age. . . . But human life is impossible without them, and God in his mercy preserves them. . . . Our relation to the structures has to contain both the judgment that is inevitable in the searing light of the cross, and also the patience which is required of us as witnesses of the resurrection. . . . We are . . . patient revolutionaries who know that the whole creation, with all its given structures, is groaning in the travail of a new birth, and that we share this groaning and travail, this struggling and wrestling, but do so in hope because we have already received, in the Spirit, the firstfruit of the new world (Rom. 8:19–25).[59]

Advocacy requires that the Church live faithfully as a social reality informed by the Trinity, to engage in an ongoing social critique within society, and to speak out of its own lived experience. The practice of transformational advocacy is rooted in humility, informed by God's love, and emanates from a deep desire to see the statesperson's life flourish as God intended, and to take a step of faith to make changes to society that will cultivate shalom.

And What of Results?

The foregoing argues that advocacy is "merely" the natural action of a faithful Church. Just as God's advocacy emanates from God's nature, the Church engages in witness because it represents the living body of Jesus on earth. The Church does this by announcing the reign of God—a reign characterized by the healing of relationships, the reconciliation of all things, and justice on earth.

Knowing this, we can advocate with confidence that we are speaking a vision for our collective future and the future of all the nations (peoples/*ethnē*) of the earth. And yet . . .

Hebrews 11 provides a broad historical overview of people, like us, who hoped for and lived into a promise of salvation, of healing, and of redemption from bondage. It is a story of people of whom, the author makes clear, "the world was not worthy" (v. 38). And they persevered in hope and faith. But, the author notes, "All these, though they were commended for their faith, did not receive what was promised" (v. 39 NRSV).

---

our dignity and responsibility, however intimidating the task may seem and however unnerved we are by our recognition of past failures. We are to make shalom." *Making the Best of It*, 351.

59. Newbigin, *Gospel in a Pluralist Society*, 209.

We write as (and to) a Church in the global North that is privileged economically and in terms of personal security. With that privilege comes a tendency to believe that we can, by our own efforts, bring about the change we envision. Indeed, we speak the language of success, of impacts, of changes effected by our efforts. Of course there is nothing wrong with planning for and articulating the change we seek, but ultimately, the Church's advocacy efforts—our witness—are carried out in the context of a promise. It is a promise for which, like our spiritual forebears, we wait. And in the meantime, we seek to be faithful.

May we, therefore, judge the "success" of our advocacy by the metric of faithfulness—of persistence in announcing the reign of God—remembering the "great cloud of witnesses" (Heb. 12:1) who persevered and whose faith, in our faithfulness, we "complete."

Part 3

❖

An Evangelical Practice of Advocacy

6

Transformational Advocacy Practice

Witness of the Local and Global Church and the Parachurch

> God has placed Christians in many different areas of work and
> levels of society, all of which need to be influenced and transformed
> if poverty is to be alleviated.
>
> Tearfund[1]

In the past, evangelicals have employed impressive advocacy campaigns, including the antislavery crusades of William Wilberforce during the late eighteenth century in England and the temperance movement in the early nineteenth century in the United States. Evangelicals used advocacy in these circumstances to address suffering and injustice in God's world. Not coincidentally, these were moments when evangelicals profoundly guided and shaped society. However, over the last fifty years, the faith community has been less likely to use advocacy in their efforts for social justice and against poverty.

Recently, evangelicals have been approaching a more holistic public engagement that serves as a bridge with these earlier campaigns. Evangelicals seem newly willing to pursue an array of justice issues. The evangelical public

1. Gordon, *Advocacy Toolkit*, 44.

conscience has expanded from abortion issues to include the indignities of human trafficking and sexual exploitation. Evangelicals today have added to their defense of marriage and religious freedom the rights of immigrants, the poor, and the hungry. They engage the powers on issues of HIV/AIDS, creation care, global poverty, violence prevention, and peace building. Evangelicals see God at work in all of these issues.

In fact, some key institutions within evangelicalism are journeying "upstream." They are taking root-cause approaches to address injustice and tilling the ground for transformational advocacy. Several common forces tend to drive and motivate this advocacy, and evangelical practice is usually characterized by one of three specific approaches. Using this lens, we will look at examples of each of the five types of evangelical pillar institutions that anchor the movement's public presence: local churches, denominations, relief and development organizations, parachurch networks, and educational institutions.

Motivations behind Advocacy

Before examining how the various types of evangelical actors have been engaging in advocacy, it is important to look at what factors motivate these actors to do so. Motivations for individuals and institutions alike fall into one or more of these three categories: (1) one has been affected, indirectly or directly, by injustice; (2) one has a convicting sense of biblical call; (3) one is searching for ways to have greater impact and effectiveness. Often evangelicals and other Christians have been moved by one or all of these circumstances to pay attention to advocacy.

Affected

From our relationships or by our own social location we may experience injustice and be moved to action. Maybe it is the circumstance within which you find yourself that subjects you to injustice, suffering, marginalization, or alienation. Possibly your sister lost her job and fell into entangling debt and debilitating misfortune. Maybe you have an uncle whose family went hungry after being cut off of SNAP (food stamp) benefits when federal budget cuts hit. Perhaps your church has a sister relationship with a congregation in the global South, and on a mission trip you felt compelled to take action by what you saw. It could be that during missionary service in Uganda, you were exposed to circumstances and conditions that profoundly challenged our North American "first world" assumptions and lifestyle. Perhaps you are involved in church planting in an inner city and found yourself confronted with socioeconomic problems with roots in structural issues that had no easy answer. Many Christians who are called to advocacy have moved toward it after being directly affected or moved by something that personally touches them.

Biblical Call

From Scripture we learn that our story and God's story are interwoven and God's plans for reconciliation involve you and me. Reading Scripture and reflecting upon it deepens our sense of connectedness and responsibility toward others. When we understand that God became incarnate in the world because of his infinite love for us, we desire to respond to that love in a befitting manner. This biblical stirring motivated by God's love for us compels us to steward all of the influence with which God has gifted us. At a profound heart-level we understand that God intended this love for all God's children—especially the foreigner, the orphan, and the widow (Deut. 14:29)—that all of them might experience shalom and that the creation might flourish (Gen. 1:28). Because each of the pillars we explore in this chapter is grounded in faith, each pillar takes its leading from Scripture.

More Profound Change

Direct service programs, works of mercy or compassionate ministries, and relief and development efforts all have key roles to play in authentic Christian witness. Lives are touched and transformed in the places where we meet people, especially when there is brokenness. While recognizing the importance of charitable efforts, we come to the conclusion that charity has limitations. One friend says, "We cannot food bank our way out of hunger." If we are to propose more lasting solutions, confront the stubborn challenges to change, and vary and multiply works of mercy, we need an approach to advocacy that reaches beyond our direct-service ministries.

In the book *Faith-Rooted Organizing*, Alexia Salvatierra and Peter Heltzel share the importance of integrating advocacy into development:

> Community development strategies reach beyond mere charity to engage people in solving the problems in their neighborhoods. What does not typically get addressed by such strategies are the barriers created by unjust policies, laws and social structures. . . . Sooner or later, those engaged in community development hit a wall. . . . Transforming a community requires more than neighborhood development; it demands courageous organizing and persistent strategic advocacy.[2]

2. Salvatierra and Heltzel, *Faith-Rooted Organizing*, 8.

As we walk the road of incorporating advocacy, creating disciples who understand advocacy's value and purpose, we acknowledge it is necessary to keep the government systems and corporate practices accountable as they undoubtedly influence and impact the people and communities with whom we minister.

Basic Advocacy Approaches

While motivations get people and organizations involved in advocacy work, there is still a question of how to go about that work. There are three essential methods to advocacy. Advocacy can be done *for* those affected by injustice, *with* those affected by injustice, and *by* those affected by injustice. We will see evidence of these methods in the local church, denominations, relief and development organizations, parachurch networks, and educational institutions. Each advocacy method has appropriate scenarios, advantages, and disadvantages, and we review each in what follows.

Advocacy For

In the *advocacy for* approach, advocates are not directly affected by injustice, yet they are moved to do something. They may have easy access to decision makers. *Advocacy for* could look something like this: A women's group of a local church in Kansas returns from a short-term mission trip in the Democratic Republic of Congo. The church women feel moved to take up the cause of Female Genital Mutilation (FGM) occurring in Congo. Through this trip, the church women learn that although FGM is illegal in Congo, women's rights are violated there every day. They meet Congolese women and hear their stories of terrible abuse and violations and even death. Maybe these church members have access to a US senator from Kansas in charge of deciding US foreign aid funding toward Congo. The church women decide to engage in advocacy efforts with their senator and other US lawmakers to influence the shape and conditions attached to this aid to Congo and raise the profile of the women victims in that country, influencing the enforcement of stated Congolese laws. In this case, the Congolese women have neither access to lawmakers nor the safety to voice their concerns in this way. Engaging in advocacy for, in this instance, is akin to the scriptural concept found in Proverbs: "Speak up for those who cannot speak for themselves, for the rights of all who are destitute" (31:8).

On the flip side, advocates in this method may be considered outsiders because they are not directly impacted and therefore may lack important perspectives. Caution ought to be exercised when doing *advocacy for* so as not to overstep boundaries to speak for others without being given authorization to represent a group. Another disadvantage is that doing *advocacy for* does not leave room for capacity building and increasing the number of affected voices around the table.

Advocacy With

In the *advocacy with* method, collaboration happens between those affected by injustice and with those concerned about the situation. Coming alongside those most affected by injustice and partnering with them in solidarity can be a powerful force. Those directly affected can speak with authority about firsthand experiences. The other party in this equation—those who feel concerned—may have more resources and access and therefore be able to echo in larger chambers what they have heard. Take Annie, a mother and longtime congregant of a local church, who tells her pastor that with her meager part-time wages she can't afford to put food in her cupboards. The pastor of the church knows Annie and about a dozen other local families who are under- or unemployed and facing similar and all-too-familiar hardships since the recession hit. Along with Annie, the pastor and other church members try to change the systems failing members in the community. They join forces with other Christian antihunger advocates from Bread for the World[3] and begin to write letters to Congress to stabilize school lunch funding and unemployment benefits, or they call for stronger minimum-wage standards. *Advocacy with* makes a powerful impact. As with any true partnership, those "concerned" yet not directly affected need to be careful not to control the advocacy agenda. *Advocacy with* enables the capacity building of those who are often voiceless or marginalized.

Advocacy By

In the *advocacy by* approach, agents of change are those who most directly experience injustice. This approach enables a woman on the margins to tell her own story. In some cases, those who are most affected by injustice take the greatest risk by confronting injustice. Where human rights are abused or

3. Bread for the World is a collective Christian voice urging our national decision makers to end hunger and poverty at home and abroad. Bread members send letters and emails, make phone calls, and visit their members of Congress about legislation that addresses hunger in the United States and around the world. Bread equips its members to communicate with Congress and to work with others on advocacy. It educates members on hunger-related issues and inspires members to be legislative activists as a way of putting their Christian faith into action. http://www.bread.org/.

violence permeates society, people who are truth tellers about injustice can experience backlash or, even worse, cruel retribution for challenging authorities. Telling one's stories can be an incredibly powerful tool. An illustrative example of *advocacy by* is found in Benin in 2012:

> Reducing maternal mortality is something women in the Union of Evangelical Churches of Benin (UEEB) are passionate about.
>
> In order to engage all the people of Benin, and in particular the political and administrative authorities in this struggle, these women organised a march with the support of Micah Challenge Benin, which ended in reading out petitions to the Mayor of the town of Djougou, as well as the local health minister, Ouaké-Copargo. This was on Thursday, 23rd February, 2012.
>
> More than five hundred Christian women were mobilised for the advocacy campaign. These women who come from the districts of Atacora and Donga, wished to express their outrage at the lack of attention women receive from health workers during their pregnancies. They have also criticised the authorities for the inadequate health infrastructure and the under-qualified staff. "This is the reason why women are dying!" said the President of the UEEB. The campaign is called "Birth Without Risk of Death."
>
> The first stop for the women was Djougou town hall where the message was brought to the Mayor. Upon receiving it, he made a commitment to forward it to the district heads of Atacora and Donga as well as the President.
>
> He congratulated and encouraged the women of Micah Challenge for the importance of the message and showed support for the community of Djougou, who he said were acting in the interest of the whole country.[4]

One limitation in *advocacy by* can be that stories may be less effective when presented separate from a wider analysis or without a context of broader social science research to undergird the anecdotal evidence. This is in no way a critique of individuals telling their stories but rather a suggestion of the need to position stories in a larger structural narrative of the problem.

Each of these three approaches is effective in particular situations. It might be appropriate to use a mixture of the three methods of advocacy at various times during the advocacy process.[5] Our goal in laying out the motivations and methods of advocacy is not to lock local churches, denominations, relief and development organizations, parachurch networks, or educational institutions in to specific categories or boxes. Rather, we hope to describe the varying contexts for advocacy and the need for discerning what the appropriate advocacy response would be given the pillar's role within evangelical life. This framework

4. Kpetere, "Improving Maternal Health in Benin."
5. Watson, *Advocacy Toolkit*, 8.

helps to illuminate our exploration of evangelical Christians' articulations of and motivations toward advocacy and to engage issues beyond using compassion or charity approaches. As local churches, denominational structures, and these other pillar evangelical institutions embrace transformational advocacy, the road leads toward a fuller sense of Christian discipleship: a pursuit that aligns us and our relationships with God's character as an advocate.

Evangelicals Practicing Advocacy

Evangelicalism in the United States has grown into one of the most powerful social movements geared toward influencing a limited set of issues and electoral party politics. As we look at this social movement with an eye toward identifying where this narrow focus is being transcended, we see it happening slowly but surely in five main group actors, or institutional "pillars": the local church, denominational bodies, relief and development agencies, parachurch networks, and educational institutions. In many cases these evangelical expressions are interconnected. However, each type of group occupies a distinctive place in evangelical life and has an important role in laying foundations for transformational advocacy as core to its identity and mission to the world.

While each of the five institutions faces challenges in its nascent attempts at integrating advocacy discipleship into outreach and missions, the following examples demonstrate how evangelicals are beginning to weave nontraditional advocacy approaches into long-standing mission and ministries. As they do so, the Church and its members are becoming more equipped to partner with God's work to alleviate suffering and brokenness in the world.

The Local Church

The local church is the heart of evangelicalism. Local churches are part of God's plan for community, fellowship, sharing love, and attending to each other's immediate needs. The local church is a body of believers and can use its prophetic voice, especially for and with those who are the most vulnerable or marginalized in society.

But what does it look like to be good stewards of the local church's prophetic voice? How has the local church opened itself to grow its missions and ministries to engage in advocacy? The short answer, we have seen, is that evangelical churches have been skeptical about engaging aspects of faith life beyond the personal, spiritual, and charitable realms and have often, as a result, held a simplistic or moralistic perspective on poverty. Many evangelicals wonder if root-cause poverty advocacy is an appropriate part of Christian discipleship. Local churches that move beyond the "if" question confront an even bigger question of "how to" engage in advocacy faithfully, as Christians. The following four characteristics demonstrate why the local church holds a special and unique capacity for transformational advocacy.

First, the local church is a praying body. Local congregants pray together as a community; they convene worship services and preach the good news. In order for Christian advocacy to reach its fullest potential, it absolutely must be connected to prayer. Christian advocacy seeks to partner in God's redemptive work in the world. God uses the local church to help extend and build up the kingdom, which includes preaching, praying, caring for those in need, defending the cause of others, speaking out against injustice, working for change, and attending to God's creation. To engage in Christian advocacy and not simply activism, we need God involved in the process![6]

Second, the local church is present in the community—grassroots based— and engaged in personal relationships that gift the local church with moral credibility and legitimacy within the community context. Therefore, the local church has abundant relational resources. Marginalized people seek out local churches for a vast array of compassionate ministries.[7] This access allows for listening to firsthand stories of those affected by injustice. Relationships and personal stories move hearts and minds. They also provide for a deeper and up-close understanding of the injustices marginalized members of the community face.

Congregations are particularly active in helping recently arrived immigrants.[8] Jenny Hwang, World Relief's vice president for advocacy and public policy, has fielded local church calls from across the country with inquiries about what to do next for struggling undocumented immigrants. World Relief offers support to immigrants and refugees throughout a network of US offices in partnership with local churches. "Calls came from pastors from Chicago, Seattle, and other nontraditional immigrant-receiving communities like rural Georgia. No matter what these churches did to help their newly arriving neighbors, they couldn't help them get right with the law," Hwang shared.[9] These churches developed relationships with immigrants who weren't just living in their neighborhoods but also attending their services. Churches started to understand the limitations and challenges facing their new friends

---

6. Gordon, *Advocacy Toolkit*, 23.
7. See Chaves, *Congregations in America*; Ammerman, *Pillars of Faith*; Ammerman, "Congregations"; Wuthnow, "Mobilizing Civic Engagement."
8. Warner, "Religion and Migration."
9. Jenny Hwang, interview by Krisanne Vaillancourt Murphy, September 3, 2014.

because of current immigration laws. This compelled World Relief to publicly advocate for comprehensive immigration reform and equip churches with tools to not just serve immigrants on the ground but engage government around immigration policies.

As pastors and church members taught ESL (English as a second language) classes or arranged legal services for immigrants, church folk were emboldened and readied to speak out. Personal relationships and an openness toward growing discipleship led congregants to listen more closely to accounts of these injustices—enough to be moved themselves—and then use their credibility to share heartbreaking stories of suffering people within their communities. It compelled them to also pursue comprehensive immigration reform with Congress.

Third, the local church is responsive to the world around it. Often the launching pad for congregant outreach activities such as tutoring, short-term mission trips, canned-goods collections, and job training, the local church offers concrete ways for believers to engage in compassionate ministry. Congregations are rooted in the local community and have allegiances with other people that transcend ethnic, geographic, or socioeconomic barriers, interconnecting the lives of people with a communal perspective that extends far beyond the believers in the church building, the local community, and even the nation. But compassionate ministry calls for an understanding that advocacy can be a concrete way for God's love to be present.

The Bridge Community Church (Wesleyan) of Logansport, Indiana, provides an example. It wanted to respond to the immigrant suffering in the surrounding community. The Bridge Community Church opened a legal clinic to help immigrants navigate the confusing immigration process while pushing national decision makers for comprehensive immigration reform. Leading up to 2014, the US Congress failed to take action on immigration reform. President Barack Obama announced an executive order in November 2014 that gave millions in the United States who lack documentation an opportunity to apply for temporary legal status. The Bridge Community Church became the first Board of Immigration Appeals site for the Wesleyan Church in the United States, a legal clinic to help immigrants apply for this new status. The pastor, Rev. Zach Szmara, recalls how his church became part of a solution in the suffering caused by a broken immigration system:

> There have been times we've missed the mark as the Church in North America and sat on the sidelines when God was calling us to engage and transform our culture. I am deeply grateful and extremely proud that so many different churches, leaders, denominations, and organizations have made a very profound

decision to engage immigrants and immigration in a biblical, Christ-focused, and Kingdom-minded way. We are better together.[10]

Fourth, the local church is a trusted source of shared information. The church shares information inside its walls—within its body of believers—and it also shares stories of people affected by injustice more widely—regionally, nationally, or internationally. Like in The Bridge Community Church example above, local churches are connected to a wider network and are recognized as a credible source of information. The Bridge Community Church led the way for the Wesleyan denomination—and dozens of other congregations in the broader Wesleyan tradition—to learn how to accompany immigrants and advocate for systems change. Local churches have ministry groups that champion causes, explore topics, and gather together for activities such as small Bible studies, mothers' or men's groups, and social ministry teams. These channels provide mechanisms to share, teach, instruct, and disseminate information, which facilitates meaningful advocacy.

In sum, churches offer a reason for hope and purpose behind efforts to restore both personal and societal brokenness. Personal relationships, stories, and the involvement of the local church can critically and broadly inform the advocacy campaigns, especially when church communities are moved to advocate from a place of discipleship. The local church is the heart of evangelicalism, as it holds a preeminent place in the evangelical community. Yet most local evangelical churches have little experience articulating advocacy messages and making them operational. Local churches benefit from the trust that comes with a long-term presence in a community, and the faithful prayers of congregants for their neighbors. When a local church values advocacy in its forming of disciples, it can respond compassionately and immediately to suffering and can ready its disciples for appropriate advocacy actions as part of church mission and ministry.

Denominational Bodies

Denominations are the umbrella or ecclesial structures designed to credential pastoral leaders and connect local churches.[11] If local churches have a grassroots, relational role in advocacy, then denominations have a higher-level, formal-advocacy function. Denominational bodies influence and represent church members in official ways through interactions with other religious and secular bodies. Yet the denominational body also has a platform to instruct its

---

10. Drury, "Wesleyan Church Joins."
11. Ammerman, "New Life for Denominationalism."

own church body through organizational, educational, and spiritual practices. Denominations have two distinctive roles in relation to transformational advocacy: a representative function and an instructive function.

In their representative function, denominations create committee structures geared to represent the denomination outside of its own body. The Wesleyan Church's statement on global poverty provides an excellent example of a denomination using its representative function. In January 2006 the International Board of the Wesleyan Church drafted and adopted a position statement on global poverty that articulated the biblical principles guiding the church's responsibility to the poor. The statement denounced "systemic evil" that enslaves people in poverty. The prophetic role of the church was supported by scriptural texts such as Nehemiah 1, Psalm 82, and Micah 6:8. The Wesleyan Church called on national and international political structures—namely, national governments and the United Nations—to support the established poverty targets of the Millennium Development Goals (MDGs), a set of eight goals adopted in 2000 by 186 countries for a fifteen-year period to galvanize efforts to end extreme poverty.[12] The denominational structure thus served as a mouthpiece for its members, trying to influence international government bodies.

In their instructive function, denominations can offer guidance to the local church about what it believes and how to interpret the world around it. By planting churches, strengthening educational institutions, credentialing pastoral leadership, publishing curricula and media, and coordinating ministries, denominations can equip the church to engage the world. How the denominational body views and practices advocacy either promotes or discourages advocacy's place in Christian discipleship among its churches.

The Wesleyan denomination's statement on global poverty, again, provides a useful example. In its instructive function, the document invited the Wesleyans worldwide to a deeper level of responsibility and relationship with poor people. Using the International Board's statement as its guide, the North American General Conference of the Wesleyan Church adopted its own declaration on global poverty that included a call to engage in appropriate public policy advocacy, suggesting the Wesleyan Church be "proactively engaging with other churches, agencies, governments and non-government organizations who share our vision for community transformation . . . promote good stewardship, accountability and justice in society, and hold our respective governments and the United Nations to account."[13] After the International Board drafted its global poverty statement,

12. Wesleyan Church, "Wesleyan View of Global Poverty."
13. Wesleyan North American General Conference Global Poverty Statement, adopted in Orlando, Florida, June 11, 2008.

the North American Wesleyan Church listened to the concerns from brothers and sisters from the global South about the poverty in their midst and responded.

Another example of how denominations use representative and instructive functions to support transformational advocacy is evidenced in the Christian Reformed Church of North America (CRCNA, also known as the CRC). The CRCNA's concern for advocacy dates back to the late 1990s, when the denomination's Board of World Missions and its relief and development arm, now called World Renew, had a historical mission focus in Sierra Leone. After almost twenty years of intensive church planting and integrated rural development work in the Kuranko region of the country, Christian Reformed Church missionaries Paul and Mary Kortenhoven had to flee from their community because it was overrun by rebels. Their model development program and church plant had made impressive gains in literacy and in health and food production, and their church was growing with local evangelists. Yet the political turmoil threatened to destroy all the development and evangelization work they had done, bringing millions of dollars of CRC investment to naught.

After much vigilant study, analysis, and discernment, it became clear that the rebel activity in Sierra Leone was intimately linked with an illicit diamond market and related warlord activity. The denomination began to understand another compelling aspect of its mission efforts. Instead of mission in the traditional sense of the global mission field, they employed "mission by advocacy." The CRCNA's newly formed Office of Social Justice and the Kortenhovens engaged their congressional representative from Western Michigan, Representative Vern Ehlers, about conflict diamonds. Fueled by the firsthand stories from CRC missions and by extensive experience in the development field of Sierra Leone, and undergirded by denominational support, the CRC helped to make Western Michigan's congressman a champion in the House of Representatives on the international Kimberley Process—an initiative jointly sponsored by industry, civil society, and government to certify diamonds. In 2003 the Kimberley Accords were signed, putting in place a certification process to stem the flow of conflict diamonds that were funding wars against legitimate governments.[14]

In 2004 the CRCNA Synod endorsed the Micah Call, an evangelical invitation to Christians to "be agents of hope for and with the poor, and to work for others to hold our national and global leaders accountable in securing a more just and merciful world."[15] The call beckoned international and national

14. See Van Harmelen, "Diamond War"; Kimberley Process, home page.
15. Edwards, McLachlan, and Jackson, *Use by 2015: Micah Challenge Insights from a Ten-Year Experiment.*

decision makers of both rich and poor nations to fulfill their public promise to achieve the MDGs and cut global poverty in half by 2015.

In its instructive function, the CRCNA encouraged churches to participate in the Micah Challenge—the global evangelical advocacy campaign seeking to hold their governments accountable to halve poverty by 2015 and to end extreme poverty.[16] This endorsement of the Micah Call spawned advocacy activities throughout the CRCNA. Church members and students alike sent Congress thousands of "Lend a Hand" handprints pledging to end extreme poverty by 2010.[17] Small-group studies sponsored by the CRC's World Renew and by Micah Challenge USA led CRCNA members to study a curriculum called *Live Just.ly*, which moved participants toward choosing lifestyles of biblical justice.[18] According to Peter Vander Meulen, director of the CRCNA's Office of Social Justice, the denomination's instructive and representative functions toward advocacy made an impact:

> The good results of the Micah Challenge mobilization are still reverberating in my neighborhood. We have a world with far fewer hungry people than in 2000. There are re-energized church members who have seen Christ's "good news to the poor" put into global goals and actions. And there are renewed—more equal relationships among followers of Christ around the world.[19]

In conclusion, how advocacy is conceived and interpreted at the denominational level either helps or hinders greater involvement in advocacy for disciples and congregants alike. Employing the representative and instructive functions proved fruitful in focusing local Wesleyan churches on global poverty and immigration reform. Similarly, by using these two functions, the CRCNA raised new advocacy standards for its congregations while contributing to the historic international promises made through the Millennium Development Goals and Kimberley Accords. When used well, both the representative and instructive functions can respond to marginalized brothers and sisters, deepen Christian discipleship, support transformational advocacy practices, and expand the mission of the Church to the world around it.

Relief and Development Organizations

Relief and development organizations are central to evangelicals' response to global poverty due to these organizations' programmatic work with the

16. The Christian Reformed Church in North America Synod endorsed Micah Call, 2004.
17. "Calling All College Students!"
18. Fileta, "Live Just.ly."
19. See also Edwards, McLachlan, and Jackson, *Use by 2015*, 15.

most vulnerable and suffering people in our world and their commitment to integrating the spiritual element into their programs. Relief and development programming, whether focused on child and maternal health, HIV/AIDS, microfinance, refugee resettlement, or disaster relief, offers a channel for the Church to engage struggling, impoverished communities around the globe and opens a window into the joys and challenges of those living on the margins of society.

Local churches offer crucial support to these organizations, providing donors, members, volunteers, mission participants, and prayer support for development efforts.[20] Similarly, denominations are linked with relief and development efforts,[21] as we saw with the Christian Reformed Church's sponsorship of World Renew.

Supported by these other pillar institutions, relief and development organizations have been positioning themselves to live further into the biblical call to pursue justice and devoting more of their resources to implementing advocacy with, for, and by those most affected and to providing opportunities for churches to learn from this kind of work. When the Church engages those living on the margins, through volunteer support, financial donations, or child sponsorship, or even when it simply listens to a community's realities through stories, the Church takes a first step toward building solidarity, an essential biblical principle, and it is a step that leads its actions toward being geared to justice and the common good.[22] In these same ways, through their work and ministry, relief and development organizations are an entry point into a profound Christian witness, the witness of transformational advocacy of a much wider Church. As they come across injustice, Christians are forced to decide, just as local churches and individual evangelicals are, whether to engage in "third-generation" advocacy, and if so, how.

And evangelical relief and development agencies *have* started to respond to the injustices they come across by integrating advocacy into their programming responses, and what might be called "socio-spiritual entrepreneur" individuals and local churches have started to create evangelical advocacy organizations to tackle specific issues. Through both of these types of response, relief and development organizations are helping to define and operationalize transformational advocacy, even as they encounter the limitations of each of these modes.

RELIEF AND DEVELOPMENT: TOWARD INTEGRATED ADVOCACY

As relief and development organizations integrate advocacy into their programming, professional staff, field practitioners, the donor base, and

20. Reynolds and Offutt, "Global Poverty and Evangelical Action"; Wuthnow, *Boundless Faith*.
21. Ammerman, *Pillars of Faith*.
22. Monsma, *Healing for a Broken World*, 75.

grassroots community partners all are called to advocacy witness. The organization treats advocacy as an integral component of its overarching goals. It moves beyond connecting volunteers with individual needs toward a more holistic advocacy that reflects system-change thinking at every level. Integrated advocacy empowers all stakeholders to respond to their call and steward their influence, local and global and vice versa. Relief and development organizations engage in advocacy systems in the local context where programs are implemented, with grassroots donors, and within its spheres of influence at the national and international policy levels to shape long-term policies and structures and address root causes of poverty. Integrated advocacy deepens relationships and creates opportunities for discipleship.

World Relief is a relief and development organization that has recently integrated advocacy into its programs. Beginning with organizational structure, in 2013 World Relief elevated its head advocacy staff position to the organization's executive team in order to embed advocacy into every part of the organization's work. This move further tied World Relief's humanitarian program to its advocacy mission focus. In 2014 World Relief adopted a comprehensive integrated advocacy campaign called #WagePeace, through which World Relief supporters make a commitment "to pray, advocate and/or give to create awareness around conflict and support peacemakers as individuals who are change agents in their communities."[23] By asking not just traditional advocates but donors and church partners to raise awareness of and advocate for common themes of peace, this campaign has become an important, effective, and practical tool for church and support-base engagement for World Relief. Again, no longer can advocacy be absent from the transformational development paradigm.

World Vision, too, has integrated advocacy into its mission, with its first-ever global advocacy campaign, called Global Child Health Now. The campaign, with a goal of reducing preventable child/maternal deaths, was launched globally in 2009 at the United Nations in New York City, in Geneva, and in Nairobi, Kenya. Looking back, we see that this global advocacy campaign touts impressive results:

> The Christian witness found in the advocacy activities of Global Child Health Now campaign included grasstop faith leaders "lobbying" members of Congress and children writing letters to United States policy makers. Higher level advocacy included coordinating messages directed at powerful international

23. World Relief, "Wage Peace."

institutions like the United Nations General Assembly, the G8, G20 and World Health Organization.[24]

World Vision's efforts to pass the Water for the World Act are another example of integrated advocacy. World Vision engaged its entire donor base— nearly one million US Christians—in advocacy for a bill in the US Congress that sought to improve US foreign assistance related to water, sanitation, and hygiene programs. Over the course of one year, World Vision donors contacted every single member of the US Congress (House and Senate—535 representatives) through emails, postcards, phone calls, in-district visits, and even op-eds in local papers. These World Vision actions added to the crescendo of advocacy efforts conducted by other like-minded organizations, making this advocacy effort effective and formidable. The bill became law on December 19, 2014, helping ensure that millions of dollars in US foreign assistance for clean water gets to the most vulnerable and hard-to-reach communities around the world. This is a strong example of the impact that is possible when the US church integrates advocacy into its understanding of missional engagement in the world.[25]

As with other relief and development agencies, World Vision's stance on advocacy has evolved significantly. Even though World Vision was founded in 1950, it wasn't until the early 1980s that World Vision USA began to formalize its professional government relations staffing. And it took roughly another twenty years for World Vision to hire staff to educate and mobilize its vast support base. One early and energized World Vision grassroots contingent began with Seattle Pacific University students and a campus advocacy group called Acting on AIDS. In 2004 these college students sought to change the US response to the global AIDS epidemic. World Vision took this campus-based advocacy model to scale and formed ACT:S, a network of college-aged activists involved in pressing global-poverty advocacy issues, such as the passage of the Trafficking Victims Protection Reauthorization Act of 2013, the organization of World Water Day, and other global poverty campaigns. Today some thirty thousand students across the United States are linked to World Vision's broader global youth movement, which engages youth in developing nations in similar global-poverty-related activism.[26] Before this time, the typical World Vision grassroots donor, though deeply engaged in supporting child sponsorships, was not otherwise connecting through World Vision to do advocacy.

24. Robert Zachritz, email to Krisanne Vaillancourt Murphy, March 10, 2015.
25. Amanda Mootz, email to Krisanne Vaillancourt Murphy, March 9, 2015.
26. Ibid.

As they integrate advocacy into their programs, evangelical relief and development organizations have also built advocacy capacity from the grass roots. In some cases, this has become part of the general asset-mapping models exercised in the development field as part of building long-term community sustainability. World Vision, for example, has been equipping and encouraging a strengthened and engaged civil-society engagement across the globe through its Citizen Voice and Action (CVA) program, a social accountability approach that promotes engagement between communities and government to improve health, education, and other services.[27] World Renew uses such an asset-based approach to all programming and grassroots advocacy, and capacity building is key in its long-term program implementation in twenty-eight countries. More recently, World Vision has begun biblical-advocacy training workshops with local churches around the country. Chaz Nichols, director of outreach at Westwood Community Church in Excelsior, Minnesota, was a participant in such a workshop training and had this to say about the experience:

> Advocacy is something practical we can all do right now, whether it is emailing our elected decision makers on specific issues, visiting a legislator's office, or making phone calls to local representatives. The Spirit-led and Bible-based practical training provided by World Vision created a greater awareness of needs and provided strategies for the issues God brings to us.[28]

EVANGELICAL ADVOCACY ORGANIZATIONS

Evangelicals are beginning to create advocacy organizations to tackle specific, difficult, nontraditional issues. One of the most encouraging is the Association for a More Just Society (AJS), a Honduran- and US-based organization created in 1998 whose vision is expressed as "Christian communities doing justice and mercy close to home and globally."[29] AJS is focused on two main areas of work—peace and public security, and anticorruption—with a clear statement of its strategy:

> AJS supports efforts in Honduras that promote the interests of the most poor in legislative projects, defend the rights of the most vulnerable in judicial processes,

27. World Vision, "World Vision's Social Accountability Approach."
28. Robert Nichols blog, February 19, 2015. Quoted in Beyond 5 blog, "Five Steps to Bring Justice Advocacy Training to Your Church."
29. Association for a More Just Society, "AJS." Another organization that deserves mention is International Justice Mission, whose resource book and encouragement of local churches into advocacy we review in the next chapter. We do not present a case study on it here because the thoroughly important issue that it is addressing, sex trafficking, is one that evangelicals have taken up significantly.

increase the awareness and democratic participation of churches to practice the Biblical teachings on justice, and publish journalistic investigations on issues that affect the poor of Honduras.[30]

This vision and strategy are not just academic or theoretical statements. In fact, AJS and its focus grew out of consternation concerning injustice that evangelicals living in one of the most violent and dangerous neighborhoods of the capital of Honduras were experiencing: corruption, murder, and other crimes were going unprosecuted, and some people were threatening violence and claiming that they would not be punished for it. After much prayer and with enormous trepidation, these "brave Christians," as they labeled themselves for self-encouragement and accountability, began to hire clean and wise former police officers and prosecutors to work the community, identify those perpetrating crimes, and testify against them; then, with brave, principled, and committed police officers, prosecutors, and judges, they began to bring the criminals to justice. The success has been enormous, with conviction rates of those committing crimes in the neighborhoods skyrocketing, murder rates plummeting, and AJS being looked to nationally and internationally as a model to imitate in tackling corruption and impunity. It serves as Transparency International's partner in Honduras; is spearheading a coalition called "Let's Transform Honduras," made up of evangelical and other religious organizations, that seeks to "improve services and fight corruption in the areas of employment, health, education, corruption, and crime through investigations, social auditing, and advocacy"; and has expanded its own work to tackling corruption in land rights, education, and public health.[31]

Taking a step back from our exploration, it is clear that responding to suffering and debilitating poverty is at the core of both relief and development mission and the newly emerging evangelical advocacy organizations. For this reason these agencies serve as a primary conduit for local churches and denominations to address global poverty. But how do we arrive at an integrated or transformational advocacy? As you recall from chapter 1, depoliticized forms of advocacy such as personal or brand advocacy and professional advocacy can be effective within certain contexts, but individually they are bound by limitations that keep them from making greater impact toward aligning our witness with God's. Personal advocacy can lead to changed individuals, but it fails to address the systems that perpetuate suffering. Professional advocacy

30. Ibid.
31. Association for a More Just Society, "Let's Transform Honduras." Also Ver Beek, presentation at Eastern University; Van Beek, presentations at Faith and Development Conference. For more information about the work and results, see AJS main website: http://ajs-us.org/.

functions at a high level to shape policy, but even though informed by faith values, it is done in isolation and falls short of connecting grassroots supporters so they can witness and use their voices to influence for change. AJS is an example of solid grassroots advocacy capacity building in the program field, an organization that equips people in local communities to seek good governance, political transparency, and development sustainability. Yet even this approach alone misses the mark in fostering solidarity between the people in the development field and grassroots supporters.

When working to its full potential, integrated advocacy builds upon the personal, professional, and grassroots forms of advocacy and takes one additional step. Integrated advocacy recognizes the importance of advocacy at every level of relief and development mission, from the boardrooms in which decisions are made to the communities in which they are operationalized. Integrated advocacy connects the local and the global and builds solidarity. As we saw in the World Relief example, in order to raise advocacy's importance within its mission, the organization elevated its chief advocate to its executive team. And World Vision invited grassroots donors to engage in advocacy and integrated advocacy to employ *advocacy for*, *advocacy with*, and *advocacy by* approaches. As relief and development organizations incorporate, apply, and practice these approaches, and as evangelical advocacy organizations are created, these agencies serve as an incredibly compelling witness toward transformational advocacy.

Parachurch Networks and Associations

Parachurch networks lay important foundations for transformational advocacy in the evangelical community. They connect churches, NGOs, and civil society actors. Typically convening collections of church or ministry bodies aligned around a common mission, these networks provide a forum to elevate conversations on emerging issues that shape the institutions within their networks. Parachurch networks perform internal formation and external messenger functions similar to those found in the instructive and representative functions of denominations. But they do so for a wider-reaching Christian audience.

Although many parachurch ministries are at work in advocacy, we would include among the leaders the National Association of Evangelicals (NAE), Evangelicals for Social Action (ESA), the Christian Community Development Association (CCDA), the Accord Network, the Justice Conference, the Micah Network, the World Evangelical Alliance, Red Letter Christians, the Lausanne Congress, Sojourners, the Evangelical Partnership for the Common Good, and the Evangelical Environmental Network. We give an account of the first four of these because in some way they either have engaged in significant advocacy activity outside of traditional issues or are now wrestling with a decision as to whether to do so; in general, they bring together a diverse set of actors who are having intentional discussions about the ins and outs of advocacy.

NATIONAL ASSOCIATION OF EVANGELICALS

Like umbrella institutions in general, the National Association of Evangelicals (NAE) can greatly influence how advocacy is understood and conducted. An organization of networks representing more than forty-five thousand local churches from forty different denominations, the NAE has a board of directors from many denominations, including Assemblies of God, Church of the Nazarene, Foursquare Church, Open Bible Churches, Salvation Army, and Vineyard USA.[32]

The NAE is one of the few evangelical bodies that has attempted to articulate a comprehensive rationale for public policy engagement. In 2001, almost sixty years after it was founded, the NAE began a project to educate its members about functioning in the public policy arena. The evangelical leadership association set out to establish a set of principles to guide evangelical engagement in public policy, to move beyond professional staff lobbying toward encouraging its denominational church members and their grassroots constituencies to develop a more integrated understanding of advocacy and of the NAE's advocacy methods and principles. The project attempted to study the Bible and study the world with the explicit purpose of having something to say about it. "Evangelicals have failed to engage with the breadth, depth, and consistency to which we are called," says the introduction to *For the Health of the Nation: An Evangelical Call to Civic Responsibility*.[33] The document continues, "As Christian citizens, we believe it is our calling to help government live up to its divine mandate to render justice (Rom. 13:1–7; 1 Pet. 2:13–17)."[34] *For the Health of the Nation* recognized that only about half of evangelical Christians vote, confirming skepticism often attributed to evangelicals about engaging government. Furthermore, of that engagement, the most well-known concerns have been "pro-life and family issues" mostly to the exclusion of global poverty-related matters such as "disaster relief, refugee resettlement, HIV/AIDS, slavery, sexual trafficking, and prison rape."[35]

32. See National Association of Evangelicals, "Denominational Members."
33. National Association of Evangelicals, *For the Health of the Nation*, 2.
34. Ibid., 3.
35. Ibid. As stated previously, the authors of this book support advocacy across the whole range of issues.

Historically, evangelicals have attempted to change the world by changing one life, one heart at a time. Ron Sider, one of the document's authors, writes that for the "last three decades evangelicals have jumped into politics without reflecting on how to do it well."[36] *For the Health of the Nation*'s purpose was thus to produce a set of principles for public policy engagement and begin to articulate a common framework for evangelical public policy engagement—a political philosophy appropriate for the US context. Key principles of the document focus on poverty-related justice matters, such as showing compassion for the poor and vulnerable, protecting human rights, seeking peace, restraining violence, and protecting God's creation.[37] The authority of *For the Health of the Nation* is limited because its framers lacked explicit authorization to draft it; furthermore, it is difficult to reach average believers/disciples with the document's message in such a way that they actually use the framework as a template for advocacy engagement. Nevertheless, the principles set forth in the document outline an instructive platform for evangelicals to engage in common action, defining the kinds of biblically based holistic social concerns evangelicals need to address. Because evangelicals have a wide range of perspectives on public policy issues, *For the Health of the Nation*'s unifying claims represented a landmark shift. It declared that a true Christian response to the suffering and brokenness in the world transcends party politics and is biblically rooted in the aforementioned principles. In light of the biblical principles for policy advocacy, it required a more holistic response to stewarding citizenship in the public realm.

Evangelicals for Social Action

One of the major players in developing the NAE's *For the Health of the Nation* was Ron Sider, who was also one of the cofounders of Evangelicals for Social Action (ESA) in 1978. ESA and its publication *Prism* have been leaders in the evangelical community by modeling many aspects of transformational advocacy, including taking on a host of nontraditional issues, many times to the dismay of more conservative evangelicals. ESA has advocated for antiwar approaches in US foreign policy, a nuclear freeze, economic sanctions on South Africa, economic justice, measures to alleviate poverty, and care for the environment, as well as taking stances on more traditional issues such as religious freedom and abortion. ESA has also done significant work to explore the importance of integrating evangelism and social action and, under the new leadership of Paul Alexander and Al Tizon, has continued to live up to its legacy.[38]

36. Sider, "Shaping Up for the Public Square."
37. Ibid., 24.
38. For a good history of ESA, see Sider's brief summary on ESA's website: "ESA's History."

The Christian Community Development Association

Focusing primarily on domestic impoverished communities, the Christian Community Development Association (CCDA) has a unique potential for transformational advocacy. This parachurch network draws together local churches, communities, and ministries involved in development. For more than twenty-five years CCDA has gathered Christian leaders deeply engaged in the work of grassroots-level local neighborhood rebuilding. Dr. John Perkins formed CCDA in 1989, drawing on his rich racial-reconciliation work and knowledge of the history of the civil rights movement. His experience in grassroots community development led him to develop an incarnational philosophy based on "relocation, reconciliation and redistribution" to "express the love of Jesus in America's poor communities."[39] Perkins's incarnational philosophy was expanded later to become the "8 key components of Christian community development," a concept that is deeply rooted in biblical principles and that evolved from his years of living and working among the poor.[40]

From the earliest days of CCDA's incarnational ministry, this core philosophy has helped to ground Christian community development efforts to humanize problems of poverty and marginalization, revitalizing some of the most broken neighborhoods in the United States. What began with Dr. Perkins and a handful of other grassroots Christian leaders has been carried on by Noel Castellanos, the leader of CCDA since 2007.

For many years the practitioners of Christian Community Development (CCD) were guided by a model framework for ministry that focused on (1) proclamation of the gospel and formation of leaders, (2) compassion ministries, and (3) restoration and development. Later, Castellanos added a fourth characteristic to the incarnational model of ministry: confronting injustice. This updated framework introduces another critical element that has become foundational in the work of CCDA—namely, the importance of confronting brokenness at a systemic and structural level.

> Because I was incarnated in the community, living side-by-side with my undocumented brothers and sisters, I became acutely aware of their situation. . . . I was already convinced that as Christians, we were called to love and serve the poor in their distress, but now, I was beginning to see more clearly that the most vulnerable people in our world were often victims of oppression and injustice. It was not just individuals who needed to be confronted with their sin, but broken and fallen systems needed to be changed and confronted as well![41]

39. Christian Community Development Association, http://www.ccda.org/about.
40. Lisa Watson, email to Krisanne Vaillancourt Murphy, February 7, 2015.
41. Castellanos, "When Love Demands Justice."

Castellanos's testimony shows how incarnational ministry based in local communities led CCDA to incorporate root-cause, integrated advocacy into the CCD model. The CCDA's role as key member of the Evangelical Immigration Table, a broad coalition of evangelical organizations and leaders advocating for comprehensive immigration reform from a biblical perspective, demonstrates this shift at the national level. CCDA represents the countless stories of people within its ministries who are suffering under an unjust immigration system as it urges national policy decision makers to work together to pass immigration reform.[42]

Over its history, many neighborhood CCD ministries have engaged in *advocacy by* and *advocacy with* at the local or state level on issues such as education, community public transportation, or affordable housing. CCDA's historical involvement in local communities brings an immense cache of powerful stories about poverty and injustice that can influence national policy conversations. Because advocacy is a natural extension of community development experiences, CCDA has enormous potential to move toward firmly integrating advocacy into the CCD model of ministry.

To that end CCDA is beginning to look strategically at national advocacy actions that can make an impact on the development ministries happening in neighborhoods across the United States. In 2014 CCDA hired its first staff person for advocacy and policy engagement to build the network's capacity for national, coordinated advocacy engagement around the pressing justice issues that resonate with a majority of CCD communities: immigration reform, education, and mass incarceration. While seeking biblical justice is certainly nothing new for CCD workers, the witness and ministry of advocacy at the larger, national-network level is a tool they have picked up on only recently.

Accord Network

The Accord Network is an example of how parachurch networks are hesitant to adopt and operationalize root-cause advocacy. From its beginning in the late 1970s, the Accord Network (until 2010 it was known as the Association of Evangelical Relief and Development Organizations, or AERDO) convened a group of biblically based development practitioners working among the poor internationally.[43] Historically, collective advocacy action within this network had been limited, and it wasn't until the network members organized and lobbied Congress around the President's Emergency Plan for AIDS Relief (PEPFAR) in 2008 that it embarked on a successful advocacy campaign with

---

42. EIT website.
43. Accord Network, "Accord Network."

global impact. (See the appendix.) Accord Network members lobbied on behalf of this historic legislation to combat HIV/AIDS in Africa and also used the opportunity to secure government funding for vital HIV/AIDS programming sponsored by some Accord member bodies. This was a successful collaborative advocacy effort. Yet this first foray into policy advocacy was short-lived.

In 2010 when AERDO changed its name to the Accord Network, the network also broadened its mission to be "a catalyst for learning, collaboration and building Christ-centered unity around the shared vision of eliminating poverty."[44] In doing so, Accord sought to develop and advance a more integrated understanding of advocacy among its membership. In its instructional function Accord took initial steps to educate member organizations about the role that Christian advocacy plays in eliminating poverty—expanding the perspectives on how practitioners from relief and development organizations in the Accord Network were addressing poverty and advocacy in the development field every day.

By 2012 the advocacy conversation within Accord grew, but slowly. Accord acquired Micah Challenge USA as a program. Micah Challenge led a new "Accord Advocacy Alliance," and this alliance's members worked together to fully define advocacy. After much deliberation, the network drafted but never adopted the following definition of advocacy: "challenging ourselves and our leaders to change attitudes, behaviors, and policies that perpetuate injustice and deny God's will for all creation to flourish."[45]

It became clear as Accord further explored advocacy and began using a root-cause or integrated definition of advocacy that this kind of advocacy was less operationalized within its relief and development member bodies than it was in Accord's leadership. This was particularly true of the support bases of these organizations. Much more work would need to be done to break through from the "teach people to fish" mode to the "challenge the company polluting the river" kind of perspective. In discussing how to move toward holistic development to fully address poverty, unjust systems, and root causes, the network has included advocacy in the discussion.

In 2012 Accord adopted Principles of Excellence in Integral Mission, a text that is helping the network further integrate advocacy into its programming.[46] These eight principles set standards for the organizations in the network by describing what excellent relief and development work looks like. Advocacy found a place in the principles:

44. Accord Network, Origins of Accord Network, http://www.accordnetwork.org/history.
45. Jason Fileta, email to Krisanne Vaillancourt Murphy, February 25, 2015.
46. Accord Network, "Principles of Excellence."

No. 5: We recognize the whole system of poverty. We see the whole system of individual, spiritual, structural and relational barriers that can keep the community trapped in poverty. From our organizational competency areas, our efforts at advocacy and empowerment address both immediate needs and the long-term systemic causes of the problems we seek to address.[47]

While this specific principle clearly recognizes that systems and structures contain barriers to overcoming poverty and affirms root-cause advocacy as an appropriate response, just how willing member agencies will be to appropriate this significant shift in advocacy learning remains to be seen.

In regard to defining advocacy and aligning with the Principles of Excellence, Micah Challenge director Jason Fileta reflects, "It became apparent in the Accord Advocacy Alliance that though we had varying ideas about the nature of advocacy, the principle of excellence recognizing systems of poverty was indeed the standard of practice we must hold ourselves to." Yet there are encouraging signs to note. In terms of implementation, Fileta says, "Organizations that traditionally used advocacy only to fundraise included legislative calls to action in advocacy campaigns. And organizations that only engaged in advocacy at a grasstops level considered how they could engage their grassroots base in advocacy for the root causes of extreme poverty."[48] Clear outcomes from this evolving advocacy conversation within Accord Network have yet to appear. However, the formalized connection between Micah Challenge and Accord, the inclusion of advocacy in the eight principles of excellence in integral mission, and the regular grassroots advocacy summit as part of the annual Developing Excellence Forum continue to pry openings for integrated advocacy within the network. Advocacy that is articulated and elevated in these settings encourages relief and development organizations to collectively approach a more holistic poverty alleviation framework and to add "advocacy" as a third characteristic to what we know today as simply the "relief and development" sector.

Thus parachurch networks pave an important path toward transformational advocacy for member bodies—providing leadership instruction as to what is possible for related public policy engagement. *For the Health of the Nation* expanded what is commonly considered appropriate policy engagement for the NAE's vast network of evangelicals—extending its membership's concerns from primarily pro-life and family issues to include a host of global and poverty issues. But principles that have been put on paper have limited effect if they do not also reside in the hearts and minds of disciples in the pews. As

---

47. Ibid.
48. Jason Fileta, email to Krisanne Vaillancourt Murphy, February 24, 2015.

mentioned, CCDA expanded its incarnational ministry development model to include "confrontation of injustice" and identified root-cause issues like immigration reform, education, and mass incarceration as its national focus areas, and in doing so it took a huge step in the direction of transformational advocacy. Advocacy is becoming a deeper, more meaningful, and more integral part of the collective ministry and mission practice of hundreds of community development organizations around the country.

Given that advocacy has been so commonly misunderstood or even neglected by the evangelical community, much work lies ahead. Within parachurch networks, advocacy needs to be brought to the fore and explored, so that common misunderstandings and barriers can be removed. When Accord Network worked to articulate a holistic definition of advocacy, the process led the network to uncover the limitations of advocacy approaches that relief and development organizations used. When Micah Challenge, a well-known global poverty advocacy campaign, became part of Accord, the network opened the possibility that root-cause poverty advocacy could be adapted to relief and development practices among its member bodies. That change is slow.

CCDA also affirmed a certain strategic engagement with advocacy when it hired policy advocacy staff to guide its national body. It signaled that national system-change advocacy—confronting injustice—could be an integral piece of its CCD model. Ultimately, as parachurch organizations open their networks to integrate root-cause advocacy, Christians can be empowered to respond to their call and steward their influence at every level of practice, thereby becoming more faithful to God's call.

Educational Institutions

Colleges, universities, and seminaries possess extraordinary potential to introduce the concept of root-cause advocacy to young adults, graduate students, and seminary students. When educational institutions embrace advocacy and make it part of their programs—inside or outside the classroom—students gain a reference point to integrate advocacy into their discipleship. Christian colleges, universities, and seminaries have a strategic role in helping students develop their worldview. Educational settings can provide an environment where faith commitments and justice concerns intersect with research and learning practices, firmly rooting practices for the next generation of evangelical leaders.

Houghton College's student-led Faith and Justice Symposium is an excellent example of a Christian college that incorporates Christian advocacy into its programming for student discipleship and formation. Through its recently inaugurated Center for Faith, Justice and Global Engagement, Houghton embraces a Christ-centered education that focuses on biblical justice in the global and local community contexts. Dr. Ndunge Kiiti is Houghton's Kenyan-born professor of intercultural studies and leads the center. Kiiti says the center "uses many ways to discuss issues and advocacy: music, art, panel discussions, Chapel service, workshops, social media, lectures, discussion groups, classroom applications such as papers as well as a service component."[49] Since its inception in 2010, the center's annual campus-wide symposium offers an opportunity for students and faculty to build on the relationship between their faith commitment and justice concerns within the framework of research, teaching, and praxis.[50] The symposium feels different than other similar evangelical projects in that it incorporates both justice and compassion and grapples with how they are intimately related. The symposium hosts speakers from the global South, challenging the thinking of students and faculty alike. According to Kiiti, this myriad of entry points into advocacy approaches "allows for students to understand advocacy from different lenses and also facilitates tapping into student populations otherwise unlikely to engage."[51]

In 2013 the theme of the center's annual symposium was "Global Poverty and Hunger: Unveiling the Connections, Seeking the Solutions." Houghton College president Shirley Mullen describes the core value of this kind of holistic student learning: "As we humbly and earnestly seek to know how we can make a difference in our world, we are at the same time being changed into the kind of people who can be used by God to make that difference."[52] The center offers space for students to become the kind of people who see the connection between faith, politics, and poverty issues. Furthermore, President Mullen continues: "The Symposium embodies Houghton's commitment to be a community that learns together how to partner responsibly with all those who seek to carry out God's redemptive and transforming work in our world."[53]

The promotion of advocacy from administration leadership makes a difference for how a school understands and engages advocacy. President Mullen writes: "God calls us to be advocates for life—not for a season. As believers, we are to be there for the 'stranger' (Deut. 15), for the 'widow and orphan' (James 1:27), for those who 'are in prison, naked, and hungry' (Matt. 25:35). The challenge for college students, and for each of us, is to allow advocacy to become a way of life."[54] When school officials embrace the value of advocacy

49. Ndunge Kiiti, email to Krisanne Vaillancourt Murphy, February 12, 2015.
50. Mullen, "Global Poverty and Hunger," 2.
51. Ndunge Kiiti, email to Krisanne Vaillancourt Murphy, February 12, 2015.
52. Mullen, "Global Poverty and Hunger," 2.
53. Ibid.
54. Mullen, "On Faith."

and create space for students to engage root causes of injustice, the school encourages more holistic, practical experiences and disciple making. Thanks to exposure to the symposium and to supportive faculty and administration, six Houghton students extended their symposium learning by attending an anti-hunger lobby day in Washington, DC. Students met with members of Congress to voice their concerns about global poverty. Moeun Sun, a Houghton junior who organized the symposium and participated in the trip to Washington, DC, reflected, "Although efforts from the bottom up are needed with grassroots movements and awareness, without engaging—and in some cases challenging power systems already in place—sustainable change cannot happen."[55]

Other evangelical schools have led the way in incorporating advocacy into their core curricula, a process that is growing significantly and for which Asbury Theological Seminary, Eastern University, and Bread for the World cooperated to establish a website to make materials available for these kinds of courses.[56] Eastern University, with its motto of "Faith, Reason, and Justice," has for years had core courses and concentrations in advocacy, public policy, and human rights as part of its decades-old MBA in Economic Development and MA in International Development. Eastern's Palmer Seminary, thanks in large part to the work of Ron Sider in founding and hosting Evangelicals for Social Action out of that seminary, also has a long-standing Master of Theological Studies concentration in Christian faith and public policy. At the undergraduate level, all first-year Eastern University students are required to take a course called INST 150: Introduction to Faith, Reason, and Justice, which includes twenty hours of service learning.

Denver Seminary offers a similar course called Advocacy for Social Justice in the justice and mission concentration of its Master of Divinity program. Other seminaries, among them Asbury Theological Seminary, have classes related to advocacy such as public theology and development theory courses. Calvin College's annual student-led Faith and International Development Conference also regularly challenges attendees on matters of advocacy, helped in no small measure by the fact that one of the cofounders of the Association for a More Just Society (AJS), Kurt Ver Beek, is a faculty member at that college.

Political science departments in undergraduate institutions may not offer specific courses in advocacy, but they do provide students with training in political theory and political systems, both of which are important building blocks for thoughtful advocacy efforts. Political science departments have been

55. Ibid., 5.
56. Asbury Theological Seminary, Bread for the World, and Eastern University, "Evangelical Advocacy," http://www.evangelicaladvocacy.org/.

around for a long time, but courses directed specifically toward advocacy are a new direction for evangelical colleges and seminaries, and they show that inroads into academic advocacy training are being made.

On the flip side, educational institutions risk common pitfalls when they fail to implement effective advocacy programs. Most evangelical academic institutions have established a "culture of compassion," paying great attention to service and experiential learning, well-known anchors for being faithful in the academic environment, an environment that can affect students powerfully. But when an educational environment avoids or ignores advocacy or the importance of addressing systemic injustice at the curricular level—when it keeps students focused on the river basin while ignoring the bend farther up—advocacy's importance becomes marginalized. When Christian schools do not integrate advocacy programming into regular curricula, student exposure to advocacy is often sporadic and limited, likely wrapped up in a particular faculty member's interest in a specific topic or a singular campaign. When the only interaction with advocacy is outside of the classroom, students might interpret the college as saying that advocacy is either irrelevant to education or simply a certain faculty's "pet project" to be tolerated.

Furthermore, service learning or short-term mission programs that only offer direct-service experiences without broaching root-cause approaches to ministry limit a student's ability to consider the basis for advocacy and to ultimately actualize his or her Christian witness and discipleship. All of this detracts from the place advocacy deserves at the core of our faith and as part of a biblical mandate to steward the image of God.

Christian colleges, universities, and seminaries can foster environments where faith and justice complement academic research and coursework, leading the way toward holistic, transformational advocacy praxis. Young adults need exposure to meaningful advocacy outlets to understand the important place of advocacy, inside and outside the classroom. Houghton, Eastern, Denver, and Asbury are four of the roughly 120 member schools in North America that constitute the Council for Christian Colleges and Universities offering Christ-centered education. Few have advocacy outlets within their institutions. Yet with so many Christian educational institutions that offer courses, symposia, lectures, experiential education, and other interdisciplinary experiences, the inclusion of advocacy could potentially undergird the next generation's questions and responses to the root causes of poverty and injustice. This complement to academic learning provides important meaning for our Christian discipleship. But advocacy needs to be incorporated into formal curriculum in order to deepen the notion of transformational advocacy in all aspects of life. Ultimately, advocacy praxis challenges us and prepares us to partner with God to address injustices in the world and participate in God's ongoing redemptive and restorative work.

Learning to Practice Transformational Advocacy

Transformational advocacy is a planned, intentional process of exploring and naming the injustices embedded in human structures and institutions that constrain the flourishing of creation, and then challenging ourselves and our leaders to remedy those injustices. The evangelical church's public presence is found in movements and expressions of local churches, denominational bodies, relief and development agencies, parachurch networks, and educational institutions. These five institutions form the sturdy pillars that support evangelical public life and institutional life in the United States.

Evangelicals are reawakening to justice witness in public life. A widening array of social issues is grabbing their attention: human trafficking, sexual exploitation, immigration, HIV/AIDS, creation care, hunger, global poverty, violence prevention, and peace building. In this chapter we have demonstrated how each of the five evangelical institutions is beginning to journey upstream and around the bend to find out how the bodies turned up in the river.

Building upon their impressive history in compassionate ministries, evangelicals are incorporating advocacy in core missions and ministries, stewarding their influence and using their prophetic voice to change public policy and address root causes. Rising above the familiar skepticism that has restricted them to only engaging society in the personal, spiritual, and charitable realms, evangelicals are beginning to adopt advocacy as an integral part of Christian discipleship. They are becoming increasingly interested in and curious about transformational advocacy and finding it to be a form of faithful service.

As local churches connect compassionate ministries and justice, they witness with incredible power among a wider faith network to how broken systems perpetuate suffering. How advocacy is interpreted or engaged in by denominations (or the larger Church) can either help Christians in churches to find, or hinder them from finding, meaningful expression of Christian discipleship through advocacy. Because of the central role that relief and development organizations play between Christians and churches in the global North and the global South, these agencies can steward advocacy influence at many levels: personal, professional, and grass roots both in the program field and among grassroots donors. Parachurch networks are redefining advocacy by articulating a transformational, root-cause advocacy. They can establish a new relevance for advocacy within the (domestic or international) development models and the Church's public presence. Lastly, as educational institutions are forming the next generation of evangelical leaders, these leaders have an opportunity to incorporate advocacy into academic pursuits as well as introduce meaningful connections and advocacy actions. This exposure can challenge young adults to partner in God's plan to address injustices and in God's redemptive and restorative work in the world.

7

Challenges and Tensions
in Transformational Advocacy
and Steps for Overcoming Them

As committed evangelicals engage in advocacy work on issues that are expanding the traditional boundaries of their public engagement, they face seven kinds of challenges, which can be divided into three categories. The first category, composed of one variable, is the challenge of integrating discipleship and evangelism with advocacy. This variable lies at the heart of a distinctively evangelical approach to advocacy and also, one would hope, at the heart of any approach adopted by people who call themselves followers of Christ.

The second category has to do primarily with the nature of knowledge and analysis from both a sociological and a theological standpoint and is composed of three variables:

1. the existence of different assumptions and principles about how people, organizations, and societies work and should work in the world, and what role God plays in all of this;

2. the limits of knowledge about the complexities of the issue on which one is advocating;

153

3. corresponding differences of opinion on the best policy or action steps to take to tackle the issue.

The third category involves practical and strategic tensions and contains three variables as well:

1. whether to enter into partnerships on advocacy initiatives, based on factors such as access to resources and shared morals and beliefs, and if so, then with whom to partner;
2. the question of what level to work at to tackle the issue (local, regional, national, international) and the issues of elitism and of the power that is created and used within the advocacy movement itself;
3. the tension created at the local-church level between, on the one hand, a history and preparation that have been narrowly focused on advocacy for a limited set of issues and, on the other hand, electoral party politics and the kind of preparation, gifts, and skills needed to expand the advocacy focus and make it more faithfully independent.

These categories—which we may call "spiritual," "epistemological," and "praxis"—and their variables all overlap. Evangelicals seeking to follow a biblically based approach to advocacy must consider these prayerfully, since the way they deal with these kinds of challenges significantly affects whether their advocacy glorifies Christ.

Integrating Discipleship and Evangelism with Advocacy

As evangelicals and their institutions struggle to understand how best to integrate discipleship and evangelism into their social outreach and missions to the poor and vulnerable, so also they struggle to know how best to integrate discipleship and evangelism with advocacy. Seldom are any of the main evangelical institutional actors—churches, denominations, relief/development agencies, parachurch networks, and educational institutions—focused on the importance of that integration in their advocacy activities. To some extent this may be because in their reflections and actions they are focusing primarily on achieving their concrete goal of policy change, but that confirms our point. We are not talking about integrating spiritual motivations into an organization's work or about publicly acknowledging those motivations. In fact, organizations often do integrate their motivations, work, and publicity, stating publicly that they do their work because of their Christian beliefs. We are talking about an integration that influences the very process of advocacy itself beyond just the drive to engage in it, integration that speaks fully to the importance of the witness involved in *how* advocacy is carried out and that looks for opportunities for discipleship and evangelism in that process. This integration is missing, and its lack poses the largest challenge for evangelicals who are involved in social care and in all efforts to change unjust systems.

As evangelical organizations try to integrate real advocacy into their missions, they struggle with five major issues: a tension between evangelism and discipleship, a tension between pursuing goals and ensuring a God-glorifying process, and three tensions related to what can be called "mission drift," superbly analyzed by Greer and Horst in their recent book on how and why evangelical agencies stray from their original integrative vision and mandates.[1] The first of these three is a tension in hiring staff, between the criterion of a candidate's expertise and that of his or her commitment to integrating discipleship and evangelism into advocacy; the second, between the desire for integration and the desire to please donors who may be uncomfortable with aspects of the integration; and the third, between the desire for integration and the need to respond to implicit or explicit pressure from partners with whom one wants to or feels the need to engage but whose own objectives militate against an integrative approach.

Tension between Evangelism and Discipleship

A tension between evangelism and discipleship in the evangelical community in the West has stalled the integration of faith into advocacy and social-change efforts by evangelicals with the result that their faith does not penetrate this work deeply.[2] Traditionally, evangelicals have reached out in mission mainly in order to "save" the lost, focusing only secondarily on discipleship; that is, they have focused on "making converts" as opposed to "making disciples."[3] More and more evangelicals have criticized this approach to mission, in large part because of mounting evidence that those who profess to be saved are not showing signs of behaving differently from the rest of the population.[4]

How and why does the separation of evangelism from discipleship prevent evangelicals from engaging in advocacy differently than others? Primarily by truncating their view of how to relate to others spiritually. Believers regard

1. Greer and Horst, *Mission Drift.*
2. A significant portion of the concepts expressed here either is taken from or builds on Bronkema, "Challenges and Promises."
3. See, for example, "Eastbourne Consultation."
4. See, for example, "New Marriage and Divorce Statistics."

nonbelievers as objects of salvation, seeing discipleship as a pursuit for believers and of secondary importance for nonbelievers, something to be tackled after Christ is accepted. This view of nonbelievers constricts the range of spiritual conversations between evangelicals and their secular colleagues, and among evangelicals themselves vis-à-vis their work with their secular colleagues, thereby limiting the depth of evangelical mission effectiveness. These conversations are more likely to be about how to get a person to "believe in Christ" than about what it means to "follow Christ" in all that one does, and especially what it means in one's language and behavior in advocacy work itself. In short, this focus on evangelization as separate from discipleship drives evangelicals toward thinking about integration only in terms of the former and not the latter as a spiritual goal, short-circuiting the range of ways that evangelicals can integrate their faith and relate spiritually with others in the advocacy arena. This focus also limits their own self-critical reflections about what discipleship means for evangelicals themselves in their work for justice.

Tension between Success and Process

When we truncate our spiritual goals, we will pray and think less deeply and our witness will penetrate less deeply, which should concern us because in advocacy, as in life in general, effectiveness of witness should always be our primary goal as followers of Christ. This limitation should concern us even more when combined with a second tension that hampers integration of faith: that between the advocacy goal and the process through which that goal is achieved, a tension that tempts advocates to place the goal above the process. While the advocacy objectives set forth by evangelicals are laudable and should be pursued, the question is whether the ways they are engaging those issues glorify God in all aspects and facilitate, rather than hamper, the role of the Holy Spirit in using that witness to convict others. As 1 Corinthians 13:3 states, "If I give all I possess to the poor and give over my body to hardship that I may boast, but do not have love, I gain nothing." As we engage with passion and commitment and fire for justice in our advocacy efforts, are we doing so with love for others, including those who seem to oppose us? Are we engaging with them in a way that honors them? Again, 1 Corinthians 13 (vv. 4–7) is instructive: "Love is patient, love is kind. It does not envy, it does not boast, it is not proud. It does not dishonor others, it is not self-seeking, it is not easily angered, it keeps no record of wrongs. Love does not delight in evil but rejoices with the truth. It always protects, always trusts, always hopes, always perseveres."

It is in the process, not the particular issues, where evangelicals are called to stand apart and stand out, and this is why so many—both evangelicals and others—are disappointed with evangelical engagement in the public sphere. There will always be believers and nonbelievers who agree with our take on the issues and the solutions that we present, and there will always be those who disagree with us. Advocacy, because it deals with injustice, power, and brokenness, is fraught with challenges to maintaining loving relationships with a variety of actors. Our analysis and solutions in this arena will rarely be what make us different, will rarely be what get us labeled followers of "the Way."

What will—in the best of cases—set us apart and gain for us this label will be that we follow 1 Corinthians 13 in word and deed as we engage in the process of advocacy. In the worst of cases, when we fail to follow these principles, we will open ourselves to justified accusations of not living up to our commitment to the Lordship of Christ. We will always be tremendously tempted to use weapons of the world in the battles of advocacy, since those weapons seem most likely to succeed. These can range from spinning the analysis of issues and of proposed solutions in ways that do not honor arguments and data from the other side that point to legitimate insights, to painting our adversaries in less-than-flattering terms, as well as a host of other weapons not fitting for Christians. Such practices not only damage our witness, they also hurt us and our relationship with Christ as they habituate us into behavior that can only be called sinful, and which after a while, as Scripture warns us, seems normal and even acceptable to us when we engage in the political sphere (Ps. 81:11–14; Rom. 1:28–32). Using false weapons also, of course, cuts off the vital path for integrating our faith into our advocacy activities.

Mission Drift: Relations with Staff, Donors, and Partners

The desire for success in advocacy, as in any other endeavor, affects not only an organization's process of executing its mission but also how it marshals resources. Three resources are particularly important for organizations involved in advocacy: staff, donors, and partners. Each can present particular challenges to the integration of discipleship and evangelism into advocacy work, and each can contribute to a "mission drift" away from the mission of witness.

First, the desire for success leads to a temptation to hire people for their expertise first and their faith second. This temptation is normal, and organizations often succumb. Time and time again Christian relief/development/ advocacy organizations face decisions like whether to work in closed countries and hire non-Christian staff and whether to hire those with experience and knowledge that are much needed to ensure the success of projects even though they are not Christian or don't show evidence that they are committed to and passionate about their faith. We are not judging those who prayerfully discern

God's leadings in these difficult decisions and hire staff who are less-than-committed disciples of Christ. We are, however, pointing out that a lack of full devotion to Christ on the part of staff can prevent an organization from fully integrating discipleship and evangelism into its advocacy. Often, especially when combined with the tension between evangelism and discipleship which limits that integration to evangelism, staff who are less than committed will very much shy away from even wanting to talk about such integration because they do not feel comfortable with proselytizing, or even because it may be specifically prohibited by law in the context in question.

Second, both donors and partners may insist that an organization tone down the integration of faith into advocacy. This is especially true, again, in a situation where the tradition has put forth evangelism as the only way to integrate faith. The desire for success and greater impact leads to the temptation to access funds from a larger and larger pool of donors, as well as to ally oneself with partners—be they in civil society, business, or government—who can increase the effectiveness of lobbying efforts. Generally, in exchange for their help, such allies demand changes in behavior, language, and rhetoric, all of which can blur the focus on faith. As a result, of course, the organization is likely to be less and less intentional in adhering to and planning for the integration of discipleship and evangelism into advocacy, and this is likely to make its advocacy look more and more like any other efforts out there.[5]

Conclusion: A Way Forward in Transformational Advocacy

How, then, is it best to deal appropriately with these challenges and tensions so as to foster the mature evangelical advocacy that we are calling for? We must be aware of them and face them. First, we must resolve to make faithful witness and discipleship the primary goal of our advocacy endeavors, and subordinate the goal of success to this primary goal. This does not mean that doing all one can to achieve the advocacy goal is unimportant. Far from it. But it means that the process toward achieving that goal must be primary. We believe that not only will this be more effective in the long run; it is also more biblical. Advocacy "wins," as with any social-change work, are not everlasting. They can be undermined or overturned, at times rather quickly. What endures is the trust and respect built up over time, and that will tend to open doors that successes will not. Our command is to be faithful and leave

5. See Greer and Horst, *Mission Drift*, for other factors leading to mission drift. See also the literature on what distinguishes faith-based programs from others, including Jeavons, "Identifying Characteristics"; Jeavons, *When the Bottom Line Is Faithfulness*; Jeavons, "Religious and Faith-Based Organizations"; Sider and Unruh, "Typology of Religious Characteristics."

the results in God's hands. And, biblically speaking, setting the goals in this order is right along the lines of Jesus's response to the question of which was the greatest commandment, which was to be faithful to God through witness: Jesus replied:

> "'Love the Lord your God with all your heart and with all your soul and with all your mind.' This is the first and greatest commandment. And the second is like it: 'Love your neighbor as yourself.' All the Law and the Prophets hang on these two commandments." (Matt. 22:37–40)

The second step, really a subset of the first, is to consistently and constantly create and use opportunities to engage others as part of our advocacy in "discipleship discussions" to ensure that the process by which we advocate is consistent with biblical principles and values.[6] By intentionally integrating faith into advocacy along evangelical lines, we will open up opportunities to discuss faith and share the gospel that complement the traditional focus on evangelism and allow us to be more open to the multiple ways the Spirit would guide us in our relationships with others that involve sharing and learning. This is not to say that speaking the gospel message is our only motive for engaging in advocacy, since Scripture is clear that we need to be driven by love for people and to "do good works, which God prepared in advance for us to do" (Eph. 2:10). But Scripture is also clear that we must be intentional and "prepared to give an answer to everyone who asks [us] to give the reason for the hope that [we] have" (1 Pet. 3:15). Advocacy is no different than any other sphere of life in this regard.[7]

Third, we must reflect on and enshrine a way for ensuring that the staffs of evangelical organizations focus on discipleship as part and parcel of the process of advocacy and also encourage such a focus in relationships with donors and partners. We can do this by clearly thinking through our guidelines on spiritual requirements for staff, ensuring strategic actions for the nurturing of their spiritual life and that of the organization as a whole, and training them explicitly on methods of integrating discipleship and evangelism with their advocacy work. We should also institutionalize this area as one to be regularly evaluated internally in the organization, with concrete metrics established that will guide that process of assessment. Just the process of creating metrics itself

---

6. For a similar argument in the development field geared toward Christian NGOs, see Bronkema, "Firm Foundations."

7. We therefore reject the unhelpful dichotomy inherent in the statement "In any case, Christians should never forget that lobbying is secondary to evangelizing" (Bandow, *Beyond Good Intentions*). We are to be faithful to all aspects of the ministry that God sets before us.

will help institutions more intentionally integrate discipleship and evangelism with advocacy, as will the periodic practice of the evaluation itself.

What Policy Is Best? Epistemology and Theories of Change

Why would people disagree so fundamentally on the best way to shape laws and policies to protect the vulnerable and encourage society to flourish in all of its aspects? Setting aside the fact that much opposition to advocacy work and proposals comes from those who are benefiting from the violation of rights or from particular structures in place, those seeking the common good still disagree significantly about how to tackle injustice and structure society to allow for the best moral and material outcomes. In fact, advocates will often mostly agree on the end goal, the end vision, but will hold very different or even contrary opinions about which kind of policy will get you there.

The reasons for this are three: stakeholders can have very different assumptions about what motivates and drives people, they can affirm very different normative and value principles and propositions, and their knowledge and beliefs can vary concerning the cause-and-effect relationships that may justly be inferred on the basis of social science analysis. All of these are inherently combined in just about any kind of approach to advocacy, and to social change in general, and any difference in any of these can lead to significant differences in terms of the types of policies for which one would advocate. Let's look briefly at each of these.

First, the details of many policies revolve around what policy makers think will either move people to action or prevent them from acting. Some will think that fear is the best motivator, others will assume that people are mostly motivated by positive incentives, others will consider values and principles, and so on. As a result, some will propose policies that rely more on the threat of punishment, others will propose policies that rely more on the promise of rewards, and still others will rely on policies that appeal on moral grounds. So, for example, on the issue of abortion, where most people agree that it should be reduced, if not eliminated, they still disagree on how best to achieve that. Some would seek to do so by making it a crime (threat of punishment), others by providing incentives to keep the baby by paying mothers not to have an abortion, while others would tackle it by supporting funding for programs that seek to persuade mothers to not abort the baby on moral grounds and seek to provide alternatives such as adoption.

Second, those involved in proposing policies as a solution to social wrongs and ills may have very different beliefs about what is right and wrong and what is most worthwhile. So, even though a policy may be deemed effective as a means, some people might think, on principle, that it is wrong, that the ends themselves should not be pursued. This is different from the assessment of value. Some may also disagree, for example, when tradeoffs are involved, on what should take priority, on what is most valuable, and that does not have to do with whether it is right or wrong. These normative and value-laden frameworks very often have religious and spiritual roots, with differences emanating from the various theologies and religious worldviews that underpin them. For Christians, unfortunately, this at times has meant that people consider their opinions and the stances of their party on issues and policies to be God-ordained, leading to serious problems of discipleship and witness. As US senator John Danforth put it so well in his call for a different kind of evangelical engagement in politics:

> If we are convinced that our opinions on social and political issues are the law of God, then people who oppose our opinions become opponents of God. If, in contrast, we recognize the limits of our own understanding of God's truth, while acknowledging that our opponents are trying, as we are, to do God's will, we are able to be ambassadors of reconciliation. In that case, our faithfulness in politics depends less on the content of our ideology than on how we view ourselves and treat each other. Faith in politics has more to do with the way faithful people approach politics than with the substance of our positions.[8]

Third, and related to the first two, people often approach a policy dialogue with very different types of knowledge and beliefs about social structures and about cause and effect in social change; in short, they engage in different kinds of "social science" analysis. The main reason for this is that unjust situations are complex and hard to understand; each person brings different assumptions, principles, normative frameworks, and criteria of valuation to the myriad variables involved and the relationship between them. The various "schools" in the disciplines of economics, political science, sociology, anthropology, and theology reflect the complexity and attempt to both make sense of that complexity and come up with policy recommendations that accord with an understanding and perspective based on those variables considered most important. The result is policy research and recommendations that are often at odds with each other and contending for power of explanation and

---

8. Danforth, *Faith and Politics*, 21. It is imperative that we scrutinize our advocacy efforts to make sure that they are not sourced by ideologies. People on both sides of the political divide allow ideologies, rather than God's character, to guide their thinking. For this reason, as stated earlier in this book, Karl Barth argues that we need to say "No!" to ideologies so we can say "Yes!" to faithful political engagement.

application, and for none of which there is ever any absolute and incontrovertible proof, no matter what any side claims.

The result, then, is that evangelicals and people of all stripes can and do disagree with good reason on the root causes of injustice, and even more so on the best policies for dealing with it,[9] especially since policies can have significant unintended consequences that not infrequently can cause other problems beyond the issue being tackled. This leads to a tension in several ways. First, it means that not only those on opposite sides of an issue but even allies and partners will often differ as to which one of a host of possible strategies and proposals is best. Second, it means both individual advocates and advocacy groups will be tempted to trumpet their own analysis, knowledge, and understanding as superior to that of the other side, and not consider carefully and prayerfully all of the arguments being presented. In responding to this temptation, advocates will tend to seek simple answers, answers based on a one-size-fits-all social science ideology rather than a careful deliberation and an understanding that contexts are different and that policies and approaches that work well in one place may be completely ineffective and counterproductive in others. This tends to lead to arrogance and to a blindness that hampers the perception of truth, and that begins to place a premium on "experts" rather than those who are closer to the situation and affected by it the most. This combination of tendencies toward ideology, arrogance, and top-down approaches is dangerous, not only materially but morally and spiritually as well. Unfortunately, it rears its head often in advocacy debates and processes, and here, again, evangelicals should stand apart.

How should we deal with the desire to push our own agenda and policies and defeat competing ones, with the tendency to do so in ways that go against our being the witnesses God would have us be? The answer to this, as are the answers to all of the tensions identified in this chapter, is found in the Bible and can be summed up in two words: humility and love. It is no coincidence, given our awareness of the limits to our knowledge, that the theme of humility is one of the capstones of the 1 Corinthians 13 passage on love (vv. 8–12 ESV):

> Love never ends. As for prophecies, they will pass away; as for tongues, they will cease; as for knowledge, it will pass away. For we know in part and we prophesy in

9. The observation that people of faith will disagree is not new. See, for example, Boyd: "The way of the kingdom of the world is always complex, ambiguous, and inevitably full of compromises. Hence, kingdom people who share the same core faith and values can and often do disagree about how their faith and values should inform their involvement in the kingdom of the world." *Myth of a Christian Nation*, 15.

part, but when the perfect comes, the partial will pass away. When I was a child, I spoke like a child, I thought like a child, I reasoned like a child. When I became a man, I gave up childish ways. For now we see in a mirror dimly, but then face to face. Now I know in part; then I shall know fully, even as I have been fully known.

While it may be difficult, an evangelical approach to advocacy demands that we listen to all arguments with humility. We should seek copious dialogue and try hard to evaluate and assess the truths that might be on the other side, looking for whatever might be good about them that we can learn from. With both words and actions, we should honor and love the people who are asserting them,[10] always acknowledging and putting forth the strongest arguments of the other side, rather than relegating them to "straw arguments" or spinning them in a way that is not true to the best they have to offer. This is especially true when we are on the opposite side of those who also claim Christ, as made clear by 1 Thessalonians 5:14–23:

And we urge you, brothers and sisters, warn those who are idle and disruptive, encourage the disheartened, help the weak, be patient with everyone. Make sure that nobody pays back wrong for wrong, but always strive to do what is good for each other and for everyone else. Rejoice always, pray continually, give thanks in all circumstances; for this is God's will for you in Christ Jesus. Do not quench the Spirit. Do not treat prophecies with contempt but test them all; hold on to what is good, reject every kind of evil. May God himself, the God of peace, sanctify you through and through. May your whole spirit, soul and body be kept blameless at the coming of our Lord Jesus Christ.

By doing this, we will make great strides toward being above reproach, toward building a reputation as fair and trusted interlocutors of advocacy, toward standing out and apart from the ways of the world and opening up the doors for people, even those who oppose us, to be witnessed to, as Peter exhorted when expanding on a point made by Jesus in Matthew 5:16: "Live such good lives among the pagans that, though they accuse you of doing wrong, they may see your good deeds and glorify God on the day he visits us" (1 Pet. 2:12).[11] And it is through such processes that we, the people advocating, grow in conformity to Jesus Christ.

10. For a similar argument on love and honoring each other, see Danforth, *Faith and Politics*, especially chap. 2 ("Christian Love and Practical Politics") and pp. 222–28. See also Bartley, *Faith and Politics after Christendom*, 214, for his use of the term "loving witness," "a witness that incorporates such values as love, generosity, grace, and forgiveness as political as well as personal virtues."

11. Jesus in Matt. 5:16, following the Beatitudes, says: "In the same way, let your light shine before others, that they may see your good deeds and glorify your Father in heaven."

Tensions from Praxis: Partners and Participation

Tensions also arise from the relationships demanded by the practice of advocacy itself. These practical tensions come from three main sources, which overlap to a significant degree with the ones already identified, but in different ways. The first is whether to enter into alliances with other actors who are seeking the same advocacy result, either donors or other organizations actually involved in advocacy work, and if so, how. At times, a donor is also an organization involved in advocacy work. The second is the degree to which one's organization engages in a participatory approach with those who are affected by the advocacy issue, enabling their voices to be the ones directing the course of the advocacy efforts rather than designing and carrying out advocacy plans based on "expert" or "elite" knowledge. The third is the degree to which the local church is encouraged and equipped to respond to God's call to participate, and often lead, processes of transformational advocacy, as opposed to feeling confused about its calling, giftedness, and mandate when faced with situations of injustice or requests for it to join ongoing advocacy efforts.

The Tensions of Partnerships and Alliances

All who are engaged in advocacy will face a choice of whether to enter into partnerships and alliances with others working on the same advocacy issue. This is particularly true for evangelicals, who take seriously the biblical admonition found in 2 Corinthians 6:14–15 (ESV): "Do not be unequally yoked with unbelievers. For what partnership has righteousness with lawlessness? Or what fellowship has light with darkness? What accord has Christ with Belial? Or what portion does a believer share with an unbeliever?"

This difficult choice is faced not only by evangelicals but also by secular organizations that, like Christian organizations, are driven by particular values and struggle with decisions about how closely to ally themselves with other secular or religious organizations of which they are wary. Advocacy organizations often face four main types of difficult decision-making processes: deciding whether to enter into a partnership with others who don't share the same principles and values and/or who are engaged in other activities or are taking stands on other issues with which one disagrees either morally, analytically, or strategically; coming to agreement on the exact nature of the objectives to be achieved that will solve the problem that has been identified; coming to agreement on methods and strategies; and deciding what roles and responsibilities the partners or allies will play. In all these processes the tensions can be exacerbated by the issue of which partners control which kinds of resources.

First, any advocacy organization considering allying itself with other organizations will be strongly tempted to partner with donors and actors who have significant resources and power in order to have more chances of success. However, some of these donors and partners may have made their money or may be accessing money whose origin is morally questionable, ranging from the production and sale of alcohol to involvement in the gambling industry. They may also be taking stances in their own advocacy work that an evangelical organization may find normatively problematic, such as an affirmation of gay marriage or a position favoring the restriction of the freedom of religious organizations to hire based on religious grounds. Even though that might not have a bearing on the issue for which the partnership is being formed, entering into a direct relationship with partners who do not share the evangelical organization's values and principles as applied to other areas should cause great concern, no matter what those partners bring to the table. This tension becomes even more problematic when a coalition is formed that includes both these kinds of partners and many other groups and organizations that take stances compatible with those of the evangelical organization in other areas, because such a coalition dilutes the direct relationship with those with whom the organization has value-laden problems, especially where the coalition is led by people and organizations with whom the organization has tremendous moral compatibility. How, then, is it possible to make a faithful decision on whether to enter into or join a partnership in these kinds of situations?

Second, even when an organization enters into partnerships with those who are completely committed to the same overall perspective, assumptions, principles, and even analytical tools, the two groups may still differ on how to solve the problem. One side may urge new legislation and the other a reform of current policies, both of which also can trigger differences about the exact content of new legislation or its reform; one side may push for reform, while the other prefers enforcement of existing rules and policies; or the partners may differ in yet another way. These differences arise frequently, because of the epistemological conditions reviewed above.

Third, and often related to the first situation, even if organizations considering partnership agree on overall objectives and goals, they may disagree very strongly on methods and strategies. They may disagree not merely about "technical" matters—that is, over what actions will be effective—but about moral matters as well. For instance, they may differ concerning whether to use street protests to pressure authorities into change and whether to use particular tactics involved in protests, such as simple marches or nonviolent resistance; concerning what kinds of language, messaging, and marketing to employ for the cause; concerning whether or not to engage authorities and other powers-that-be in negotiation; and concerning whether to mobilize particular segments of the population in forms other than protest, such as letter-writing campaigns or lobbying, and if so, how. Again, these differences are rooted in the different sociological and theological knowledge and perspectives that the partners bring to the table.

Fourth, there can be tensions around what roles and responsibilities are assigned to each partner. Usually the partners will all have organizational interests at stake in the advocacy action as well, meaning they want what they do and the visibility they achieve through doing it to redound to their advantage by strengthening the organization overall or even specific programs, or strengthening its reputation and the networks it belongs to. Partner organizations, therefore, may have competing interests that cause tensions when duties are being assigned.

In summary, in advocacy partnerships inherent tensions crop up that have to do with differences in values, goals, strategies, and allocation of roles and responsibilities. Often the issue of control over resources such as money, staff time, contacts, networks, knowledge, and expertise exacerbates these tensions, since resources are always at play as the partners dialogue and negotiate around how best to approach the advocacy work. Those with more resources, obviously, have more power both implicitly and explicitly if they should choose to use it, using their resources as leverage to get what they want. This can be particularly frustrating when organizational interests predominate over the interests of effectiveness, leading to increasingly bad feelings and relationships between the actors. It is crucial for evangelicals engaged in advocacy to be aware of and deal prayerfully and faithfully with these tensions.

Getting It Done versus Listening to Those Affected

An organization may also be tempted to drift into elitism in three ways. First, it may start to relate more to representatives of the state and its advocacy partners than to the people affected by the issue. Second, and related to the first, the power of decision making can become concentrated in organizations that are close to centers of power, like Washington, DC, or state capitals, with the result that actions are planned and implemented by an even more restricted number of organizations and individuals. Third, and as a result of the first two, policy solutions, strategies, and actions may be designed by those with power rather than those affected by the issue, with the result that the voices of those affected by the issue are not heard during planning and implementation. They also do not learn how to carry out the advocacy activities themselves and thus do not do so; consequently, power is further entrenched in organizations that already have it, and those who have little already are further disempowered.

This danger of elitism is very much known by those who have looked at and had experience in advocacy matters.[12] And the benefits of listening to the poor and the dangers of dismissing the poor as lacking knowledge and wisdom are very much emphasized in Scripture. Consider, for example, this passage in Ecclesiastes:

> I have also seen this example of wisdom under the sun, and it seemed great to me. There was a little city with few men in it, and a great king came against it and besieged it, building great siegeworks against it. But there was found in it a poor, wise man, and he by his wisdom delivered the city. Yet no one remembered that poor man. But I say that wisdom is better than might, though the poor man's wisdom is despised and his words are not heard. The words of the wise heard in quiet are better than the shouting of a ruler among fools. Wisdom is better than weapons of war, but one sinner destroys much good. (9:13–18 ESV)

Local Church Involvement

We have seen that evangelical churches and their members have been actively encouraged and mobilized to advocate concerning a limited set of social/civic issues. In fact, some have characterized the evangelical movement as having the strongest, best, and most widespread capabilities for advocacy of all religious groups because of the range of strategies, actors, networks, and resources they have developed over the years:

> American Evangelicals have built "the largest, best organized grassroots" social movement network of the last-quarter century. Thus, such well-funded groups as the Family Research Council, Concerned Women for America, Focus on the Family, and the Traditional Values Coalition draw upon the resources of a host of conservative Protestant denominations and the extensive network of nondenominational megachurches, local activist groups, alternatives schools, Christian colleges, parachurch organizations, broadcast ministries, and publishing houses. Lobbying activity thus is melded into the multifarious social movement activities of institutional development, electoral mobilizations, litigation, media campaigns, and demonstrations.[13]

12. In fact, Myers gives this type of warning as well at the end of the pages he dedicates to advocacy (*Walking with the Poor*, 274).

13. Fowler et al., *Religion and Politics in America*, 145. The quote in the first sentence is from Putnam, *Bowling Alone*, 162.

In the development of this movement, a heavy emphasis was placed on "a kind of citizen education. Conservative evangelical groups have invested enormous resources in 'leadership schools' and various voter awareness programs that explain such matters as where to register to vote and how to attend a caucus. . . . In other cases, citizen awareness programs constitute basic civic education."[14] Ironically, however, while this evangelical movement has influenced elections and party politics tremendously, "It has been largely unsuccessful in winning major policy change around its core."[15] And, perhaps even more perniciously, the gearing of this function of citizen education toward political-party ends exacerbated and continues to exacerbate the conditions that have led to the limited focus of evangelical advocacy and the demise of discipleship among evangelicals in the advocacy and political arena. Through this education and the networks that reinforce it, evangelicals are not taught to think critically and deeply, are exposed to limited and poorly explained alternative viewpoints, are encouraged to make fun of and even demonize those with other points of view, and are discouraged from tackling issues of injustice that don't fit their traditional categories, hearing those issues portrayed as "liberal" or as secondary.

The result is that when the local church, whether in the form of a congregation or in the form of an individual in the congregation, is confronted with a kind of injustice that has not been deemed important, relevant, or appropriate for evangelicals to tackle, that congregation or individual is confused and unready to respond to the Spirit's call. Not only does the church become paralyzed and conflicted over whether to address the problem because it is "out of the box" of issues sanctioned by the evangelical social movement; even if it does decide to act, the advocacy know-how, resources, and networks it has available for figuring out how to tackle the problem are of little use. In large part, the advocacy training in this network was geared toward mobilization, not toward doing research on issues in order to understand the problem and design specific ways to tackle it, which requires gifts of critical analysis, discernment, organization, and administration. Moreover, because this situation is due to an issue being outside the traditional evangelical focus, few people in the evangelical networks can help. It is no accident, therefore, that young evangelicals who face the problem of homelessness in their cities, extreme poverty in mission trips, and police discrimination against their African American friends in schools are confused and unprepared to react as Christians to these issues, since in their churches

14. Fowler et al., *Religion and Politics in America*, 146.
15. Ibid.

they have never heard sermons on these subjects; nor should it surprise us that they then tend to drift away, seeing their churches as irrelevant and meaningless in tackling key issues in society. And it is also no accident that authors and speakers like Shane Claiborne and Jim Wallis tend to be so popular with these audiences, or that the Justice Conference has exploded in attendance in recent years. It is particularly poignant that when these young evangelicals attempt to draw their congregations into discussions and actions around nontraditional issues, they are often ostracized and shut down because the Church as a whole is not ready to prayerfully discern God's call in this area.

While partnership with and engagement of those affected can be incredibly difficult, they also can be incredibly rewarding, since they are the locus of relationships that give meaning and purpose to so much of what Christians do. Our suggestions for overcoming the challenges and tensions involved with this dimension of advocacy are fairly straightforward and may seem too simple. But we cannot stress their importance enough. There are no concrete, technical solutions that can be applied to every situation. Rather, evangelicals must pray for discernment and pray that they will be faithful as they engage those who are affected. Unfortunately, too often evangelicals impulsively reject cooperation and collaboration with not only unbelievers but also other Christians with whom they do not see eye to eye, declining to "enter into coalition with ecumenical, interfaith, or secular civic groups, even where they share common concerns and goals. . . . Evangelicals instead establish their own organizations."[16] This rejection has a long history, one that as far back as 1947 was identified by Carl F. H. Henry in his poignant call for taking a more prayerful and thoughtful approach to partnership:

> There are Fundamentalists who will insist immediately that no evangelical has the right to unite with non-evangelicals in any reform. . . . Apart from denominational problems, it remains true that the evangelical, in the very proportion that the culture in which he lives is not actually Christian, must unite with non-evangelicals for social betterment if it is to be achieved at all, simply because the evangelical forces do not predominate. To say that evangelicalism should not voice its convictions in a non-evangelical environment is simply to rob evangelicalism of its missionary vision. It will be impossible for the evangelical to cooperate for social betterment with any group only when that group clearly rules out a redemptive reference as a live option for the achievement of good ends.[17]

16. Steensland and Goff, "Introduction," 20.
17. Henry, *Uneasy Conscience*, 80–81.

As others have exhorted since then, "Christians need to work with nonbelievers"[18] in affairs that involve the state, in an approach of "humble cooperation and respectful provocation."[19] And, to go back to Henry's clarion call to action almost seventy years ago:

> While the evangelical will resist the non-evangelical formulas for solution, he assuredly ought not on that account to desist from battle against world evils. Just because his ideology is unalterably opposed to such evils, the evangelical should be counted upon not only to "go along" with all worthy reform movements, but to give them a proper leadership. . . . More vigorously than the humanists and religious modernists press their battle, the evangelical ought to be counted upon in the war against aggressive conflict, political naturalism, racial intolerance, the liquor traffic, labor-management inequities, and every wrong. And as vigorously as the evangelical presses his battle, he ought to be counted upon to point to the redemption that is in Christ Jesus as the only adequate solution.[20]

An evangelical organization or individual never knows what partnerships God may lead one into, and the key is to choose faithfulness over the temptations of the resources that might seem more likely to guarantee success. It is absolutely essential for evangelicals engaged in advocacy to make clear from the start the values that trump all else in terms of methods, and to shy away from alliances that will compromise those values. But they must always do so with deep, prayerful consultation with the Lord, since he might surprise us with his calls to partnership. The same goes for the other tension of allocation of responsibilities: a prayerful consideration of the situation and a measured, humble language and approach to dialogue around this will do wonders for witness.

To solve the tension of elitism, on the other hand, will require forcing ourselves to pay special attention to what is going on at the local level, to constantly consult with those affected by the issue, and always to look to create opportunities for them to participate in the planning and implementation of advocacy activities. It may take a lot of time, and we will constantly be tempted to just do it ourselves. However, the success of the advocacy effort will ultimately depend on the quality and strength of local engagement, which brings us back again to the key role that the local church must play in these efforts (note, of course, that the local church can also fall into elitism vis-à-vis the people it is serving). In the end, evangelical advocacy and its approach

18. Bandow, *Beyond Good Intentions*, 227.
19. Keller, *Generous Justice*, 158.
20. Henry, *Uneasy Conscience*, 77–78.

based on love means that advocates need to trust the people affected to be the best arbiters of what is most appropriate, and to take the time and care to build relationships with them and enter into a dialogue of mutual learning with them. This is not always easy or straightforward, which is why falling into top-down approaches is so tempting. But it is an approach that not only provides dignity and respect for those involved; it also unquestionably tends to be the most effective technically in the long run and, more important, is the approach that gives the best witness in many ways.

Finally, the solution to the tension of an evangelical church that is confused and unequipped to tackle advocacy issues that are outside the traditional ones is to prayerfully and strategically work with local churches and the actors and networks of the evangelical grassroots social movement to prepare and equip them for the call to transformational advocacy. Some actors are already doing this, the most prominent, strategic, and active one being International Justice Mission (IJM). In its 2012 resource book by Jim Martin, *The Just Church: Becoming a Risk-Taking, Justice-Seeking, Disciple-Making Congregation*, IJM calls on churches to educate themselves on the biblical dimensions of justice issues, to apply that theology to their current context and environment, and to create a justice task force to identify issues in the community and gifts and talents in the church that God may be calling the church to apply to those issues. Replete with theology and practical tools for researching and engaging, this book challenges all in the evangelical community who are seeking to faithfully respond to God's mandate to love him and love our neighbors.[21]

While some might think that advocacy should be reserved for specialists, with others in the church supporting that work through prayer and giving,[22] and while questions of technical proficiency will arise in any social outreach—including whether to measure our impact, and if so, how, and how we use that information to improve our actions[23]—we believe that prayerfully responding to injustice is a matter of discipleship for church and individuals alike. We know that responding to God's call to tackle injustice is not easy; we face that tension in our own lives, work, and churches. We cannot say that the churches we attend or that we as individuals have always been, or continue to be, as faithful as we should be in this area. We wrote this book for ourselves as much as for you, and we hope that you will join us in an intentional journey of prayerfully discerning God's call on your time and efforts in transformational advocacy whenever that call arises.

21. J. Martin, *Just Church*.
22. Stackhouse, *Making the Best of It*, 340–44.
23. Moberg, *Inasmuch*.

Conclusion

We opened this book with the claim that evangelicals have not developed sufficient theological resources or practical know-how to undertake advocacy in God-honoring ways. We have tried to provide both theology and know-how, so as to equip the evangelical community to more effectively fulfill their call to be Christ's witness in the world.

We define evangelical or transformational advocacy as *an intentional act of witness by the body of Christ that holds people and institutions accountable for creating, implementing, and sustaining just and good policies and practices geared toward the flourishing of society.* This definition highlights the central role that local congregations can play in advocacy. It also emphasizes that when evangelicals undertake advocacy, they engage with those who hold power. This can be a scary prospect even for those who are well prepared. We believe, though, that a biblically consistent witness to the world must include such actions.

For the last half-century such intentional acts have been done by evangelicals far too infrequently. But today there are signs that evangelicals, especially younger ones, are waking up to opportunities for transformational advocacy. We ourselves have contributed to these efforts.

An Evangelical Theology of Advocacy

We live in a world of competing ideologies, swirling interests, and overlapping political and economic spheres that impinge upon the lives of people everywhere, but especially the lives of people trapped in poverty around the world. As the African proverb so colorfully expresses it, "When elephants fight, the grass gets trampled." In other words, when world powers collide or ideologies get fought over, it is often the people on the underside of history who suffer most. Enter advocacy. Christian thought in the West has developed in such a way as to leave evangelicals anemic with regard to structural evil: from the Enlightenment heritage, to pietistic reaction, to the fundamentalist/modernist divide, along with a host of theological renderings of the political realm (as noxious, ambiguous, or unredeemable), leading to a variety of responses, from subtle forms of gnosticism, to escapism, to neo-Constantinian collusion, all endorsed (for different reasons) by biblical support. As a result, not only do evangelicals disagree with non-Christians about the nature of institutions but they also disagree sharply with each other, often falling out sharply along political lines. This reveals two things. First, that our theology follows political ideologies rather than the other way around. Second, that our disunity leads to ineffectiveness in witness.[1]

But all is not so bad as this may seem. Evangelicals possess a wide range of theological resources for engaging the political realm, drawing upon traditions found in Lutheran, Reformed, Anabaptist, and Wesleyan-Holiness thought, as well as upon later influences from the Pentecostal movement: traditions on doctrines such as the Trinity, creation, image of God, covenants, blessings, justice, incarnation, the life and death and resurrection of Jesus Christ, the Holy Spirit, church, and the coming restoration of all things. Such theological assets position evangelicals favorably to not only react to what is happening in public life but also generate new creative ways of thinking about "politics," the state, and/or justice for those trapped in poverty.

What is more, the growth of Christianity around the world is bringing new ways of looking at the integration(s)[2] of evangelism and social action through a dizzying array of lenses, many of these unencumbered by the Enlightenment divide between public truth and private faith and predicated upon a larger cosmology. Scholars (but no less churches and parishioners) in Asia, Latin America, and Africa, along with indigenous and ethnic communities in North America, are helping reframe not only the answers to questions about holistic mission but also the questions themselves, in ways that (we hope) will strengthen what we have presented here.[3] Our posture in the West needs to

---

1. Of course we are not suggesting that all evangelicals should endorse the same candidate or subscribe to the same political party. That would be reductionism at its worse. We rather argue that our unity in Christ and what the kingdom of God means for politics should be greater than any ideological differences; for it is our unity in Christ that best positions us for public witness (John 17:23).

2. For surely, there is more than one way to integrate.

3. For example, evangelicals in Latin America possess a long history of critically thinking about structural evil, as seen, in part, by their active involvement in shaping the Lausanne Movement toward holistic or integral mission.

be one of active listening and receptiveness to what these communities have to teach us.

Finally, changes are also taking place in the West as younger evangelicals react against some of the historical baggage that has left the churches uncertain about social engagement. Short-term missions are exposing young people all around the world to the pernicious effects of global poverty. Gatherings such as the Justice Conference, Passion, Christian Community Development Association (CCDA), and smaller meetings associated with evangelical colleges, mission organizations, and the rise of church-planting networks are all providing evangelicals with new lenses to look at and engage the world. Even the word "justice," which in previous eras carried pejorative connotations of "judgment," is being reframed in positive, world-transforming ways by the likes of modern-day prophets such as Walter Brueggemann, Gary Haugen, Ron Sider, and Nicholas Wolterstorff. Evangelicals are slowly becoming more involved in advocacy work that has for the most part been the purview of more mainline Christian denominations, especially through faith-based NGOs such as World Relief, International Justice Mission, and Bread for the World.

But with these areas of growth come concerns. Despite the burgeoning literature associated with justice, public theology, international development, and holistic mission, and notwithstanding the herculean efforts of practitioners all around the world, we pause again to ask: have we adequately used our theological resources to address the multidimensional nature of structural evil, especially as it is sourced by deep "social imaginaries," and further tangled by overlapping spheres of politics, economics, ethnicity, and religion, particularly as these institutions aspire to autonomy, inscribe identity, or demand worship? We suggest not, and thus the need for beginning to articulate a theology of advocacy with tangible points of relevance for the church.

Here is our basic premise. First, advocacy has a subject and that is the Triune God. As long as we begin with the human condition, no matter how pure or noble our efforts, our theologies will inevitably prove vulnerable to the cultural readings of our day and therefore susceptible to prevailing ideologies. Another way of saying the same thing: if advocacy merely responds to the injustices in the world, then it could easily become a fad, or worse yet a weapon used to divide, assuage guilt, play god for others, or advance one's own political agenda. But by beginning with God, we seek to reframe everything according to a new standard.[4] God's advocacy flows out of his Triune nature

---

4. We fully understand that even "God" can easily become something understood within cultural lenses and therefore hijacked for personal gain. We have endeavored, however, to guard against this by allowing God's advocacy to establish and critique modern-day varieties.

to love, create, bless, empower, and, after sin entered the world, redeem, serve, and send himself through a completely different kind of power in the world, a power that takes on full humanity, unites disparate parts into new wholes (Eph. 2–3), heals, and redeems the world from the inside out. Ultimately, we see this advocacy in Jesus Christ. He refuses to allow religious or political interests to prevail, dying on the cross to defeat the "powers," while ushering in a new kind of power into the world, what Marva Dawn refers to as the tabernacling of God. And this life is now accessible to the Church through the Holy Spirit, our Advocate.

Second, despite robust theologies of sin that have been a trademark of the evangelical movement from the beginning, we have shown how evangelicals struggle with the corporate, structural form of sin in the world, especially as it crystallizes in the shape of modern-day institutions. The individualism of Western evangelicalism has not only influenced how people think about the gospel but also shaped how they understand sin, limiting it to largely personal, moral dimensions.[5] What is more, the prevalence of "social imaginaries" abounds and compounds the problem. For some the very mention of structural evil smacks of Marxism, socialism, liberation theology, and theological (and political) liberalism along with all the assorted baggage that comes with these terms, while for others it suggests contamination of the gospel by the public realm. These are hurdles we need to clear if we are going to move with the gospel into all arenas of life (Eph. 1:10).

Thus we must use the language of "powers" to talk about institutional evil in a way that acknowledges its inner and outer, spiritual and material coordinates. Evangelicals have too frequently struggled with this kind of language, spiritualizing it and thus trying to absolve themselves of any public responsibility. But the "powers" are real and assume institutional forms. They arise out of creation, the gift of "image bearing" in the world, and, as such, are not independent of God, but under the Lordship of Jesus Christ (Col. 1:15–17). In very natural ways, these institutions assume a kind of "spirit" or "ethos" over time through human collectivity that exceeds the sum of the parts. But when these entities become unmoored from God's rule, they become unwieldy, dangerous, and potentially evil. And, over time, people accept them as the new normal: the way things are rather than the way things ought to be. When this happens, institutions and structures assume power in the world: taking upon themselves godlike status that claims "freedom" (autonomy), the ability to

---

5. We want to affirm the heritage of framing the gospel (and sin) in personal ways, but want to suggest that personal sins never remain personal but feed larger wholes, ultimately influencing things such as institutions or structures.

create (give identity), and the right to receive worship (love, or demanding a particular kind of loyalty that does not question their authenticity).[6] When institutions or structures act in such ways, they become "demonic": unbridled and unmoored from God's purposes and therefore dangerous and destructive.

This leads to the third point. Although God could accomplish his mission in any number of ways, he chooses to witness to these "powers" through the church (Eph. 3:10). It has been far too convenient to disparage the Church, decry its institutional form as a lingering vestige of Constantinianism, or else run away from the Church through language of "justice" or the "kingdom of God." The Church nevertheless remains God's chosen instrument of witness to the world, which means, among other things, that advocacy takes place through a different kind of power: an embodiment of God's rule in a new shared humanity, a humanity that has its own "spirit" or "ethos" (which is one of the reasons that unity is such a prominent theme in Scripture) defined and expressed by holy love. This new humanity, what we call the Church, gives and receives gifts, sends and gathers, forgives and asks for forgiveness, all the while growing through the Holy Spirit and living its "spirit" openly before the world. Said in another way, the "complicated wickedness" that Wesley spoke about can be countered only by a "complicated goodness," embodied through diverse communities of witness in the world: people who image God's rule together, in social, economic, and political ways.

In Ephesians, Paul lays before readers the stark reminder that God's "intent was that . . . through the church, the manifold wisdom of God should be made known to the rulers and authorities in the heavenly realms, according to his eternal purpose that he accomplished in Christ Jesus our Lord" (3:10–11). Lesslie Newbigin says it best:

> The principalities and powers are real. They are invisible and we cannot locate them in space. They do not exist as disembodied entities floating above this world, or lurking within it. They meet us as embodied in visible and tangible realities—people, nations, and institutions. And they are powerful. What is Christ's relation to them? To recapitulate briefly: they are created in Christ and for Christ; their true end is to serve him; some do—for the New Testament speaks of good angels who perform his service; but they become powers for evil when they attempt to usurp the place which belongs to Christ alone. In his death Christ disarmed them; he has put them under his feet; they must now serve him; and the Church is the agency through which his victory over them is

6. But the perception is different from the reality. These "powers" never become autonomous, but just give humans that impression; they never truly give identity, but distort what is already there; they are incapable of giving love, and can only receive what humans give them.

made manifest and is effected as the Church puts on the whole armor of God to meet and master them.[7]

We believe that the Church holds the powers to accomplish this mandate, powers that come to us through the incarnation, life, death, and resurrection of Jesus Christ, applied to us through the Holy Spirit, our Advocate. Living such realities openly allows us to say "No!" to all culturally defined idolatries, so that we can say "Yes!" to faithful engagement with the world, while offering the world a different understanding of reality.[8]

Finally, we believe advocacy is an act of discipleship. As image bearers, we represent God to the world, and, as we do so, we grow in conformity to Jesus Christ. Anyone who has shared something meaningful with another person knows how both parties grow through the exchange. How much more with the character of Jesus Christ! As we witness to the "powers," not only do we hope to change the structures but we also position ourselves to change: to grow into conformity with Jesus Christ, while doing so with other image bearers. Charles Mathewes says it this way: "Properly undertaken, public engagement can be a struggle for conversion, conversion of one's loves and the loves of one's interlocutor."[9] This is to acknowledge that as we undertake advocacy *for, with,* and *by* others, we open ourselves to what we can learn from other people, while constantly testing and purifying our own affections (Ps. 139:23–24). This posture, we believe, is foundational for advocacy work because of the fundamental "spirit" that it fosters. The Church will not change the world by force or might, but by being faithful to the person of Jesus Christ, growing to be like him as we witness to God's reality before the institutions of our world. Or as Richard Mouw says,

> The responsible patterns of power to which the Scriptures call us are characterized by faithfulness, which involves mutual accountability and responsibility; freedom, not *from* institutional structures but *for* the shaping and preserving of structures that promote mutual integrity; love, which is manifested in sacrificial service, sharing, and mutual support; and hope, which realistically assesses the potential for future growth together.[10]

We further believe that this is not some utopian pipe dream, nor a triumphalistic enterprise, but representative of what James Davison Hunter calls

7. Newbigin, *Gospel in a Pluralist Society*, 207–8.
8. Newbigin continues: "Our relation to the structures has to contain both the judgment that is inevitable in the searing light of the cross, and also the patience which is required of us as witnesses to the resurrection." Ibid., 209.
9. Mathewes, *Theology of Public Life*, 297.
10. Mouw, *Political Evangelism*, 45.

"faithful presence."[11] God calls us to advocacy, even as he advocates for the world. Therefore, the Church does not retreat into false, sterilized ghettos or force its agenda by rolling up its sleeves to flex its muscles. Rather it witnesses, it advocates to the institutions, telling them that there is another way of being human in the world. This new humanity comes to us by the One who created the powers and holds them all together: Jesus Christ.

An Evangelical Practice of Advocacy

Just as the Church is at the center of our theological approach to advocacy, so too do local congregations stand at the center of our vision for living out transformational advocacy. Many evangelical churches are already responding to poverty and injustice in their communities, usually by conducting service-oriented ministries or through community development. We want churches to wake up to how powerful advocacy can be in solving the problems that they have already identified. Even the notion that advocacy can be an option for these kinds of issues is often just not on evangelicals' radar.

When churches consider advocacy, they should do so in the same spiritual context that governs the rest of their activities. It should be bathed in prayer. It should be well thought out and theologically informed. It should be consistent with the church's overall witness in the community and incorporated within the existing processes of the congregation. Although advocacy as an activity may be new to a congregation, advocacy should not be seen as a new agenda. Rather, it should be used to heed the same biblical call that has directed the body of Christ for the last two millennia.

While our vision is for advocacy to be embedded in the life of the congregation so that local congregants can use their spiritual gifts, callings, and skills, at times other types of organizations can help. These include denominational structures, relief and development (and advocacy) organizations, educational institutions, and evangelical umbrella networks. Evangelical businesses, media corporations, professional guilds, consultancies, and the vast array of other, more corporately oriented organizations can play a role as well. Evangelical organizational involvement in transformational advocacy can depend on the nature and scope of the problem as well as the power or institution toward which advocacy is to be directed.

A few examples may show how effective linkages between evangelical organizations can be in advocacy efforts. The International Justice Mission

11. Hunter, *To Change the World*.

(IJM), for example, regularly visits Christian college campuses across the United States. These and other efforts ground the IJM, which is based near Washington, DC, in grassroots evangelical institutions that can provide them with greater public support and thus greater leverage in the public sphere. The IJM mobilizes and creates advocacy opportunities for those with whom its personnel come into contact. Second, evangelical megachurches also develop partnerships that can help with advocacy for the poor. Willow Creek Community Church, for example, has played a role in the Del Camino Connection since it began. This network of churches runs through North and South America and creates space where issues of poverty and need are regularly part of the discussion. Willow Creek also has developed partnerships in the greater Chicago area that open doors for advocacy ministry, one of which is with the Greater Chicago Food Depository. This kind of collaborative work allows resources to be channeled more effectively and creates more opportunities for voices to be heard than might exist for a single organizational entity. In spite of potential problems with partnerships within and beyond the evangelical community, it is hard to imagine transformational advocacy being done without them.

Everyone can participate in advocacy, but some types of advocacy do require specialized skills. This can be the case when economic or social policies need to be evaluated or created. It can also be true when advocacy brings people into physically dangerous situations. A third area in which specialized knowledge can be necessary is the international relations arena. Decisions about whether and how to engage in one of the globe's conflict-ridden hotspots like the Middle East or to deal with complicated issues like how to nurture clean energy industries requires wisdom, prayer, *and* high levels of expertise. In such areas our vision for evangelical advocacy emphatically does *not* include the waving of placards by evangelicals who do not understand the issues and who look foolish in front of a news camera. This kind of response is not God honoring, hurts the cause evangelicals intend to support, and ultimately also damages the overall witness evangelicals hope to have in the world.

The more difficult areas in which advocacy is needed are precisely where discipleship is especially important. For those called into a vocation of advocacy, such discipleship should occur alongside rigorous formal education at the collegiate, master's, and even doctoral levels. In the mid-1990s Mark Noll called for an evangelical life of the mind—cultivating this is a critical prerequisite for evangelicals to seriously engage in policy issues. What evangelicals who take this path *cannot* do is abandon the spiritual disciplines and their local communities of faith along the way. Rather, they must be nurtured by local bodies of Christ and shepherded by older evangelicals who have traveled such paths before. Those individuals will then be equipped with special skill sets and received wisdom to engage the relevant institutional powers. They will likely also be called to educate and inform the evangelical community at large, not just on the issue but also on the most appropriate ways for the body of Christ to engage with them in their efforts to be salt and light in the world.

Some evangelicals might be concerned that overemphasis on advocacy could distract churches from their call to proclaim the gospel of Jesus Christ. This *can* be a danger when advocacy is done poorly. Losing the spiritual vitality and missional focus of the movement is always a concern, and increasing the emphasis on advocacy does create opportunity for distraction. The threat exists from the local level all the way up to the national identity of the movement. To avoid such mission drift, we must be firmly rooted in theology. If we keep our eyes on Jesus (to paraphrase an old hymn) while we do advocacy, we will not be distracted from our call to proclaim Christ's message. Rather, it will be a valuable and contributing strategy of holistic gospel proclamation.

Moving Forward

The modern evangelical movement embraced the fight against poverty from its beginnings in the mid-twentieth century. Although these efforts were sometimes backgrounded, evangelicals made steady progress in understanding how to address poverty with increasing effectiveness. In recent years, concerns about poverty have become more visible in evangelical identity; the mainstream academic community has charted evangelicalism's social engagement literally around the world. We likewise celebrate the commitment, persistence, and achievements of evangelicals on this front.

Even as we celebrate, we identify a blind spot: evangelicals remain reluctant to acknowledge or address the role of power in poverty. Abuse or misuse of power is often *the main cause* of poverty in communities around the world. But evangelicals have consistently elected to work around this central issue in the solutions for poverty they offer. That they have been so successful in combating poverty largely without engaging power structures is a testament to evangelical resourcefulness and commitment.

But it is not enough.

We urge evangelicals to take up the biblical call to confront the powers and principalities of this world. We acknowledge that there will be costs to heeding this call and that our commitment must be serious and sustained. Dietrich Bonhoeffer's life and words ring in our ears as we make this call. But we have also shown that such activities are not herculean tasks for the body of Christ but rather natural and logical components of the mission of the Church in the world—the natural outworking of the Church simply being the Church.

APPENDIX

Case Studies in Evangelical Advocacy

In this appendix we highlight current examples of evangelical advocacy efforts. We acknowledge and celebrate these efforts while also exploring how the ideas presented in this book might intersect with them. We provide discussion questions at the end that are intended to help readers begin to imagine how they might craft advocacy efforts on equally important topics.

We see the critical reflection and subsequent integration of learning as foundational to evangelicals' ability to effectively witness to the gospel in their advocacy. Therefore, we encourage all organizational staff, pastors, and individual advocates to prayerfully reflect on their own recent experiences and the commitments articulated in this book. The same impulse that called Martin Luther to defend orthodoxy in a time of the church's error should also call us to reform our public witness in order to more faithfully image God in his world. We hope that this appendix will help the reader begin that process of prayerful self-reflection.

In the light of that reflection, we call all those who are new to advocacy to find or create opportunities in their local congregations, schools, or other institutions to undertake Christ-honoring advocacy efforts. Jesus's words ring true today: "The harvest is plentiful, but the workers are few" (Luke 10:2). The fields of advocacy are replete with opportunities for faithful Christians to call the world toward justice and righteousness. Whether in rolling back the evil of slavery, ending world hunger, or stewarding the environment, we have much work to do. Dietrich Bonhoeffer, a true inspiration to many evangelicals, wrestled late in his life with the decision to involve himself in a plot that he knew would draw him into difficult situations. He did not allow the possible ensnarement before him to prevent wise, prayerful action. In his estimation the sinfulness of the world cannot serve as a believer's pretext for inaction. Rather, the eminent theologian chose action. We should follow this example and, with humility in prayer, step forward to advocate.

The examples below represent faithful Christians' attempts at advocacy. They are impressive, but they are not perfect. We offer the following analysis of these campaigns in a charitable spirit, seeking our mutual improvement in thinking and practice. We introduce each campaign and then generously evaluate it in light of the commitments laid out in this book. We have also included a range of discussion questions to foster more thorough reflection on these recent efforts. Although the case studies are brief and much more could be written on each of them, we encourage readers to use them, along with the discussion questions, to reflect on the potential that evangelical advocacy has to impact the world for Christ.

Example 1: Human Trafficking

The knell of slavery has sounded many times in history: when Moses petitioned Pharaoh to release the people of Israel; in 1807 when William Wilberforce and company successfully outlawed the slave trade in Britain; and on January 1, 1863, when Abraham Lincoln issued the Emancipation Proclamation.

Yet today there are more slaves than at any other time in human history. It is estimated that between 30 and 40 million people are enslaved globally, and that the slave industry generates profits of over $150 billion annually.[1] Such exploitation takes two central forms.[2] The first and most common is labor exploitation, often in the form of debt bondage. The second is sexual exploitation, often referred to as commercial sexual exploitation. Regardless of the form slavery takes, the fundamental relationship between a master (owner, boss, or pimp) and slave (worker, employee, or "prostitute") remains one of exploitation for gain.

Human trafficking is one of the issues that evangelicals have been most active about in the advocacy world. Groups such as the International Justice Mission, founded in 1997, mobilized evangelicals by increasing awareness at the local level. In June 1999, evangelicals were working alongside women's

1. International Labor Organization, *Profits and Poverty*, 13–15.
2. The Global Slavery Index (maintained by Walk Free) estimates that there are 35.8 million people in some form of slavery, with India, China, and Pakistan having the highest gross totals (2014 Index).

groups, child advocates (such as the UN Children's Fund), and other religious voices (such as Michael Horowitz of the Hudson Institute) to spearhead the legislation that became the Trafficking and Victims Protection Act (TVPA).[3] The National Association of Evangelicals rallied leaders together to declare that "the God-given dignity and integrity of each individual compels us to take action to combat evil . . . , [and] experience also teaches us that strong legislation and higher priority attention by our own government can reduce the incidence of the international sex trade."[4] Alongside feminist groups and the UN Children's Fund (UNICEF), such support was instrumental in the passage of the bill. The act not only defined the crime of human trafficking, thereby making it possible to hold perpetrators accountable, but also established the Trafficking in Persons (TIP) Office within the State Department to coordinate the US government's efforts against trafficking. The TVPA was a landmark declaration by the United States indicating that human trafficking will not be tolerated.

By 2008, the TIP Office had supported a number of antislavery initiatives around the globe, spreading its limited funding to programs it deemed effective. Yet World Vision and International Justice Mission (IJM) wanted to combine a focused approach on enforcing local anti-trafficking law with providing survivor aftercare, which would involve civil society and NGOs.

Women of Vision, a coalition of groups around the country who raise support and awareness for international poverty issues through World Vision, helped in raising grassroots support for this idea. Students were mobilized through the Urbana 2009 youth convention in Urbana, Illinois; 2009 was the first year when the student missions groups at the convention had an advocacy track (sponsored by World Vision and Sojourners with a focus on anti-trafficking efforts). As a result, in fall 2010 college students around the country generated more than five thousand phone calls to their members of Congress asking them to make the needed changes. IJM made the Child Protection Compact Act the main ask for their annual lobby day both in 2009 and in 2010, organizing hundreds of meetings for passionate constituents with their elected officials. For two years everyday citizens, most of them evangelical Christians, pushed Washington to make the changes. While the reform bill eventually stalled in committee, over the span of the campaign it gained support from 117 representatives and 27 senators.[5]

3. UNICEF-sponsored letter to congressional leaders, August 4, 2000.
4. National Association of Evangelicals letter to congressional leadership, June 16, 1999.
5. We are indebted to the staff of World Vision and International Justice Mission for their detailed recounting of the history of the campaigns they ran. This entire section is drawn from personal correspondence and interviews conducted throughout the fall of 2014 by Jared Noetzel.

In 2011, the Department of Health and Human Services (HHS) denied the US Conference of Catholic Bishops' (USCCB) request to continue receiving government funds to provide services to survivors of trafficking in the United States, as USCCB had been doing since 2006. This was due to the Catholic organization's refusal to provide a full range of reproductive health services, including those prohibited by Catholic social teaching. Many religious freedom advocates and conservative members of Congress objected to such a decision, and TVPA's reauthorization stalled.[6] Hundreds of anti-trafficking advocates suddenly found themselves in the middle of a different discussion.

When the legislation stalled, 150 NGOs, including Sojourners, World Vision, Catholic Relief Services, the Mennonite Central Committee, and IJM, signed a letter urging congressional leaders to renew the law in order to "continue the fight to end modern-day slavery in our generation." Even as public attention to this issue waned during the presidential election of 2012, Senator Patrick Leahy pushed conversations on TVPA again, in part due to the pressure from groups such as Women of Vision and college students.

What stands out about evangelical activism in anti-trafficking efforts is its cooperation with broad coalitions, its consistent advocacy when political negotiations seem to stall, and its engagement with religious freedom concerns together with other issues of exploitation and oppression. While organizations like IJM and World Vision are involved in relief efforts that impact those who have been trafficked, they have done this alongside advocating.

Example 2: Immigration Reform

Immigration has been an ongoing issue in the United States since the founding of the nation. Few would dispute that immigrants have shaped American history. In fact, the US federal government started regulating migration into the country before the turn of the nineteenth century. The first version of our current immigration system became law in 1925, when Congress set annual quotas for the entrance of migrants. Throughout the rest of the mid-twentieth century, immigration law reflected a desire to limit non-European immigration. The radicalized quota system was eliminated in 1965, and in 1986 Congress legalized all previously unlawful entries before 1982. At the same time, the legislators made it illegal to hire anyone without proper documentation and created a visa category for temporary agricultural workers. Legislation in

6. Jerry Markon, "Abortion, Birth Control Access at Issue in Dispute over Denial of Grant to Catholic Group," *Washington Post*, November 11, 2011.

1990 more than doubled the migrant limit and sought to increase the diversity of the immigrant stream. In 1996 Congress made nonresident immigrants ineligible for any kind of public assistance programs (food stamps, Medicaid, etc.). These efforts represent the long-running debate over how to best regulate immigration.

In that debate, evangelicals have historically supported tougher regulation of immigration, focusing specifically on the importance of upholding the rule of law and, more recently, securing the US border. Nonetheless, evangelicals have played a unique role in the relatively recent history of US immigration reform advocacy. Thirty years ago migrant workers and undocumented immigrants remained concentrated in a limited number of states and cities. Because of this geographic consolidation, the general population of the United States, and by extension many in the evangelical church, had little occasion to interact with immigrants. More recently, economic and social forces have drastically changed the factors that pushed immigrants to leave their native country.

Today, first-generation immigrants live all over the country. They work in the tomato fields of Alabama and pick strawberries in Oregon. They labor in Chicago's suburban industrial plants and throughout the service industry in Boston. Many churches and individual believers interact with immigrants regularly, but that was not always the case. The substantial new interactions result primarily from evangelical churches' missional desire to serve their surrounding communities. Motivated by the call of Matthew 28, church leaders have pursued various strategies to share the gospel of Jesus Christ with their new neighbors. These new relationships, facilitated by their community ministry, have encouraged evangelicals to reflect on the broken immigration system, including the factors that push immigrants to leave and the dynamics that pull them toward the United States. As a result of this commitment to community, many evangelicals have developed relationships with immigrants.

In response to the increasing presence of immigrants in their lives, evangelicals began to take a more serious stance on issues affecting the immigrant community. In 2009 the National Association of Evangelicals passed a resolution calling for comprehensive reform of the immigration system. Seeking to provide biblically sound thinking on current issues, the NAE routinely delivers public statements on issues of religious liberty, poverty, family, and human rights. The 2009 immigration resolution included the usual scriptural guidance as well as the most specific policy recommendations the NAE has ever made on any issue. The NAE's board of directors called for a secure border, "sound, equitable process toward earned legal status for currently undocumented immigrants," and serious enforcement of the law with an eye toward due process.[7] Galen Carey, vice president of government relations at the NAE, said, "The 2009 resolutions would not have been adopted if it would have been rejected by [the NAE's] membership."[8] That acceptance was grounded in the shared biblical understanding of the dignity of every person, the acceptance of the "stranger and foreigner" found in the Old Testament, and the commandment to love and care for neighbors with an emphasis on the marginalized. At the same time, the NAE affirmed the scriptural call for order and that Christians should uphold and obey the law.

Just two years later, in 2011, the Southern Baptist Convention (SBC), the largest evangelical denomination in the United States and a member of the NAE, published its own resolution calling on Congress to implement, "with the borders secured, a just and compassionate path to legal status, with appropriate restitutionary measures, for those undocumented immigrants already living in our country."[9]

Bill Hybels explained the evangelical motivation for immigration advocacy best. In a message at Willow Creek Community Church, Hybels walked through the church's thinking on the issue. The church began, he said, by serving the largely Hispanic immigrant community around them. However, the ministry leaders quickly realized that many of the people they served needed legal assistance for a wide range of issues, including immigration. The church recruited lawyers from within the congregation to start taking cases. The church discovered, Hybels explained, that the legal system was stymied with a backlog of cases. Moreover, the out-of-date system continued to put people in unsustainable situations where they needed help. Seeking the root cause of the problem, the church began to consider how they could prevent the tragedies they routinely witnessed. This led the congregation to advocate for balanced, comprehensive immigration reform. In his explanation, Hybels asked his congregation, "Can we really help the poor without getting into politics?"[10] If the story of Willow Creek is typical, then the answer is "No."

In response to the converging opinion of local pastors across the United States and to resolutions by the NAE and large denominations like the SBC,

7. National Association of Evangelicals, "Immigration." The reader should note that these policy recommendations were developed in the midst of a uniquely charged political climate. Therefore, terms like "secure border" and "pathway to legal status/citizenship" often function as code words. In some cases a secure border might indicate an overt militarization of border regions. Others may use that same phrase to refer to a better enforcement of current policy without increased enforcement.

8. Galen Carry, interview with Jared Noetzel, July 2, 2014.

9. Southern Baptist Convention, "On Immigration and the Gospel."

10. Hybels, message to Willow Creek Community Church, April 13, 2014.

evangelical leaders came together to found the Evangelical Immigration Table (EIT). The coalition kicked off its advocacy with a challenge to evangelical believers across the country to commit to read forty Bible verses that address issues of immigration by distributing more than 120,000 "I Was a Stranger" bookmark guides to the verses.[11] EIT advocates hoped that average evangelicals across the country would understand the scriptural command to care for immigrants and be willing to support reform efforts. The campaign also included a video of notable evangelical leaders reading the text of Matthew 25, where Christ proclaims, "Truly I tell you, whatever you did for one of the least of these brothers and sisters of mine, you did for me" (Matt. 25:40). The EIT also supported the creation of the film *The Stranger* to demonstrate the broken immigration system's effects on a range of people in society.

One of the most pressing components of the immigration crisis in the United States is the state of the undocumented immigrants. "I have not wanted to venture into this," Hybels admitted, but "there is no sane path to citizenship these days. Twelve million people live in the US today without proper documentation."[12] As the message sank into evangelical communities, more and more pastors and laypeople began to understand the importance of a serious reform effort. To further ground their work in their faith, the EIT organizers encouraged evangelicals across the country to pray both that those impacted by the broken immigration system would be cared for and that the system would be fixed.

The EIT and the evangelical community more broadly have taken a strong, and for some a new, stand for immigration reform that includes serious public policy advocacy. Hybels, a strong supporter of the EIT, explains, "For the first time in forty years of doing ministry I've started to write op-eds pieces in newspapers. I've visited people in Congress, Republicans and Democrats. I've stood on the capitol lawn with dozens of other leaders doing press conferences, simply asking our elected leaders to come up with comprehensive immigration reform. Because they are the only ones who can fix the mess."[13] He is right; only Congress has the power to fully and permanently address a broken system that continues to create disaster for families.

Jenny Yang, vice president for advocacy and policy at World Relief, who led her organization's efforts on immigration reform advocacy, noted, "In 2006, evangelicals were polled to be the most anti-immigrant among other religious groups surveyed." In 2013 the US Senate voted in favor of a comprehensive

11. Yang, "How Evangelicals Helped Shape."
12. Hybels, message to Willow Creek Community Church, April 13, 2014.
13. Ibid.

reform bill. Yang continued, "The Senate vote . . . is reflective of the change in attitudes among Americans and particularly among evangelicals towards immigration reform. Two pastors from Arkansas put it well in saying that they serve some of the most downtrodden and vulnerable in their neighborhoods, and by passing immigration reform, we would be helping the very people whom these churches have come to serve and love."[14]

In response to the changing demographics, economic forces, and the call of Scripture to love their neighbors, evangelicals in the United States broadened their understanding of immigration. Whereas they first supported only enforcement and border security, they added to those commitments a concern for undocumented immigrants. In concert with many other voices in the United States, they called for a comprehensive reform of a broken immigration system that, in the words of the EIT principles, "Respects the God-given dignity of every person. Protects the unity of the immediate family. Respects the rule of law. Guarantees secure national borders. Ensures fairness to taxpayers. Establishes a path toward legal status and/or citizenship. . . ."[15] Those principles represent a significant change in the perspective of evangelicals, and, more important, they demonstrate the evangelical community's commitment to advocating for those in need. The foundational commitment for evangelicals, as demonstrated here, is "Love your neighbor as yourself." In this case evangelicalism in the United States coalesced around specific values to address a specific injustice. Moreover, the advocacy undertaken by the EIT had its roots firmly in the Bible. While comprehensive immigration reform has not passed at the time of this writing, it is clear that for the foreseeable future the EIT will continue to seek scripturally grounded approaches to advancing comprehensive immigration reform.

Example 3: HIV/AIDS

Evangelicals haven't always cared about public health. In fact, the evangelical church initially struggled to understand the new disease when it first appeared in West Africa and eventually took root in the Los Angeles gay community in the 1980s. Without an attachment to the community that was suffering, evangelicals quickly developed a narrative of condemnation, which left them apathetic about those who had the disease. It would take face-to-face interactions with the dying around the world to change this story and attitude.

14. Yang, "How Evangelicals Helped Shape Immigration Reform."
15. Evangelical Immigration Table, "Evangelical Statement for Principles of Immigration Reform," http://www.evangelicalimmigrationtable.com.

Fast-forward thirty years. Every major evangelical relief and development organization, as well as many evangelical churches, addresses HIV/AIDS in some fashion. We hold conferences on how to deliver better assistance to communities stricken by the virus, how to prevent its spread, and how to best care for the ravages left in its wake. Evangelicals continue to make a difference across the globe on HIV/AIDS. Although they were slow to take on the issue, a combination of firsthand testimonies from health practitioners and missionaries, open-minded evangelical students, trusted relief and development organizations, and church leaders willing to garner wider support in the evangelical world worked together to mobilize evangelicals on this issue.

Evangelicals began discussing HIV/AIDS before the turn of the millennium. *Christianity Today* reported on HIV/AIDS as early as 1997, and the NAE had made a statement about the virus back in 1988.[16] Samaritan's Purse had encountered HIV/AIDS throughout the 1980s and 1990s through their health-focused work around the world.

According to Ken Casey, who directed World Vision's HIV/AIDS program, program staff "woke up" when it became clear that the virus was undoing their work.[17] After sponsoring a Barna Group survey of evangelicals' willingness to give toward HIV/AIDS relief, Richard Stearns, president of World Vision, wrote, "A scant 3 percent of evangelicals said they would definitely give for AIDS education and prevention, compared with 8 percent of non-Christians. Why the evangelical reluctance on this issue?"[18] As the director of evangelicalism's largest relief and development organization, Stearns struck at the heart of the matter with his simple question.

By 2000 the overseas mission hospitals Samaritan's Purse supported were reporting an overwhelming demand for HIV/AIDS services, and their staff in the United States knew they needed to do something. It had become clear that these practitioners, both African nationals and missionaries, had a message they needed to share. The US staff convened a committee of medical professionals to discuss how to proceed. Initially, the committee thought they would bring missionary medical professionals together in North Carolina, but at one meeting Franklin Graham encouraged the group to move the nascent conference to Washington, DC. Because of the testimony of those on the ground, he and others in the organization had realized that US evangelicals need to get past the anti-HIV/AIDS stigma.

16. Woong Shin, "Are Culture Wars Over?"
17. Quoted in Rebecca Barnes, "The Church Awakens," *Christianity Today*, January 1, 2005.
18. Richard Stearns, "Mercy Impaired," *Christianity Today*, September 3, 2001.

In planning what became the Prescriptions for Hope conference, Samaritan's Purse decided to invite three key groups of people: practitioners, both national and missionary from around the world; US political leaders; and the media. In the end, more than a thousand people gathered in February 2002 at the Washington Hilton to hear from African leaders and medical missionaries who had been fighting the virus for years. Some of the most influential members of Congress also attended, including the staunch conservative Senator Jesse Helms and Senate majority leader Bill Frist. Both senators had substantial influence over foreign-assistance funding dedicated to global health. Ken Isaacs, who directed the conference, remembers clearly the moment that Jesse Helms stood up to speak. Speaking in reference to the lack of action by the United States to address the disease in Africa, the aged senator from North Carolina said simply, "I have been wrong." Because the media outlets showed up, that commitment stuck. In response to the passionate presentations from an array of committed Christian health practitioners from the global South, Jesse Helms became a champion for US intervention to address HIV/AIDS.

Holly Burkhalter, an organizer for the secular anti-AIDS group Physicians for Human Rights (PHR), attended the conference and was shocked by how committed the participants were to the issue. "They were on fire for treatment," she said, adding that she was struck by how many representatives from the developing world were present. She and her colleagues in various secular organizations had long been fighting to get treatment included in HIV/AIDS policy. According to Burkhalter, Jesse Helms's comments at the Prescriptions for Hope conference marked the first time that such a policy became politically plausible. Six weeks later Helms and Frist stood in the Rose Garden with President George W. Bush as he signed into law the first US funding dedicated solely to combating HIV/AIDS overseas, $500 million to prevent mother-to-child transmission. Looking back on the conference, Isaacs conveyed that the participants did not have any specific policy "ask." Rather, their message was simple: the church was already addressing the issue, and the government needed to get involved.[19]

Major evangelical relief and development organizations played a key role in demonstrating the efficacy of faith-based AIDS interventions. However, their authority to speak came directly from health practitioners around the world. This credibility was matched with the scriptural case made by many in the anti-HIV movement that Christians should engage with the issue. The evangelical community's willingness to push for both US government funds and a coordinated approach to countering the virus was a critical step forward. As

19. Ken Isaacs, interview with Jared Noetzel, July 17, 2014.

they began to better understand the scope of the problem, they increasingly grasped the importance of the US government's involvement. However, those closest to the problem knew that this initial success would not fully address the scope of the pandemic. They had to press further.

Enter Bono. The U2 front man had been deeply involved in the Jubilee 2000 movement and was in the early stages of launching his new organization, DATA (Debt, AIDS, Trade, Africa), yet he saw the importance of deploying his charisma and name recognition to awaken the evangelical grass roots for AIDS advocacy. The rock star had traveled extensively and, like the development and health practitioners, had seen firsthand the devastation of HIV/AIDS. In December 2003, as part of his seven-stop "Heart of America Tour," Bono visited Wheaton College, one of the bastions of evangelicalism in the United States. To a packed house of twenty-four hundred students and faculty, he made an impassioned plea replete with gospel quotations, appeals to the commonness of humanity, and a stark call to the Church to fight for justice. Eileen Campbell, an organizer for PHR at the time, described Bono's speech at Wheaton as a watershed moment.[20] Reflecting on the evening, Brittany Noetzel, a Wheaton graduate who attended, said:

> It was a formative moment where I was encouraged—perhaps for the first time— to take definitive action toward accomplishing social good on behalf of those who lacked the kind of power I had. Bono made it seem possible that we could achieve something great in the fight to stem the AIDS epidemic. He respected us for the role we could play, and he respected our underlying reasons for caring, namely our faith in God as creator and healer.[21]

If grassroots medical and development professionals steered the evangelical conscience toward HIV/AIDS, then Bono put the movement on its feet. *Christianity Today*'s March 2003 cover included a picture of him holding hands with a young African girl, with the succinct caption, "Rock star calls the church to fight Africa's AIDS epidemic." But could a few committed missionaries, activists, and a rock star make a difference?

President George W. Bush was widely seen in the evangelical world as a man of deep Christian faith. In 2002, after the president committed the first $500 million to prevent mother-to-child transmission, he reportedly went to his deputy chief of staff, Joshua Bolten, and said, "Go back to the drawing board and think even bigger."[22]

20. Eileen Campbell, interview with Jared Noetzel, June 26, 2014.
21. Brittany Noetzel, email to Jared Noetzel, June 27, 2014.
22. George W. Bush, *Decision Points* (New York: Crown Publishing, 2010), 338.

Bolten and Anthony Fauci, the director of the National Institute of Allergy and Infectious Diseases, together took the lead in devising the White House's "bigger" plan to combat HIV/AIDS. The president's speechwriter and advisor Michael Gerson, also an evangelical, later partnered with Bolten and Fauci to advance the plan. At a key juncture, the president and his economic advisors wanted to know whether or not the metric-driven, country-focused plan could succeed. They called on renowned medical experts including, among others, Dr. Paul Farmer, a noted Harvard Medical School faculty member and global health advocate, and Dr. Peter Mugyenyi, a Ugandan doctor who had years of experience treating the disease in his native country, to convince the adminis-tration.[23] Grassroots pressure had encouraged President Bush to consider how the US government could lead the intervention efforts, and now a decision had to be made. In January 2003 during the State of the Union the president an-nounced a bold new initiative: $15 billion, including $10 billion in new funding, to combat the spread of HIV/AIDS. The President's Emergency Plan for AIDS Relief (PEPFAR) took its place in history as the largest investment ever directed at combating a single disease. In March 2003 the House of Representatives introduced legislation to authorize the program, and by the end of May of that year the Senate agreed and the president signed PEPFAR into law.

Between 2001 and 2004 US evangelicals shifted profoundly in their stance toward HIV/AIDS. The Kaiser Family Foundation, in a 2011 report, said, "The trend has been towards a decline in reports of attitudes . . . such as the view that AIDS is a punishment—which has dropped 27 percentage points since 1987."[24] But the ground for this change in attitudes and support was cre-ated by decades of work by missionaries, international voices, and others in healthcare. Franklin Graham organized a conference to lift the voices of those long-serving healthcare workers, Bono campaigned across Middle America to rally students, and average evangelicals in the pews stood up. Debbie Dortzbach, who ran World Relief's AIDS program, put it best in 2004 right after PEPFAR passed: "Ironically . . . an agent of death . . . is bringing life to the Body."[25]

Conclusion

Taken together these stories demonstrate the impressive reach of recent ad-vocacy efforts undertaken by evangelicals. From addressing the HIV/AIDS

23. Harold Varmus, "Making PEPFAR," *Science and Diplomacy*, December 1, 2013.

24. Kaiser Family Foundation, *HIV/AIDS at 30: A Public Opinion Perspective*, June 1, 2011.

25. Agnieszka Tennant, "Q & A: Deborah Dortzbach," *Christianity Today*, September 1, 2004.

pandemic to supporting a comprehensive reform of the US immigration system, evangelicals have shown up over the past decade and a half in areas of public discourse that surprised many. The most consistent theme across the three examples is the influential impact of being connected to the people most directly experiencing injustice or marginalization. For example, Bill Hybels and Willow Creek Community Church would have never become engaged in advocacy for immigration reform if they had not had a direct connection with their community through legal counseling services. And because African and missionary medical professionals testified to the impact of HIV/AIDS at the Prescriptions for Hope conference, real change happened. In all these cases, we can appropriately celebrate the privileged position that those closest to the reality took. At the same time, each of these campaigns failed to elevate these individuals to a position of leadership within the advocacy movement. Overall the immigration reform movement did the best job of putting the local level first, but many current efforts to address slavery and HIV/AIDS in the evangelical church do not regularly put affected communities at the front of their advocacy efforts. We encourage all those involved in advocacy to pay special attention to what is going on at the local level, constantly consult those affected by the issue, and create opportunities for their participation in planning and implementing advocacy activities. Of course, this effort should also strive to rely on local churches as a primary mechanism for that involvement.

In our assessment the formulation of goals and strategies in light of Scripture, keeping God as a subject throughout, forms the basis of any distinctively Christian advocacy campaign. In each of the campaigns described here, theological reflection and biblical values guided decisions about strategy and goals. However, the degree to which Scripture played the defining role varied. For the immigration campaign, the first action taken focused entirely on Scripture—reading forty verses related to immigrants—and coalesced into a foundational concept of "welcoming the stranger," an inherently biblical concept. On slavery, advocates cite a range of biblical motivations for the work they do. At present the campaign does not have a central, unifying theological theme to undergird it. That is not to say that advocates have not reflected on Scripture or sought to discern their callings theologically. However, the degree to which that process is foregrounded in the public aspects of any campaign is, in our opinion, an essential point of evaluation. To repeat an earlier question: have we adequately used our theological resources outlined above to address the multidimensional nature of structural evil?

In sharing these examples as well as in these brief reflections, we hope to inspire further reflection by seasoned and fresh advocates alike. Below we have listed questions drawn from the final chapters of the book to foster reflection both on these campaigns and on others. We encourage readers to find space in their church or school to discuss these ideas with others. At the same time, some of the points raised here cannot be fully addressed by group discussion. Rather, they require prayer and the Holy Spirit's guidance to fully digest and resolve.

Discussion Questions

Formulation

- Was prayer a foundational component of the advocacy campaign?
- Did the campaign develop and maintain a theological basis for the work?
- Did the campaign overcome the distinction between advocacy and evangelism by testifying to Christ appropriately and effectively?
- Was the advocacy effort compromised by a prioritization of ideology over theology at any point?
- Did those involved in this movement identify structural sin and work against it in their advocacy?

Implementation

- Did the advocacy campaign partner effectively within the evangelical world? How did they appropriately partner with non-evangelical entities? Did the campaign maintain its Christian character in the process of partnering with others?
- Was the campaign driven by outside agendas at any point? If so, did this compromise the nature of the advocacy effort?
- Did the campaign rely upon local churches as a primary means of advocacy? Did the campaign support or hinder the growth of local churches in their ministry of advocacy?
- Was the campaign connected to the reality of those at the local level? How did local and affected communities play a part in directing the campaign?
- How did the campaign formulate its policy suggestions? Were those suggestions based in theological/biblical values? Did they take into account the contribution of other points of view, including opposing ones?

- Did the campaign appropriately communicate policy details to ensure advocates understood the desired outcomes?
- Did campaign leadership, both executive and midlevel, maintain a humble attitude of discipleship within their local congregation and the wider evangelical community? Did the campaign encourage the same disposition among its supporters?

Bibliography

Accord Network. "Accord Network—Empowering the Christian Community to End Poverty." 2013. http://www.accordnetwork.org/.

———. "The Principles of Excellence in Integral Mission." 2013. http://www.accord network.org/integral/.

Aldrich, Joe. *Lifestyle Evangelism*. Colorado Springs: Multnomah Books, 1981.

Ammerman, Nancy T. "Congregations: Local, Social, and Religious." In *The Oxford Handbook of the Sociology of Religion*, edited by Peter B. Clarke, 562–80. New York: Oxford University Press, 2009.

———. "New Life for Denominationalism." *Christian Century*, March 15, 2000, 302–7.

———. *Pillars of Faith: American Congregations and Their Partners*. Berkeley: University of California Press, 2005.

Amstutz, Mark R. *Evangelicals and American Foreign Policy*. New York: Oxford University Press, 2014.

Anderson, Leah Seppanen. "The Anglican Tradition: Building the State, Critiquing the State." Chap. 6 in Joireman, *Church, State, and Citizen*.

Asbury Theological Seminary, Bread for the World, and Eastern University. "Evangelical Advocacy." 2012. http://www.evangelicaladvocacy.org/.

Association for a More Just Society. "AJS." 2013. http://www.ajs-us.org/ajs.

———. "Let's Transform Honduras." 2013. http://www.ajs-us.org/project/lets-transform -honduras.

Bacote, Vincent E. *The Political Disciple: A Theology of Public Life*. Grand Rapids: Zondervan, 2015.

Bandow, Doug. *Beyond Good Intentions: A Biblical View of Politics*. Turning Point Christian Worldview Series. Westchester, IL: Crossway, 1988.

Barth, Karl. *Church and State*. Translated by G. Ronald Howe. Greenville, SC: Smyth and Helwys, 1991.

————. *Church Dogmatics, Vol. 2, Part 2*. Edited by G. W. Bromiley and T. F. Torrence. Translated by Geoffrey William Bromiley et al. New York: T&T Clark, 2004.

————. *Church Dogmatics, Vol. 3, Part 1*. Edited by G. W. Bromiley and T. F. Torrence. New York: T&T Clark, 1961.

————. *Community, State, and Church: Three Essays*. Garden City, NY: Doubleday, 1960.

Bartley, Jonathan. *Faith and Politics after Christendom: The Church as a Movement for Anarchy*. After Christendom. Waynesboro, GA: Paternoster Press, 2006.

Beasley-Murray, George Raymond. *John*. Waco: Word Books, 1987.

Bebbington, David. *Evangelicalism in Modern Britain: A History from the 1730s to the 1980s*. London: Unwin Hyman, 1989.

————. "Evangelicals, Theology and Social Transformation." In *Movement for Change: Evangelical Perspectives on Social Transformation*, edited by David Hilborn, 1–19. Nottingham: Paternoster, 2004.

Benson, Bruce Ellis, and Peter Goodwin Heltzel, eds. *Evangelicals and Empire: Christian Alternatives to the Political Status Quo*. Grand Rapids: Brazos, 2008.

Berger, Brigitte. *The Culture of Entrepreneurship*. San Francisco: ICS Press, 1991.

Berger, Peter L. *The Desecularization of the World: Resurgent Religion and World Politics*. Grand Rapids: Eerdmans, 1999.

————. *The Sacred Canopy: Elements of a Sociological Theory of Religion*. New York: Anchor, 1990.

Berkhof, Hendrik. *Christ and the Powers*. Translated by John Howard Yoder. Scottdale, PA: Herald Press, 1977.

Bird, Michael F. "One Who Will Arise to Rule over the Nations: Paul's Letter to the Romans and the Roman Empire." In *Jesus Is Lord, Caesar Is Not: Evaluating Empire in New Testament Studies*, edited by Scot McKnight and Joseph B. Modica, 146–65. Downers Grove, IL: IVP Academic, 2013.

Black, Amy E. *Beyond Left and Right: Helping Christians Make Sense of American Politics*. Grand Rapids: Baker Books, 2008.

Bonhoeffer, Dietrich. *Christ the Center*. Translated by Edwin H. Robertson. San Francisco: HarperOne, 1978.

————. *Conspiracy and Imprisonment, 1940–1945*. Translated by Mark S. Brocker. Minneapolis: Fortress Press, 2006.

————. *Creation and Fall: A Theological Exposition of Genesis 1–3*. Translated by Douglas Stephen Bax. Minneapolis: Fortress Press, 2004.

————. *Ethics*. Translated by Neville Horton Smith. New York: Macmillan, 1955.

Boyd, Gregory A. "Advancing the Cruciform Revolution: A Kingdom Perspective on Evangelism." *Word & World* 29, no. 4 (2009): 407–17.

————. *The Myth of a Christian Nation: How the Quest for Political Power Is Destroying the Church*. Grand Rapids: Zondervan, 2005.

Brenneman, Robert E. *Homies and Hermanos: God and Gangs in Central America.* New York: Oxford University Press, 2012.

Bronkema, David. "Business as Ministry." *PRISM* 19, no. 1 (January/February 2012): 36.

———. "The Challenges and Promises of Spiritual Metrics: Understanding the Dynamics at Play and Guidelines for Best Practices." Chap. 1 in *Towards an Understanding and Practice of Spiritual Metrics: Measuring Spiritual Impact Faithfully and Productively in Christian Development Agencies, Missions Organizations, Schools, and Churches,* edited by F. David Bronkema, Mark Forshaw, and Ellen Strohm. Forthcoming.

———. "Firm Foundations: Christian Development NGOs, Civil Society, and Social Change." In *Local Ownership, Global Change: Will Civil Society Save the World?,* edited by Roland Hoksbergen and Lowell M. Ewert, 234–59. Monrovia, CA: World Vision, 2002.

Bronkema, David, and Christopher M. Brown. "Business as Mission through the Lens of Development." *Transformation: An International Journal of Holistic Mission Studies* 26, no. 2 (April 2009): 82–88.

Brueggemann, Walter. "From Dust to Kingship." *Zeitschrift für die alttestamentliche Wissenschaft* 84, no. 1 (1972): 1–18.

———. *Genesis: A Bible Commentary for Teaching and Preaching.* Atlanta: John Knox Press, 1982.

———. *The Prophetic Imagination.* Philadelphia: Fortress Press, 1978.

———. *Theology of the Old Testament: Testimony, Dispute, Advocacy.* Minneapolis: Fortress Press, 1997.

———. *Truth Speaks to Power: The Countercultural Nature of Scripture.* Louisville: Westminster John Knox, 2013.

Brusco, Elizabeth. "Colombian Evangelicalism as a Strategic Form of Women's Collective Action." *Feminist Issues* 6, no. 2 (1986): 3–13.

Calhoun, Craig. "Rethinking Secularism." *Hedgehog Review* 12, no. 3 (Fall 2010): 35–48.

"Calling All College Students! Get Your Campus to Lend a Hand on 10.10.10" (blog). Micah Challenge. July 21, 2010. http://www.micahchallengeusa.org/blog/item/callingallcollegestudents.

Campolo, Anthony. *Red Letter Christians: A Citizen's Guide to Faith & Politics.* Ventura, CA: Regal, 2008.

Carter, Craig A. *Rethinking Christ and Culture: A Post-Christendom Perspective.* Grand Rapids: Brazos, 2006.

Castellanos, Noel. "When Love Demands Justice." *Plough Quarterly,* no. 2 (2015). www.plough.com/en/topics/justice/politics/when-love-demands-justice.

Cavanaugh, William T. "Are Corporations People?" In Kalantzis and Lee, *Christian Political Witness,* 128–46.

Chambers, Robert. *Rural Development: Putting the Last First*. New York: Longman, 1983.

Chaves, Mark. *Congregations in America*. Cambridge, MA: Harvard University Press, 2004.

Cheong, John, and Eloise Meneses, eds. *Christian Mission and Economic Systems: A Critical Survey of the Cultural and Religious Dimensions of Economies*. Pasadena, CA: William Carey, 2015.

Cho, Eugene. *Overrated: Are We More in Love with the Idea of Changing the World Than Actually Changing the World?* Colorado Springs: David C. Cook, 2014.

Christian, Jayakumar. *God of the Empty-Handed: Poverty, Power and the Kingdom of God*. Monrovia, CA: MARC Books, 1999.

———. *Re-Thinking Christian Response to the Poor*. Sydney, Australia: World Vision Australia Resource Unit, 1994.

Clines, D. J. A. "Image of God." In *Dictionary of Paul and His Letters*, edited by Gerald F. Hawthorne, Ralph P. Martin, and Daniel G. Reid, 426–28. Downers Grove, IL: InterVarsity, 1993.

Coates, Gregory R. *Politics Strangely Warmed: Political Theology in the Wesleyan Spirit*. Eugene, OR: Wipf & Stock, 2015.

Cohen, David, Rosa de la Vega, and Gabrielle Watson. *Advocacy for Social Justice: A Global Action and Reflection Guide*. Bloomfield, CT: Kumarian Press, 2001.

Colson, Charles. Foreword to Overton, *God and Governing*.

Compassion International. "Resource Guide: Equipping Your Personal Ministry with Compassion." Spring 2015. http://www.compassionmedia.com/pdf/compassion-resource-guide-spring-2015.pdf.

Corbett, Steve, and Brian Fikkert. *When Helping Hurts: How to Alleviate Poverty without Hurting the Poor—and Yourself*. Expanded ed. Chicago: Moody Publishers, 2012.

Cox, Harvey Gallagher. *Fire from Heaven: The Rise of Pentecostal Spirituality and the Reshaping of Religion in the Twenty-First Century*. Cambridge, MA: Da Capo Press, 2005.

Crouch, Andy. *Playing God: Redeeming the Gift of Power*. Downers Grove, IL: InterVarsity, 2013.

Curry, Dean C. "Biblical Politics and Foreign Policy." Chap. 3 in *Evangelicals and Foreign Policy: Four Perspectives*, edited by Michael Cromartie. Lanham, MD: Ethics and Public Policy Center, 1989.

Danforth, John C. *Faith and Politics: How the "Moral Values" Debate Divides America and How to Move Forward Together*. New York: Viking, 2006.

Dawn, Marva J. *Powers, Weakness, and the Tabernacling of God*. Grand Rapids: Eerdmans, 2001.

Dayton, Donald W., and Douglas M. Strong. *Rediscovering an Evangelical Heritage: A Tradition and Trajectory of Integrating Piety and Justice.* 2nd ed. Grand Rapids: Baker Academic, 2014.

Diamond, Sara. *Roads to Dominion: Right-Wing Movements and Political Power in the United States.* New York: Guilford Press, 1995.

Diehl, Judith A. "Anti-Imperial Rhetoric in the New Testament." In McKnight and Modica, *Jesus Is Lord, Caesar Is Not,* 38–81.

Dilley, Andrea Palpant. "The Surprising Discovery about Those Colonialist, Proselytizing Missionaries." *Christianity Today,* January 8, 2014, 34.

Drury, David. "The Wesleyan Church Joins in Launching the Immigration Alliance." The Immigration Alliance. October 21, 2014. http://www.wesleyan.org/2699/the-wesleyan-church-joins-in-launching-the-immigration-alliance.

"The Eastbourne Consultation Joint Statement on Discipleship." Paper presented at the International Consultation on Discipleship, Eastbourne, England, 1999.

Edgar, Brian. "The Consummate Trinity and Participation in the Life of God." *Evangelical Review of Theology* 38, no. 2 (2014): 112–25.

Edwards, Joel, Vikki McLachlan, and Amanda Jackson. *Use by: 2015; Micah Challenge; Insights from a Ten-Year Experiment.* Self-published, 2014.

Ellul, Jacques. *Money & Power.* Translated by LeVonne Neff. Downers Grove, IL: InterVarsity, 1984.

———. *The Political Illusion.* Translated by Konrad Kellen. New York: Knopf, 1967.

———. *Présence au monde moderne.* Collection du Centre Protestant d'Études. Geneva: Editions Roulet, 1948.

———. *The Technological Society.* Translated by John Wilkinson. New York: Knopf, 1964.

Ellul, Jacques, and Willem H. Vanderburg. *Perspectives on Our Age: Jacques Ellul Speaks on His Life and Work.* New York: Seabury Press, 1981.

Emerson, Michael O., and Christian Smith. *Divided by Faith: Evangelical Religion and the Problem of Race in America.* New York: Oxford University Press, 2000.

Evangelical Alliance. "What Is an Evangelical?" 2015. www.eauk.org/connect/about-us/what-is-an-evangelical.cfm.

Evangelical Immigration Table. "Evangelical Statement for Principles of Immigration Reform." http://www.evangelicalimmigrationtable.com/.

Fileta, Jason. "Live Just.ly." 2014. http://www.livejust.ly/.

Flemming, Dean E. *Contextualization in the New Testament: Patterns for Theology and Mission.* Downers Grove, IL: InterVarsity, 2005.

Ford, David. *Christian Wisdom: Desiring God and Learning in Love.* New York: Cambridge University Press, 2007.

———. "Theology." In *The Routledge Companion to the Study of Religion,* edited by John Hinnells, 61–79. London: Routledge, 2005.

Fowler, Robert Booth, Allen D. Hertzke, Laura R. Olson, and Kevin R. Den Dulk. *Religion and Politics in America: Faith, Culture, and Strategic Choices.* 5th ed. Boulder, CO: Westview Press, 2014.

Freston, Paul. *Evangelical Christianity and Democracy in Latin America.* New York: Oxford University Press, 2008.

Friedmann, John. *Empowerment: The Politics of Alternative Development.* Cambridge, MA: Blackwell, 1992.

Garr, W. Randall. "'Image' and 'Likeness' in the Inscription from Tell Fakhariyeh." *Israel Exploration Journal* 50 (2000): 227–34.

Gitari, David. "You Are in the World but Not of It." In Kalantzis and Lee, *Christian Political Witness*, 214–31.

Gitari, David M., and Ben Knighton, eds. *Religion and Politics in Kenya: Essays in Honor of a Meddlesome Priest.* New York: Palgrave Macmillan, 2009.

Goosen, Rachel Waltner. "Defanging the Beast: Mennonite Responses to John Howard Yoder's Sexual Abuse." *Mennonite Quarterly Review* 89, no. 1 (January 2015): 7–81.

Gordon, Graham. *Advocacy Toolkit: Understanding Advocacy.* Edited by Rachel Blackman. Roots Resources. Teddington, UK: Tearfund, 2002.

Gramby-Sobukwe, Sharon, and Tim Hoiland. "The Rise of Mega-Church Efforts in International Development: A Brief Analysis and Areas for Further Research." *Transformation: An International Journal of Holistic Mission Studies* 26, no. 2 (April 2009): 104–17.

Greer, Peter, and Chris Horst. *Mission Drift: The Unspoken Crisis Facing Leaders, Charities, and Churches.* Minneapolis: Bethany House, 2015.

Grudem, Wayne. *Politics according to the Bible: A Comprehensive Resource for Understanding Modern Political Issues in Light of Scripture.* Grand Rapids: Zondervan, 2010.

Guinness, Os. "The Golden Triangle of Freedom." In Overton, *God and Governing*, 41–49.

Gushee, David P. *The Future of Faith in American Politics: The Public Witness of the Evangelical Center.* Waco: Baylor University Press, 2008.

———, ed. *A New Evangelical Manifesto: A Kingdom Vision for the Common Good.* St. Louis: Chalice Press, 2012.

Gustafson, James M. "Preface: An Appreciative Interpretation." In *Christ and Culture*, by H. Richard Niebuhr. Expanded ed. New York: HarperCollins, 2001.

Hafemann, Scott J. *Suffering and Ministry in the Spirit: Paul's Defense of His Ministry in II Corinthians 2:14–3:3.* Grand Rapids: Eerdmans, 1990.

Hart, Trevor A. *Faith Thinking: The Dynamics of Christian Theology.* Eugene, OR: Wipf & Stock, 2005.

Hauerwas, Stanley. "Church Matters." In Kalantzis and Lee, *Christian Political Witness*, 17–34.

Haugen, Gary A. *Good News about Injustice: A Witness of Courage in a Hurting World*. Downers Grove, IL: InterVarsity, 1999.

Henry, Carl F. H. *The Uneasy Conscience of Modern Fundamentalism*. Grand Rapids: Eerdmans, 1947.

Hertzke, Allen D. "Evangelicals and International Engagement." In *A Public Faith: Evangelicals and Civic Engagement*, edited by Michael Cromartie. Lanham, MD: Ethics and Public Policy Center / Washington, DC: Rowman & Littlefield, 2003.

Howell, Brian M. "Contextualizing Context—Exploring Christian Identity in the Global Church through Six Contemporary Cases." In *Power and Identity in the Global Church*, edited by Brian M. Howell and Edwin Zehner, 1–25. Pasadena, CA: William Carey, 2009.

Hunter, James Davison. *To Change the World: The Irony, Tragedy, & Possibility of Christianity in the Late Modern World*. New York: Oxford University Press, 2010.

Huntington, Samuel P. *The Clash of Civilizations and the Remaking of World Order*. New York: Simon & Schuster, 2011.

Hutchison, William R. *Errand to the World: American Protestant Thought and Foreign Missions*. Chicago: University of Chicago Press, 1987.

Hybels, Bill. Message to Willow Creek Community Church, April 13, 2014.

International Labor Organization. *Profits and Poverty: The Economics of Forced Labor*. Geneva: ILO, 2014.

Jayakaran, Ravi. *Holistic World View Analysis: Seeing Their World as They See It*. Madras, India: World Vision India, 1997.

Jeavons, Thomas H. "Identifying Characteristics of 'Religious' Organizations: An Exploratory Proposal." In *PONPO Working Paper No. 197 and ISPS Working Paper No. 2197*. New Haven: Yale University, Institution for Social and Policy Studies, Program on Non-Profit Organizations, 1993.

———. "Religious and Faith-Based Organizations: Do We Know One When We See One?" *Nonprofit and Voluntary Sector Quarterly* 33, no. 1 (March 2004): 140–45.

———. *When the Bottom Line Is Faithfulness: Management of Christian Service Organizations*. Bloomington: Indiana University Press, 1994.

Joireman, Sandra F. "Anabaptists and the State: An Uneasy Coexistence." Chap. 5 in Joireman, *Church, State, and Citizen*.

———, ed. *Church, State, and Citizen: Christian Approaches to Political Engagement*. New York: Oxford University Press, 2009.

Kalantzis, George, and Gregory W. Lee, eds. *Christian Political Witness*. Downers Grove, IL: IVP Academic, 2014.

Keener, Craig. "Scripture and Context: An Evangelical Exploration in Intercultural Hermeneutics." Paper presented at Asbury Theological Seminary, October 10, 2014.

Keller, Timothy J. *Generous Justice: How God's Grace Makes Us Just*. New York: Dutton, 2010.

Kellstedt, Lyman A., John C. Green, James L. Guth, and Corwin E. Smidt. "Religious Voting Blocs in the 1992 Election: The Year of the Evangelical?" *Sociology of Religion* 55, no. 3 (1994): 307–26.

Kemeny, Paul Charles, ed. *Church, State, and Public Justice: Five Views*. Downers Grove, IL: IVP Academic, 2007.

Kennedy, Stephen. "Justice in Evangelical Political Theology." In Overton, *God and Governing*, 108–26.

Kidner, Derek. *The Proverbs: An Introduction and Commentary*. Downers Grove, IL: InterVarsity, 1964.

Kimberley Process. Home page. 2015. http://www.kimberleyprocess.com/en.

King, David. "The Role of Religious Identity among Evangelical NGOs." Paper presented at the Social Scientific Study of Religion Conference, Indianapolis, IN, October 30, 2014.

Kisker, Scott Thomas. *Mainline or Methodist: Rediscovering Our Evangelistic Mission*. Nashville: Discipleship Resources, 2008.

Korten, David C. "Third Generation NGO Strategies: A Key to People-Centered Development." *World Development* 15, supplement (1987): 145–59.

Kpetere, Jean. "Improving Maternal Health in Benin." Micah Challenge. July 13, 2012. http://micahchallenge.org/blogs/category/guest-blog.

Lederach, John Paul. *The Moral Imagination: The Art and Soul of Building Peace*. New York: Oxford University Press, 2005.

Lewis, C. S. *The Magician's Nephew*. New York: HarperCollins, 1994.

———. *Mere Christianity*. New York: Macmillan, 1958.

Lindblom, Charles Edward. *Politics and Markets: The World's Political Economic Systems*. New York: Basic Books, 1977.

Lindsay, D. Michael. *Faith in the Halls of Power: How Evangelicals Joined the American Elite*. New York: Oxford University Press, 2007.

Lomperis, Timothy J. "Lutheranism and Politics: Martin Luther as a Modernizer, but for the Devil." Chap. 3 in Joireman, *Church, State, and Citizen*.

MacIntyre, Alasdair C. *After Virtue: A Study in Moral Theory*. Notre Dame, IN: University of Notre Dame Press, 1984.

Maddox, Randy L. *Responsible Grace: John Wesley's Practical Theology*. Nashville: Kingswood Books, 1994.

"Make Disciples, Not Just Converts: Evangelism without Discipleship Dispenses Cheap Grace." *Christianity Today*, October 25, 1999, 28–29.

Malesic, Jonathan. *Secret Faith in the Public Square: An Argument for the Concealment of Christian Identity*. Grand Rapids: Brazos, 2009.

Marsden, George M. *Fundamentalism and American Culture: The Shaping of Twentieth Century Evangelicalism, 1870–1925*. 2nd ed. New York: Oxford University Press, 2006.

Marti, Gerardo, and Michael O. Emerson. "The Rise of the Diversity Expert: How American Evangelicals Simultaneously Accentuate and Ignore Race." In Steensland and Goff, *New Evangelical Social Engagement*, 179–99.

Martin, David. *Pentecostalism: The World Their Parish*. Malden, MA: Blackwell, 2001.

———. *Tongues of Fire: The Explosion of Protestantism in Latin America*. Cambridge, MA: Basil Blackwell, 1990.

Martin, Jim. *The Just Church: Becoming a Risk-Taking, Justice-Seeking, Disciple-Making Congregation*. Carol Stream, IL: Tyndale Momentum, 2012.

Mathewes, Charles. *A Theology of Public Life*. Cambridge: Cambridge University Press, 2007.

McBride, Jennifer M. "White Protestants Aren't Aliens: Resident Aliens at 25." *Christian Century*, September 16, 2014. https://www.christiancentury.org/article/2014-09/white-protestants-arent-aliens.

McKnight, Scot. *Kingdom Conspiracy: Returning to the Radical Mission of the Local Church*. Grand Rapids: Brazos, 2014.

McKnight, Scot, and Joseph B. Modica, eds. *Jesus Is Lord, Caesar Is Not: Evaluating Empire in New Testament Studies*. Downers Grove, IL: IVP Academic, 2013.

Miller, Donald E., and Tetsunao Yamamori. *Global Pentecostalism: The New Face of Christian Social Engagement*. Berkeley: University of California Press, 2007.

Moberg, David O. *Inasmuch: Christian Social Responsibility in the Twentieth Century*. Grand Rapids: Eerdmans, 1965.

Moltmann, Jürgen. "Political Theology in Germany after Auschwitz." In *Public Theology for the 21st Century: Essays in Honour of Duncan B. Forrester*, edited by William Storrar and Andrew Morton, 37–43. New York: T&T Clark, 2004.

Moltmann-Wendel, Elisabeth, and Jürgen Moltmann. *Humanity in God*. New York: Pilgrim Press, 1983.

Monsma, Stephen V. *Healing for a Broken World: Christian Perspectives on Public Policy*. Wheaton, IL: Crossway, 2007.

Mouw, Richard J. *Political Evangelism*. Grand Rapids: Eerdmans, 1974.

Muck, Terry C., and Frances S. Adeney. *Christianity Encountering World Religions: The Practice of Mission in the Twenty-First Century*. Grand Rapids: Baker Academic, 2009.

Mullen, Shirley. "On Faith." Column in Bread for the World newsletter. January/February 2012.

———. "Global Poverty and Hunger: Unveiling the Connections, Seeking the Solutions." Symposium presentation booklet. September, 2013.

Myers, Bryant L. *Walking with the Poor: Principles and Practices of Transformational Development*. New York: Orbis Books, 1999.

———. *Walking with the Poor: Principles and Practices of Transformational Development*. Rev. ed. New York: Orbis Books, 2011.

National Association of Evangelicals. "Denominational Members." http://www.nae.net/denominations/.

―――. *For the Health of the Nation: An Evangelical Call to Civic Responsibility.* 2004. http://nae.net/for-the-health-of-the-nation/.

―――. "Immigration." 2009. http://nae.net/immigration/.

―――. "Statement of Faith." http://www.nae.net/about-us/statement-of-faith.

Newbigin, Lesslie. *The Gospel in a Pluralist Society.* Grand Rapids: Eerdmans / Geneva: WCC Publications, 1989.

―――. *The Open Secret: An Introduction to the Theology of Mission.* Grand Rapids: Eerdmans, 1995.

―――. "Stewardship, Mission, and Development." In Lesslie Newbigin Papers. Orchard Learning Resources Centre, Information Services, University of Birmingham, Birmingham, UK.

―――. "The Trinity as Public Truth." In *The Trinity in a Pluralistic Age: Theological Essays on Culture and Religion,* edited by Kevin J. Vanhoozer, 1–8. Grand Rapids: Eerdmans, 1997.

―――. *Truth to Tell: The Gospel as Public Truth.* Grand Rapids: Eerdmans, 1991.

"New Marriage and Divorce Statistics Released." Barna Group. March 31, 2008. https://www.barna.org/barna-update/article/15-familykids/42-new-marriage-and-divorce-statistics-released.

Niebuhr, H. Richard. *Christ and Culture.* New York: HarperCollins, 2001.

Noll, Mark A. *The Scandal of the Evangelical Mind.* Grand Rapids: Eerdmans, 1994.

Norwood, Frederick Abbott. *The Story of American Methodism: A History of the United Methodists and Their Relations.* Nashville: Abingdon, 1974.

Offutt, Stephen. *New Centers of Global Evangelicalism in Latin America and Africa.* New York: Cambridge University Press, 2015.

―――. "The Role of Short-Term Mission Teams in the New Centers of Global Christianity." *Journal for the Scientific Study of Religion* 50, no. 4 (2011): 796–811.

Online Etymology Dictionary. 2015. http://www.etymonline.com/.

Overton, Roger, ed. *God and Governing: Reflecting on Ethics, Virtue, and Statesmanship.* Eugene, OR: Pickwick Publications, 2009.

Pannenberg, Wolfhart. *Anthropology in Theological Perspective.* Philadelphia: Westminster Press, 1985.

Perlman, Janice E. *Favela: Four Decades of Living on the Edge in Rio De Janeiro.* New York: Oxford University Press, 2009.

Pinter, Dean. "The Gospel of Luke and the Roman Empire." In McKnight and Modica, *Jesus Is Lord, Caesar Is Not,* 101–15.

Plantinga, Cornelius. *Not the Way It's Supposed to Be: A Breviary of Sin.* Grand Rapids: Eerdmans / Leicester, UK: Apollos, 1995.

Price, S. R. F. *Rituals and Power: The Roman Imperial Cult in Asia Minor*. New York: Cambridge University Press, 1984.

Putnam, Robert D. *Bowling Alone: The Collapse and Revival of American Community*. New York: Simon & Schuster, 2000.

Ramachandra, Vinoth. "Learning from Modern European Secularism: A View from the Third World Church." *Evangelical Review of Theology* 27, no. 3 (2003): 213–33.

———. *The Recovery of Mission: Beyond the Pluralist Paradigm*. Grand Rapids: Eerdmans, 1997.

Reynolds, Amy, and Stephen Offutt. "Global Poverty and Evangelical Action." In Steensland and Goff, *New Evangelical Social Engagement*, 242–64.

Rundle, Steven, ed. *Economic Justice in a Flat World: Christian Perspectives on Globalization*. Colorado Springs: Paternoster, 2009.

Sachs, Jeffrey D. *The End of Poverty: Economic Possibilities for Our Time*. New York: Penguin, 2005.

Salvatierra, Alexia, and Peter Heltzel. *Faith-Rooted Organizing: Mobilizing the Church in Service to the World*. Downers Grove, IL: InterVarsity, 2014.

Sanneh, Lamin O. *Encountering the West: Christianity and the Global Cultural Process; The African Dimension*. Maryknoll, NY: Orbis Books, 1993.

Schlossberg, Herbert, Vinay Samuel, and Ronald J. Sider, eds. *Christianity and Economics in the Post–Cold War Era: The Oxford Declaration and Beyond*. Grand Rapids: Eerdmans, 1994.

Schmalzbauer, John. "Whose Social Justice? Whose Evangelicalism? Social Engagement in Campus Ministry." In Steensland and Goff, *New Evangelical Social Engagement*, 50–72.

Schnable, Allison. "Frames, Modes of Action, Networks: What Religion Affords Grassroots NGOs." Paper presented at the Social Scientific Study of Religion conference, Indianapolis, October 30, 2014.

Schweiker, William. "Power and the Image of God." *Theology Today* 52, no. 2 (1995): 204–5.

Shah, Timothy Samuel. "For the Sake of Conscience: Some Evangelical Views of the State." Chap. 7 in Joireman, *Church, State, and Citizen*.

Shelledy, Robert B. "The Catholic Tradition and the State: Natural, Necessary, and Nettlesome." Chap. 2 in Joireman, *Church, State, and Citizen*.

Sherman, Amy L. *Kingdom Calling: Vocational Stewardship for the Common Good*. Downers Grove, IL: InterVarsity, 2011.

Sider, Ronald J. "ESA's History: A Reflection." ESA. 2014. http://www.evangelicals forsocialaction.org/about/history.

———. "Justice, Human Rights, and Government." In *Toward an Evangelical Public Policy: Political Strategies for the Health of the Nation*, edited by Ronald J. Sider and Diane Knippers, 163–93. Grand Rapids: Baker Books, 2005.

———. *Just Politics: A Guide for Christian Engagement.* 2nd ed. Grand Rapids: Brazos, 2012.

———. "Shaping Up for the Public Square." Address at the Micah Summit, Salvation Army Center. New York City, December 8, 2014.

Sider, Ronald J., and Heidi Rolland Unruh. "Typology of Religious Characteristics of Social Service and Educational Organizations and Programs." *Nonprofit and Voluntary Sector Quarterly* 33, no. 1 (March 2004): 109–34.

Skillen, James W. *The Good of Politics: A Biblical, Historical, and Contemporary Introduction.* Grand Rapids: Baker Academic, 2014.

———. "Reformed . . . And Always Reforming?" Chap. 4 in Joireman, *Church, State, and Citizen.*

Skinner, Christopher. "John's Gospel and the Roman Context: An Evaluation of Recent Proposals." In McKnight and Modica, *Jesus Is Lord, Caesar Is Not*, 116–29.

Smilde, David. *Reason to Believe: Cultural Agency in Latin American Evangelicalism.* Berkeley: University of California Press, 2007.

Smith, Christian. "The Spirit and Democracy: Base Communities, Protestantism, and Democratization in Latin America." *Sociology of Religion* 55, no. 2 (1994): 119–43.

Smith, James K. A. *Imagining the Kingdom: How Worship Works.* Grand Rapids: Baker Academic, 2013.

Smith, Timothy Lawrence. *Revivalism and Social Reform in Mid-Nineteenth-Century America.* New York: Abingdon, 1957.

Snyder, Howard A., and Joel Scandrett. *Salvation Means Creation Healed: The Ecology of Sin and Grace; Overcoming the Divorce between Earth and Heaven.* Eugene, OR: Cascade Books, 2011.

Solzhenitsyn, Aleksandr I. *The Gulag Archipelago, 1918–1956: An Experiment in Literary Investigation.* Translated by Thomas P. Whitney. New York: Harper & Row, 1974.

Southern Baptist Convention. "On Immigration and the Gospel." 2011. http://www.sbc.net/resolutions/1213.

Stackhouse, John G. *Making the Best of It: Following Christ in the Real World.* New York: Oxford University Press, 2008.

Stebbins, Tom. *Friendship Evangelism by the Book: Applying First Century Principles to Twenty-First Century Relationships.* Camp Hill, PA: Christian Publications, 1995.

Steensland, Brian, and Philip Goff. "Introduction: *The New Evangelical Social Engagement.*" In Steensland and Goff, New *Evangelical Social Engagement*, 1–30.

———, eds. *The New Evangelical Social Engagement.* New York: Oxford University Press, 2014.

Stringfellow, William. *An Ethic for Christians and Other Aliens in a Strange Land.* Waco: Word, 1973.

Suttle, Tim. *An Evangelical Social Gospel? Finding God's Story in the Midst of Extremes.* Eugene, OR: Wipf & Stock, 2011.

Swartley, Willard M. "Jesus Christ: Victor over Evil." In *Transforming the Powers: Peace, Justice, and the Domination System*, edited by Ray C. Gingerich and Theodore C. Grimsrud. Minneapolis: Augsburg Fortress, 2006.

Swartz, David R. *Moral Minority: The Evangelical Left in an Age of Conservatism*. Philadelphia: University of Pennsylvania Press, 2012.

Swindle, Stephen M. "Pentecostalism: Holy Spirit Empowerment and Politics." Chap. 8 in Joireman, *Church, State, and Citizen*.

Taylor, Charles. *A Secular Age*. Cambridge, MA: Belknap Press of Harvard University Press, 2007.

Tennent, Timothy C. *Invitation to World Missions: A Trinitarian Missiology for the Twenty-First Century*. Grand Rapids: Kregel Publications, 2010.

Tizon, Al. *Transformation after Lausanne: Radical Evangelical Mission in Global-Local Perspective*. Eugene, OR: Wipf & Stock, 2008.

Tolkien, J. R. R. *The Silmarillion*. Boston: Houghton Mifflin, 1977.

Treier, Daniel J. *Virtue and the Voice of God: Toward Theology as Wisdom*. Grand Rapids: Eerdmans, 2006.

Upstream Journal. 2015. http://www.upstreamjournal.org/.

Upstream website. 2015. http://www.thinkupstream.net/sign_up_splash?splash=1.

US Department of Health and Human Services. "2014 Poverty Guidelines." December 1, 2014. http://aspe.hhs.gov/poverty/14poverty.cfm.

Van Beek, Jill. Presentation at Eastern University, February 23, 2015.

Van Duzer, Jeffrey B. *Why Business Matters to God (and What Still Needs to Be Fixed)*. Downers Grove, IL: IVP Academic, 2010.

Van Harmelen, Rachel Boehm. "Diamond War." Christian Reformed Church, Office of Social Justice. 2007. http://www2.crcna.org/pages/osj_kortenhoven.cfm.

Vanhoozer, Kevin J. *The Drama of Doctrine: A Canonical-Linguistic Approach to Christian Theology*. Louisville: Westminster John Knox, 2005.

———. "One Rule to Rule Them All? Theological Method in an Era of World Christianity." In *Globalizing Theology*, edited by Craig Ott and Harold A. Netland, 85–126. Grand Rapids: Baker Academic, 2006.

VeneKlasen, Lisa, Valerie Miller, Debbie Budlender, and Cindy Clark. *A New Weave of Power, People, and Politics: The Action Guide for Advocacy and Citizen Participation*. Bourton-on-Dunsmore, Warwickshire, UK: Practical Action Publishing, 2007.

Ver Beek, Kurt. Presentations at Faith and Development Conference, Calvin College, Grand Rapids, February 6–7, 2015.

Volf, Miroslav. *After Our Likeness: The Church as the Image of the Trinity*. Grand Rapids: Eerdmans, 1998.

———. *A Public Faith: How Followers of Christ Should Serve the Common Good*. Grand Rapids: Brazos, 2011.

———. "Soft Difference: Theological Reflections on the Relation between Church and Culture in 1 Peter." *Ex Auditu* 10 (1994): 15–30.

Wacker, Grant. *Heaven Below: Early Pentecostals and American Culture.* Cambridge, MA: Harvard University Press, 2001.

Walk Free Foundation. *2014 Global Slavery Index.* Australia: Hope for Children Organization Australia Ltd., 2014. http://www.globalslaveryindex.org/.

Walls, Andrew F. "A History of the Expansion of Christianity Reconsidered: Assessing Christian Progress and Decline." In *The Cross-Cultural Process in Christian History*, 3–26. Maryknoll, NY: Orbis Books, 2002.

———. *The Missionary Movement in Christian History: Studies in the Transmission of Faith.* Maryknoll, NY: Orbis Books, 1996.

Warner, R. Stephen. "Religion and Migration in the United States." *Social Compass* 45, no. 1 (March 1998): 123–34.

Watson, Joanna. *Advocacy Toolkit.* 2nd ed. Teddington, UK: Tearfund UK, 2014.

Weber, Theodore R. *Politics in the Order of Salvation: New Directions in Wesleyan Political Ethics.* Nashville: Kingswood Books, 2001.

Wells, David F. "Why Being Good Is So Political." In Overton, *God and Governing*, 7–27.

Wesley, John. *The Works of John Wesley.* 3rd ed. Thomas Jackson Edition, 1831. Reprint, London: Wesleyan Conference Office, 1872.

Wesleyan Church. "A Wesleyan View of Global Poverty." 2006. https://www.wesleyan .org/238/a-wesleyan-view-of-global-poverty.

Westermann, Claus. *Genesis 1–11: A Commentary.* Minneapolis: Augsburg, 1984.

Whaling, Frank. "The Development of the Word 'Theology.'" *Scottish Journal of Theology* 34, no. 4 (1981): 289–312.

Willard, Dallas. "The Failure of Evangelical Political Involvement in the Area of Moral Transformation." In Overton, *God and Governing*, 74–91.

———. "Rethinking Evangelism." 2001. http://www.dwillard.org/articles/artview .asp?artID=53.

Wilson, John. "Introduction." In Cromartie, *A Public Faith*, 1–10.

Wink, Walter. *Engaging the Powers: Discernment and Resistance in a World of Domination.* Minneapolis: Augsburg Fortress, 1992.

———. *Naming the Powers: The Language of Power in the New Testament.* Philadelphia: Fortress Press, 1984.

Wolterstorff, Nicholas. *Justice in Love.* Grand Rapids: Eerdmans, 2011.

———. *Justice: Rights and Wrongs.* Princeton: Princeton University Press, 2008.

———. "Theological Foundations for an Evangelical Political Philosophy." In *Toward an Evangelical Public Policy: Political Strategies for the Health of the Nation*, edited by Ronald J. Sider and Diane Knippers, 140–62. Grand Rapids: Baker Books, 2005.

Wommack, Andrew. "Discipleship versus Evangelism." Andrew Wommack Ministries. 2015. http://www.awmi.net/extra/article/discipleship_evangelism.

Woodberry, Robert. "The Missionary Roots of Liberal Democracy." *American Political Science Review* 106, no. 2 (2012): 244–74.

Woong Shin, Chan. "Are Culture Wars Over? Evangelicals and the Global AIDS Crisis." Religion, Media & International Affairs program of Syracuse University. Accessed June 26, 2015. http://sites.maxwell.syr.edu/luce/ChanWoong.html.

World Bank. "Poverty Overview." Last modified October 7, 2015. http://www.world bank.org/en/topic/poverty/overview.

World Relief. "Wage Peace." http://worldrelief.org/wagepeace.

World Vision. "World Vision's Social Accountability Approach: Citizen Voice and Action." 2015. http://www.wvi.org/health/citizen-voice-and-action-0.

Wright, Christopher J. H. *The Mission of God: Unlocking the Bible's Grand Narrative*. Downers Grove, IL: IVP Academic, 2006.

———. *Old Testament Ethics for the People of God*. Downers Grove, IL: InterVarsity, 2004.

———. *The People of God and the State: An Old Testament Perspective*. Bramcote, Nottingham: Grove Books, 1990.

Wright, N. T. *The Challenge of Jesus: Rediscovering Who Jesus Was and Is*. Downers Grove, IL: InterVarsity, 2009.

———. *The New Testament and the People of God*. Minneapolis: Fortress Press, 1992.

———. "Romans." In *The New Interpreter's Bible*, vol. 10, edited by L. E. Keck, 393–770. Nashville: Abingdon, 2002.

Wuthnow, Robert. *Boundless Faith: The Global Outreach of American Churches*. Berkeley: University of California Press, 2009.

———. "Mobilizing Civic Engagement." In *Civic Engagement in American Democracy*, edited by Theda Skocpol and Morris P. Fiorina, 331–63. Washington, DC: Brookings Institution Press / New York: Russell Sage Foundation, 1999.

Yang, Jenny. "How Evangelicals Helped Shape Immigration Reform." *On Faith*, July 1, 2013. Faith Street. https://www.faithstreet.com/onfaith/2013/07/01/how -evangelicals-helped-shape-immigration-reform/10094.

Yoder, John Howard. *Body Politics: Five Practices of the Christian Community before the Watching World*. Scottdale, PA: Herald Press, 2001.

———. *The Christian Witness to the State*. Scottdale, PA: Herald Press, 2002.

———. "How H. Richard Niebuhr Reasoned: A Critique of *Christ and Culture*." In *Authentic Transformation: A New Vision of Christ and Culture*, edited by Glen H. Stassen, D. M. Yeager, and John H. Yoder, 31–90. Nashville: Abingdon, 1996.

———. *The Politics of Jesus: Vicit Agnus Noster*. 2nd ed. Carlisle, UK: Paternoster, 1994.

———. *The Priestly Kingdom: Social Ethics as Gospel*. Notre Dame, IN: University of Notre Dame Press, 1985.

Index

spirits, the powers as, 63–64
staff, advocacy and, 155, 157–58
state, the, 94–98, 104–8. *See also* powers, the
statesperson, advocacy and the, 114
stoicheia, 89
success, advocacy and, 117–18, 156–57
symbolism, advocacy and, 75–76

tabernacling, 110–11
technique, power of, 90
testimony, advocacy and, 70n64
theology
 advocacy and, 8–12, 15, 99–101, 161, 175–79
 the church and, 107–8
 God and, 53–62, 64–70
 sin and, 62–64
transformational advocacy, definition of, 11–12
transformation paradigm, the, 33–37
trap, deprivation, 34
Trinity, the
 advocacy and, 57–59, 99–101, 175–76
 the church and, 22, 102–3
 the powers and, 80–81

upstream analysis, 7, 123–24

values, advocacy and, 160–61
vulnerable, quartet of the, 53n1

#WagePeace, 135
Walking with the Poor (Myers), 33–35, 37
Water for the World Act, 136
weakness, human, 72–73
weakness, the kingdom and, 110–11
wealth, etymology of, 63n41
Wesley, John, 21–22
Wesleyan Church, 131–32
wildness, creation and, 60n30
Willow Creek Community Church, 180, 188, 195
wisdom, theology as, 56–57, 107–8
with, advocacy as, 125
witness, advocacy and, 70n64, 178–79
world, the, 70–71
World Relief, 135
World Vision, 5, 135–37
worship, advocacy and, 112–13